S0-BOK-777

Kathy Jacobs

on PowerPoint

ALEXANDRIA LIBRARY
ALEXANDRIA, VA 22304

Kathy Jacobs on PowerPoint

Copyright © 2004 by Kathy Jacobs

All rights reserved. No part of this book may be reproduced or transmitted in any form or by any means, electronic or mechanical, including photocopying, recording, or by any information storage retrieval system without written permission from the publisher.

Written by:
Kathy Jacobs

Edited by:
Tracy Syrstad

Cover Design
Irubin Consulting

Published by:
Holy Macro! Books
13386 Judy Avenue Northwest
Uniontown, Ohio, USA 44685

Distributed by:
Independent Publishers Group

First printing:
2004
Printed in Hong Kong

Library of Congress Control Number: 2003108840

ISBN: 0-9724258-6-1

Trademarks:
All brand names and product names used in this book are trade names, service marks, trademarks, or registered trademarks of their respective owners. Holy Macro! Books is not associated with any product or vendor mentioned in this book.

About the Author

Kathy Jacobs has 20 years in the computer and training fields. She got into the PowerPoint business while developing training materials for several major companies. She founded her website, www.PowerPointAnswers.com, to help others learn from her experiences. She was named a PowerPoint MVP by Microsoft in the Spring of 2003. Kathy shares her knowledge regularly on the PowerPoint newsgroup, as well as via a number of on-line forums and mailing lists. She does consulting on developing and improving PowerPoint presentations and applications, as well as training PowerPoint users of all levels.

Dedication

To Bruce, without whom I would never had started or finished.

Acknowledgements

In the development of any book, there are more people involved than could ever be listed on an Acknowledgement page. This book is no exception. That being said, there are people and organizations without whom this book never would have been possible:

Bruce Jacobs, who read every page - more than once

Echo Swinford, who made sure I got it right

Anne Pierson, who got me started

Tracy Syrstad, who made it as clean as possible

Bill Jelen, who saw the possibilities

Austin Myers, who filled in the multimedia hole

The PowerPoint MVPs, they all know why

April Dalke, for all her support

Kate Eskesen, for being there

Microsoft and TechSmith, whose products made it happen

The PowerPoint newsgroup community, whose sharing helps us all

In addition, many people encouraged me as the book progressed. They know who they are. Their support kept me going. Without them, this book couldn't have happened.

Table of Contents

14. For Presenters: Getting Ready To Present 289

This page left intentionally blank.

Table of Tips

Table of Tips

Forward – Those Scary PowerPoint Books

I first came across Microsoft PowerPoint in its 2.0 incarnation, the first Microsoft release since the product had been acquired. It was a Macintosh product, the Windows release wouldn't show up until version 3, and it actually ran off a single floppy disc. I was working as a technical writer for spreadsheet software on the Macintosh at the time. This was in the olden days, before applications had tons of hard disk space upon which to install megabytes of help files and tutorials. Software applications usually shipped with a manual or two. Real paper and binding stuff. Hard to imagine, I know.

As a writer looking at this new presentation product, I was more interested in the manual than the actual program, and I was most interested in seeing what Microsoft had done with it. It turned out they had done a very scary thing. The manual was thick, hardcover and full color. Hardcover and full color! The thing was almost a coffee table book! My cadre of software documentation writers looked upon this development with fear and trepidation. You see, we all had trouble just justifying two color printing and spiral binding to our project managers. Microsoft products would surely start outselling us on the basis of their manuals alone! We were sure it spelled our doom.

As it turned out, the hardcover software documentation manual didn't continue as a trend for Microsoft any more than it inspired other software manufacturers to spend precious cost-of-goods money in this manner. And of course, a few years later software documentation was pretty much replaced by the aforementioned electronic help topics and tutorials. It was during that transition phase I joined that scary Microsoft organization. I became a Program Manager for PowerPoint, tasked with evolving the products design. To my surprise I found Microsoft to be populated with tremendously talented and caring individuals, constantly trying to do the right thing for their customers, only scary in their drive and resolve. And PowerPoint was a joy to work on. Great fun.

Jump forward about twelve years. I find myself having been associated with seven or so subsequent releases of the product, having designed and managed features I hope have made people's presentations better and easier to create. However, an unfortunate truism of almost any reasonably complex technical product is there will be difficult things that need additional explanation and support. This leads us to your author, to Kathy Jacobs.

Kathy is one of a heroic band of individuals known as the PowerPoint MVPs. MVP stands for Most Valuable Professional, a program Microsoft started to help directly support our users. To quote the official Microsoft definition, MVPs are individuals who are

- o Recognized: Microsoft MVPs are acknowledged by peers and also by Microsoft for their active participation in Microsoft technical communities around the globe.

- o Credible: Microsoft MVPs have demonstrated practical expertise providing the highest quality information and content.

- o Accessible: Microsoft MVPs are active technical community leaders sharing their experience with peers.

In short, Microsoft "anoints" individuals who aren't actually on the payroll with the title and responsibility of helping users of the product. These people create web sites and answer Internet newsgroup messages, write articles, and other activities all in the name of solving PowerPoint users problems and giving feedback to Microsoft. Think electronic Good Samaritan. Think digital docent.

I'm the guy on the PowerPoint team who meets regularly with the MVPs. We meet regularly on phone conferences and in the newsgroups to discuss the current state of PowerPoint usage; what's giving customers problems, where we could do a better job in the next release. The MVPs ask questions, I try to answer them or get back to them. I ask questions, they tell me what's going on in the real world. It's a great program.

It was about a year ago that Kathy Jacobs joined our little group. Right off the bat I knew Kathy was a force to be reckoned with. Kathy was not shy, not even at the start. She brought up lots of user's questions and issues, fiercely, tenaciously, and loudly! And when my answer didn't go far enough, she dug in her heels and told me, then she'd ask the question again, and again, or she might finally admit this was something I would have to get back to her on. No, she doesn't make my life easier, she makes PowerPoint's customer's lives easier. We're lucky to have her.

So Kathy's written this book and I've read it. You are well advised to consider arming yourself with it before you approach your next presentation. She's got straight facts on how to work the product, and that's good. As a bonus she starts where the program really can't; getting your thinking straight about what you want to present. That step is tremendously important. You'd be surprised how often it just gets skipped in the creation of a presentation. (Then again, maybe you wouldn't.) And she's not just doing some weird calming Zen philosophy, not a scolding about thinking before talking, or even tricks about imagining your audience naked. She has real methods that will get you organized, ordered and eventually confident you know what you're going to talk about. After that, working with the actual program is just a matter of following her clear instructions.

You're lucky to have such a good and able guide. Listen to Kathy, she'll get you through it.

Richard Bretschneider
San Jose, CA
February 28, 2004

Richard Bretschneider is an eleven year Microsoft veteran, having joined the company in 1993 to work on Microsoft PowerPoint 4. He holds three PowerPoint related patents and is currently working on the next release of the product.

This page left intentionally blank.

1. What Can I Use PPT For?

> ➢ Why PowerPoint?

> ➢ Presentation Types

> ➢ Who Uses PowerPoint?

Why PowerPoint?

I started using PowerPoint in the early 1990's as a trainer developing training materials. I needed an easy way to ensure the materials I taught were consistent from session to session and were easy to follow. Because I was training in the use of computer software, I needed to use a tool that allowed multiple computer programs to be run at the same time on a single machine. PowerPoint allowed me to not only run multiple programs, but also to swap between my presentation and the programs.

I also found myself using PowerPoint to create presentations of many other kinds, including:

- Status reports on the training classes
- Publicity presentations for classes
- Professional presentations
- Student evaluation summaries

As my familiarity with PowerPoint grew, so did my skills. I became known as a presentation expert, especially skilled at enhancing presentations.

As I consulted with other organizations, I learned of the many different ways people used PowerPoint to communicate information. The most common problems encountered by my clients are addressed in this book. In each chapter, you will find an example of how a client used PowerPoint to communicate with an audience and how using the tool helped get the message across in a more efficient manner.

Before we get to how people use PowerPoint, I want to introduce three terms I will be using throughout this book.

Presentation Types

This book will use three terms to categorize the presentations created:

- Speaker-led presentations
- Self-running presentations
- Kiosk presentations

Speaker-Led Presentations

Speaker-led presentations are usually what most people think of when they think of PowerPoint. The presentation is designed with the intent that there will always be a speaker sharing the information in the slides. The information in the slides is not complete − it is expected the majority of the information comes from the presenter. The slides should not be the focus of the audience's attention, the content should be. And if the speaker is not familiar with the mechanics of PowerPoint, the mechanics can easily become the focus.

This type of presentation still makes up the bulk of the PowerPoint work in today's business world. However, as you will see later in this chapter, people have taken the speaker-led approach and expanded it to create stand-alone presentations of all types.

Content slides, such as bulleted lists, graphs, pictures or multimedia slides, provide the bulk of the presentation material for a speaker-led presentation. Each content slide is expected to contain enough information to provide a summary of what the speaker is currently discussing or to add spice and interest to the material.

Tip 1: Slide Content Suggestions	Keep textual slide content to a minimum when developing speaker-led presentations. You don't want your audience to spend all of their time reading the slides and not listening to what you have to say.
	Everything on a speaker-led presentation should be in a font large enough for the whole room to see it.

Speaker-led presentations should be balanced. As a presenter, be careful to keep the audience interested in the content and avoid overdoing the extras, such as animations. Too many extras can cause some of the audience to stop listening to the speaker and start anticipating the next trick.

Speaker-led presentation navigation is usually via simple mouse clicks and keyboard actions. The order in which information is presented is determined by the speaker, with some influence from the audience. While there may be links to hidden slides, FAQ slides and other presentations for additional information, the path through the presentation tends to be linear.

Self-Running Presentations

Self-running presentations present enough information that the presentation can be viewed by itself without a speaker to support it. They are linear in nature, with no human intervention while the presentations are running. Movement through the presentation is automated and timed so the presentation flows on its own.

Self-running presentations should contain enough information to prevent confusion by those viewing the presentation. These presentations provide information such as:

- Schedules
- Room information
- Announcements
- Product information

- Mall kiosks
- Museum displays

These presentations are set to run unattended indefinitely. It is recommend that during the development of these presentations extensive testing is done to ensure the material is moving fast enough to keep the viewer's attention, but not so fast it is impossible for the average viewer to keep up with the changing content.

One special use of a self-running presentation is an introductory loop for other presentations. In this case, a series of slides is set up to provide introductory information. When the main presentation is ready for use, a key press or a mouse click transitions from the introduction loop to the main presentation.

Kiosk Presentations

A kiosk presentation is a non-speaker led presentation in which all movement through the presentation is done via mouse clicks and automation instead of keyboard entry. You can think of these presentations as a middle ground between a speaker-led presentation and a self-running presentation.

Kiosk presentations depend heavily on animation and automation, and are not generally linear in nature. Because the presentation provides information to a user without any outside information, the path through the presentation depends on the user instead of the designer. Each user may take a different path.

A kiosk presentation must have navigation buttons to allow the user to move from slide to slide. While some slides may be linked and have automatic transitions, there still needs to be a way for the user to move around. Since the keyboard is disabled, movement through the presentation is done by right and left mouse clicks and clickable navigation buttons. If there are no navigation buttons, the presentation must be fully automated and is considered a self-running presentation.

This style of presentation is designed to provide detailed information to one viewer at a time. In the corporate world, you might see a product announcement done as a kiosk. The information provided is summarized on the main presentation slides, with links to product detail slides, web information, FAQ slides and other information. This idea can be taken a step further by linking a number of presentations to a main menu to provide a catalog of products and services.

Who Uses PowerPoint?

Presentations can also be categorized by who is creating them and for whom they are being created. Presentation creators and their audiences include:

- Business users, including managers, salespeople and others who need to communicate with clients or other employees
- Trainers, including those creating presentations primarily to help adults learn processes, procedures or other new information
- Teachers, including anyone creating presentations to teach children or adults in a formal education situation
- Students who need to present information for a class project or assignment
- Home users who want to share information with others in a non-business environment

Business Uses

PowerPoint users in the business world need to communicate ideas to people within their company and outside of their company. These users tend to be both the most formal and the most imaginative users of PowerPoint.

A common presentation might document the need for additional resources for a project or to request the creation of a new project. PowerPoint allows users to target the information to the audience. In Chapters 2 and 3, we meet Jane who has been tasked with creating, publicizing and implementing a new project for her non-profit organization. In Chapter 5, we meet George, who needed to inform his corporation's management of a new business opportunity.

Many companies have created interactive company reports to communicate both internally and externally. Creating a single PowerPoint presentation and distributing it to all employees ensures a consistent message is presented and all employees see and hear the same words. In Chapter 9, we meet Sam, who needs to create a series of presentations to introduce a new benefits package to the members of her company.

Business users who need to share information with clients without a representative in attendance create kiosks of product, store or site information. Creating the kiosks with PowerPoint allows re-use of existing hardware and skills, while still reaching a large audience. Sam will take advantage of these ideas while creating her benefits presentations.

Corporate users create presentations to share sales data with employees and clients. The ease of data exchange between PowerPoint and the other Microsoft Office applications, along with the visuals provided by charts and graphs, can help create powerful presentations that express exactly what you want the audience to hear. In Chapter 10, we meet Lydia and learn how to integrate sales information into your presentations in the best possible manner.

By the same token, creating a single presentation about a new product and distributing it to all clients and potential clients allows for a more timely and consistent preview of the product. In addition, the presentation can be easily adapted for use as a background to a trade show booth or announcement page. In Chapter 11, we meet Bryan, who is creating a mini-CD catalog of his company's new products for employees at the branch offices. In Chapters 13 and 18, we meet Curt, who runs a consulting company. He needs to create a multi-use presentation to share his consulting services with clients around the world.

PowerPoint's template creation allows business users to develop a corporate identity that helps clients identify their products and services at a glance. In Chapter 12, we meet Rachel, who needs to integrate a corporate color scheme into her printed materials. Rachel also joins us in Chapter 16, when she takes the corporate identity one-step further and develops a series of standard templates for company employees.

Training And Teaching Uses

Because PowerPoint allows the creation of both student and teacher/trainer materials in a single file, it lends itself perfectly to the creation of speaker-led training materials.

Each slide has a notes section for additional presenter information, while the slides present information to focus student attention upon the most important points. Once class materials are created, handouts can be printed using either PowerPoint or Word. Slides, notes or outlines can also can be sent to Word for formatting and distribution.

Tip 2: CBT Examples	Looking for a great PowerPoint template for creating Computer Based Training slides? Check out this example from PowerPoint MVP Bill Foley's website: www.pttinc.com/power_point.htm#Microsoft%20 PowerPoint

Some teachers have learned to use PowerPoint's animation features to create slides in which elements move and/or change. The changing slides hold the student's interest. In Chapter 6, we meet Alicia and learn with her how to keep her students' attention and improve her classroom dynamics by adding animation to her slides.

In addition, PowerPoint's multimedia capabilities allow teachers and trainers to reach all learning styles. Information can be presented using text, sound, animations and movies. Teachers and trainers have even started taking the learning one step further and assigned students to create their own presentations to reinforce the learning from the classroom. In Chapter 7, we meet members of Daniel's classroom and help them incorporate multimedia into their biology reports.

One of the other uses for PowerPoint in the classroom is to ensure the information presented is retained. Many users have

developed PowerPoint games for this use. "Games?" you ask...
"Why on earth would people want to use PowerPoint for game
development?" Well, it is an easy way to begin interactive
programming. It is a non-threatening way to verify the content
presented has been learned. What's more, it is fun for both the
user and the presentation developer.

Samples of games available currently on the web:

- Jeopardy – Samples available at either

  www.echosvoice.com/jeopardy.htm
  www.pttinc.com/customized_software.htm

- Quiz Shows – Sample and code available at

  www.mvps.org/skp/ppt00031.htm

- Family Feud – Sample available at

  www.pttinc.com/customized_software.htm

- Tic-Tac-Toe – Sample available for download at

  www.mvps.org/skp/download.htm

- Mystery games – Template available at

  www.d124.s-cook.k12.il.us/pp_templates/
  PP_templates.htm

If you are looking for even more ideas, check out *PowerPak for
PowerPoint* from FTC Publishing – a series of PowerPoint
templates that turn lesson plans into games. While aimed at the
education world, they are adaptable to business uses as well.

Home Use

The third group of PowerPoint users create their presentations
outside of the business world. While we do not meet as many of
these users, I thought you might like to know some of the more
imaginative uses for PowerPoint at home.

Websites

PowerPoint's Save as Web Page option (called Save as HTML in PowerPoint 97) is not intended to be a web site creation tool. However, there are places where people have found it very useful to save PowerPoint presentations as web pages.

Saving presentations as web pages creates a reproducible, distributable presentation that runs on multiple platforms. PowerPoint itself runs only on Macs and PCs. Presentations that have been converted to HTML can be viewed on almost any machine available.

Photo Albums

Do you have a series of pictures from an event or trip? Do you want to share those old family photographs sitting in storage? PowerPoint is a great way to collect these photographs together, organize them and share them with others.

Once the pictures have been scanned into a folder, they can quickly and easily be inserted into PowerPoint either individually or together. Add some animation, some entrance and exit effects, captions describing who or what is in the picture, some background music or narration, and you have an interactive, electronic photograph album. Save the presentation to a CD and it can even be set up to run automatically on any machine.

Lip Syncing / Karaoke / Church Uses

Volunteers across the world are discovering the animations available within PowerPoint can be used to display the words to songs for large groups to follow. Churches are moving to PowerPoint to display music during services.

Tip 3: Churches That Use PowerPoint	With more and more churches going to PowerPoint to present sermon notes, music, announcements, and other church information, an entire industry has sprouted to meet the needs of churches.
	Several organizations sell software to make it easier to present and track church music, and inspirational backgrounds and templates for presentations. Many of these products are priced with church budgets and volunteer efforts in mind.

People working with children are using PowerPoint to teach songs using the bouncing ball methodology. While the timing problems inherent in PowerPoint need to be overcome, using PowerPoint to teach music is quite possible. In Chapter 8, we meet Wayne who creates presentations to teach his group new songs.

Resumes

As the population of computer users increases and the job market tightens, people have begun distributing electronic resumes. Many still stick to Word documents, but as the population base for PowerPoint increases, so does the number of people hoping to show off their creative skills by designing interactive, updatable resumes that are PowerPoint presentations.

Looking for work in the communications and computer markets? You can show off your PowerPoint skills by taking static brochures or flyers and translating them into interactive public relations pieces. These pieces show off not only what you have done, but also what you can do for the potential client.

You can also make a presentation that is a skeleton for an electronic portfolio. With the ability to link PowerPoint to other documents and applications, your resume becomes not just a static document, but a way to show off your wide range of skills and accomplishments.

With the distribution capabilities of PowerPoint 2003, the possibilities of PowerPoint-based resumes grow even further. CDs can show off the creative talents of the creator, with all of the information capable of being stored on a single CD for easy distribution.

VBA developers use PowerPoint resumes as a way to show their programming skills. Not only are they able to give examples of code they have written, they can show the code is clean and executable as well.

This page left intentionally blank.

2. Developing the Content

> What Do You Want To Say?

> Who Is Your Audience?

> How Do You Want To Say It?

> Creating an Outline

© UFS, Inc.

DILBERT reprinted by permission of United Feature Syndicate, Inc.

Jane runs a non-profit agency that connects people who need services with those who provide them. She has been assigned to create a program to use local teens to do yard work for members of the city's homebound population. She needs to start this project as quickly as possible by creating a series of PowerPoint presentations to introduce her program to the area.

I need help. I have experience speaking off the cuff, but am new to PowerPoint and re-creatable presentations. I need to get the project launched as soon as possible.

I have read through several of the available on-line resources, so I have a pretty good idea of what PowerPoint can do. I know that I am going to need several different presentations, but don't even know where to start the development process. I also know that I will not be the only one giving these presentations, so I need to create the most versatile presentations possible. Can you help?

Jane has several things to do before she even opens PowerPoint. She knows what she needs to say, but not to whom she needs to say it. She also wants some help making sure the messages are consistent from presentation to presentation, as she won't always be there when the information is looked at. She needs to decide:

- What main messages she wants people to take home
- Who is the intended audience for each presentation
- How she is going to present the information
- What is in each presentation (the outline)

These decisions seem trivial and obvious at first glance, but the time you take to do them correctly saves considerable time and effort later. Making the right choices up front makes your presentations much more useful and understandable by your intended audience. If you don't first decide who you are talking to and what you want to say, you may end up sharing your information with the walls instead of your audience.

People who are new at developing presentations usually spend hours building and picking just the right graphics, adding sounds, and moving between slides in the best way possible. Unfortunately, these extras are not the most important parts of the presentation. The most important part is the content. One of the stumbling blocks for presentation creators is the actual process of creating the content.

What Do You Want To Say?

Since PowerPoint is a mechanism for communicating messages, like Jane, your first decision is to determine what to tell your audience. These are your main messages.

The main messages for your presentation are a "high-level gloss" of the content you wish to convey. Different audiences may need similar messages, but some groups will need to have differing detail levels.

In a perfect world, each of these main messages becomes a section of your presentation. The more time spent defining the messages, the less re-work you need to do later on. This is not going to take hours and hours to do: determining the main messages for most presentations is fairly easy. A good way to learn how to create main messages is to think about the last few presentations or speeches you have heard. Make a two-column chart that shows each presentation and what you got out of each one.

Sample Presentation Topics	Main messages
Status	We did great at these things... We didn't do great at these things...
Sales Review	XYZ sold beyond belief this quarter ABC didn't sell this quarter
Training	Objectives for this session are...
Informational speech	Provide details on new topics

Some main messages are not as easily defined. For example, if a CEO is getting ready to present news of a layoff to a group of employees, the main message needs to be very clear. Is the message:

- You are all losing your jobs, but I am keeping mine.
- The company is not doing well, so we need to let some of you go.
- You are being laid off... Here are the benefits you will get.
- We are in a short-term cash flow situation and need to let some of you go. You will be called back in 90 days.
- We need to make some cuts in our department. The following people will be losing their jobs along with me.
- We are closing the doors and laying you all off today

Each of these approaches has been used as the main message in a layoff situation. The first one didn't go over very well. The last one didn't either. On the other hand, when the main message wasn't just

"Bye Bye," the audience was much more open to listening to why the layoffs were happening.

Layoff presentations are one area where you might not want to lead with your main point. This type of presentation takes practice and finesse to create.

So how do you determine what the main message is? The easiest way is to look at the potential content as an audience member instead of as the presenter. Think about what you would like to know about the topic instead of what you can say about the topic. I find it easier to determine this information by stating questions that need answering and then developing the answers. That is why you will see my main messages stated as questions.

In Jane's case, we know the basics of the presentation but we need to determine what the main messages will be.

What Does Everyone Need To Know?

From reading the one-sentence blurb about Jane's project, you quickly see there are some messages everyone involved in the project needs to know:

- Who will the work be done for?
- Who is providing the funding?
- Who will be doing the yard work?
- How will we measure the success of the program?
- When will the work be done?

As we researched the project, we found there are also hidden messages some of the audiences will want to know:

- Why should the project be funded?
- What equipment will we need?
- What training will we provide?
- Will the teens be supervised?
- How will the teens be assigned to projects?
- How many hours will the teens be expected to work?

- Where are we getting the volunteers?
- How will we select places to have work done?

Did We Miss Anything?

Once the basic brainstorming on the messages has been completed, it is time to review the messages with a member of the potential audience. Ask this person to review the messages as if they knew nothing about the project. Tell them you would rather have more messages than you can present, than to have missed a major message.

Chances are pretty good your reviewer will find at least one or two pieces of information you have missed. Add these messages to your list and move to the next step.

Prioritize Your Messages

Some of the messages for your presentation are more important than others. The most important messages should get certain specialized treatments in your presentation:

- Placement: The most important messages should go close to the beginning or close to the end of your presentation.
- Repetition: The most important messages should be said more than once.
- Interaction: The more interaction an audience member has with a piece of information, the more likely they are to remember it.

Once the messages and their individual priorities have been determined, the next step is to build a chart with the messages down one side and a number of blank columns following the messages. These blank columns will be filled in with the audience for the specific message.

Tip 4: Building Your Message Table	When you get the messages defined, type them into a Word table or an Excel spreadsheet. This allows easy addition of columns for the audiences defined in the next stage of your presentation development.
	An additional advantage to keeping the messages in this format is messages and audiences can be added as they are discovered during the development of the content.

Who Is Your Audience?

Now that we know what the presentation needs to say, it is time to define who needs to hear each message. The match between some audiences and some messages are obvious. In Jane's case, two of the audiences are fairly obvious from the project description:

- The homebound people for whom the work will be done
- The teens who will do the work

Two more main audiences can be determined by looking at the list of messages:

- The companies who are being asked to donate funding
- The companies who are being asked to donate equipment

Link Messages To Audiences

The next step is to determine which audience members need to hear which messages. This can be done by taking the list of messages and filling the columns indicating who needs to hear each message. For example, the four audiences would be listed in our table as the columns:

- H for homeowners
- T for teens
- F for companies providing funding
- E for companies providing equipment

After Jane's first pass at creating the table, it looked like this:

Message	H	T	F	E
How will we select places to have work done?	X	X	X	X
How will we measure program success?	X	X	X	X
How will participants be chosen?	X		X	X
Who is providing the funding?			X	X
Where are we getting volunteers?		X	X	X
Who will be doing the yard work?	X	X	X	X
When will the work be done?	X	X		
Why should the project be funded?			X	X
What equipment will we need?		X		X
What training will we provide?	X	X		
How many hours will the teens be expected to work?		X		
How will the teens be assigned to projects?		X		
Will the teens be supervised?	X		X	X

Evaluate: Did We Miss Anyone?

When Jane went through the process of defining and linking the messages and the audiences, it became apparent an entire audience and the information they needed to know had been missed.

Her hidden audience was the people who supervise the teens. So, she added a column (S for supervisor) to the table to show the supervisors and marked which messages they need to know. In addition, adding an audience may reveal messages that audience needs to hear. In Jane's case, we added two messages. The table now looks like this:

Message	H	T	F	E	S
How will we select places to have work done?	X	X	X	X	X
How will we measure program success?	X	X	X	X	X
How will participants be chosen?	X		X	X	X
Who is providing the funding?			X	X	
Where are we getting volunteers?		X	X	X	X
Who will be doing the yard work?	X	X	X	X	X
When will the work be done?	X	X			X
Why should the project be funded?			X	X	
What equipment will we need?		X		X	X
What training will we provide?	X	X			X
How many hours will the teens be expected to work?		X			
How will the teens be assigned to projects?		X			X
Will the teens be supervised?	X		X	X	X
How many hours will each supervisor be expected to work?					X
What training will be provided for the supervisors?					X

How Do You Want To Say It (Part 1)

After determining what to say and who to say it to, the next step is to determine how to present the information to each audience. There are several things to keep in mind while deciding what type of presentation to create for any given audience. These include:

- Audience
- Audience size
- Audience location

- Amount of interaction needed between the presenter and the audience
- Frequency of providing the information

Keep in mind that while you may design a presentation mainly for use in one way, you can change from non-automated presentations to automated presentations if you prepare your files correctly.

Audience Size

The first thing to consider when deciding how you want the presentation to run is the size of the audience. If the information is being presented to one person at time, the presentation should be some type of automated presentation. If it is being presented to a large group, it may need to be developed as a speaker-led presentation.

What About Middle-Sized Groups?

Some presentations need to be created to work with both single-person sessions and larger audiences. Sometimes, you may not even know if the presenter is going to be available to run the presentation.

In these cases, you should design the presentation as a speaker-led presentation. When the speaker-led presentation is complete, create a second version that can be used as a kiosk or self-running presentation. Be sure to add the feedback mechanisms to help participants gather more information and be sure to add navigation elements to help them move from slide to slide.

Aiming The Presentation At The Right Group

Presentations need to be aimed at the target audience. In Jane's case, she created speaker-led presentations for the corporate representatives to allow them to meet the members of the organization. She then created kiosk presentations for the training modules for the teens and supervisors, allowing them to work through the training on their own time. She also created a self-running presentation with information for public distribution to advertise the service and to gather names of homebound persons needing the service.

Audience Location

Another factor in your presentation design is whether the whole group is able to get together at the same time. If you are going to be presenting a set of information to a large number of people at once, create a speaker-led presentation. If the audience is spread across multiple geographic areas or if the members of the audience will not be all together at one time, create a kiosk-style presentation. If the information needs to reach a very wide audience, you may want to create a self-running presentation so they may access the information on their own.

Presenter And Audience Interaction

The amount of speaker-audience interaction also impacts the presentation design. If you are going to be presenting, you want to ensure the presentation is complete enough to cover all the information, but still leaves room for interaction with the audience. For example, a manager may not want to see all the details on every part of your presentation, but will want to see the detailed information for some parts.

Jane found this to be the case for her presentations to the corporate sponsors. She wanted to establish a connection between the presenter and the audience, so she made sure the design allowed for question and answer sessions, as well as questions during the presentation.

In other cases, such as a kiosk-style training presentation, you know that no one will be available to answer questions. In these cases, ensure enough information is provided to answer questions the participants have as they work through the material. Jane found email links from section slides allowed the teens and the supervisors to email questions. After Jane received and answered the questions, she added the information when she next updated the training.

At this point in your content development, the idea is not to answer each question that may arise during viewing. Instead, define the detail level you need for your outline. If you know one particular section of the outline needs more depth, note it on the outline. You probably also want to note whether you expect the extra details to go in the slide content or in associated notes pages.

Number Of Times To Present

Jane knew each presentation would be shown many times. She also knew she would not be doing the presenting every time. She made sure as much of the content as possible was documented in the notes.

Benefits Of Preparation

When Jane translated some of the presentations into kiosks and training modules, she found the task was much easier than she expected. All of the information Jane needed to add to the slides was already in the slide notes.

Back To The Table...

Now that Jane has defined the format of the various presentations, it is time to add this information to the messages table. Jane developed a code to represent the various presentations to be created and the style of each presentation:

Code	Meaning
G	General information for everyone in the project
S	Speaker-led presentation with information for a specific audience
T	Training for a specific audience (in Jane's case, the teens and the supervisors)
A	Automatic presentations used to generate interest and provide information to the homebound

To integrate this information into the message chart, Jane replaced each "x" in the original message table with one or more of the above codes.

Message	H	T	F	E	S
Who are we doing the work for?	G	G	G	G	G
How will we measure program success?	G	G	G	G	G
How will participants be chosen?	A		S	S	S
Who is providing the funding?			S	S	
Where are we getting volunteers?		S	S	S	S
Who will do the yard work?	G	G	G	G	G
When will the work be done?	A	T			T
Why should we fund the project?			S	S	
What equipment is needed?		T		S	T
What training will be provided?	A	T			T
How many hours will each teen be expected to work?		T			
How will the teens be assigned?		T			T
Will the teens be supervised?	A		S	S	T
How many hours will each supervisor be expected to work?					T
What training will be provided for the supervisors?					T

Creation of this table shows Jane she needs to create one large speaker-led general information presentation, a couple of targeted speaker-led presentations, a couple of automated presentations and two training presentations.

Tip 5: Number of Presentations	If you are careful when you create your message and audience table, decisions about the number of presentations should be fairly easy.
	Usually, you find the only presentation you need to add at this point is a general information presentation. Develop this presentation first and use it as a basis for all the other presentations.

How Do You Want To Say It (Part 2)

The final part of your content design is to determine your presentation's style. Some of the stylistic decisions you need to make are:

- Is the audience looking for a solemn presentation or more relaxed one?

- Are you going to take a text-focused approach or graphics-focused one?

- Will you be doing formal information sharing or will you put in some activities and games?

Some General Rules About Style

- When presenting to management, keep the main presentation brief, to the point, clear and concise. Keep the flashiness to a minimum so the participants don't feel you are wasting time. Keep backgrounds and graphics formal.

- When requesting support, keep the presentation interesting. Show what you need to show with enough flashiness to keep interest. Prepare FAQ slides to use when questions come up. Target your graphics, backgrounds and colors to the intended audience.

- When presenting to children, keep the information moving at a rate appropriate to their learning level. Use flashier backgrounds, sounds and graphics. If the audience is early elementary school children, it is especially important you stay sensitive to their reading level.

- When presenting to teens, keep in mind they are more "tech-savvy" and likely know the basic technology tricks. That is a good thing. It means presentations can use a little more glitz to maintain their interest. Provide links to extra information whenever possible to allow them to do their own discovery.

- If you have a lot of information to share during a speaker-led presentation, break it up into viewable pieces. There's more on this later in the book, but for now remember the mind can absorb only what the body can see and endure. Too much at once turns the audience off.

- If you have a lot of information to present during a kiosk presentation, make sure you provide navigation buttons so the participants can review information from earlier sections.

Creating An Outline

Now that the general information for the presentation is designed, it is time to put together an outline. If the messages list was done well, this step should go quickly.

First, decide what tool to use to generate the outline. We are going to cover three ways to develop your outline:

- Create as text files in Notepad or equivalent
- Develop in Word
- Create directly in PowerPoint

Developing outlines in PowerPoint can be the most efficient because it uses the same application all the way through the process. There are two reasons you may find other tools used: the outline is developed by someone without access to PowerPoint or the content is coming from a document or plan already created.

Since I create my message tables in Word, I create my outlines in Word as well. (When I get message tables created in Excel, I transfer that data to either Word or PowerPoint, as the client desires.)

Creating An Outline In Notepad

At first glance, this appears to be the simplest option. Merely open Notepad and type. However, with no formatting, be careful when typing the text so it is correctly imported into PowerPoint.

Lines in the text file intended to be slide titles should start directly at the left margin. From there, each tab space inward is one bullet level inward on a PowerPoint slide. When you are done creating the outline, save the file as a text file with an extension "ppt."

To open the file in PowerPoint, go to File→Open and select All Outlines as the file type option. Navigate to the folder containing the text file, select it and click open. A new presentation opens with the text content as slide content. An outline file created in Notepad looks something like this:

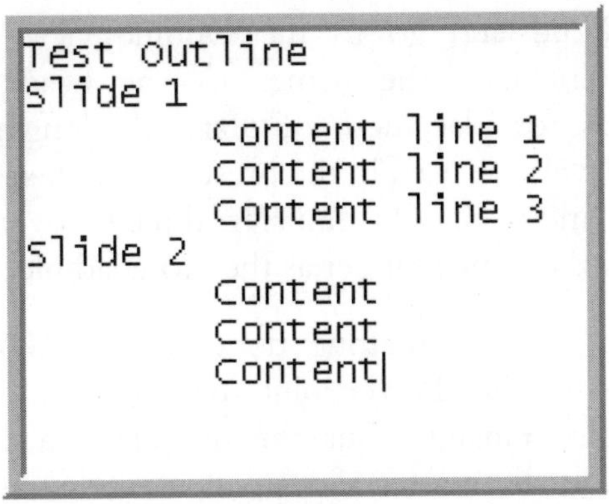

Test Outline
Slide 1
Content line 1
Content line 2
Content line 3
Slide 2
Content
Content
Content

Figure 2-1: Outline in Notepad

This file creates three slides. When viewed in PowerPoint's Slide Sorter view, the slides look like this:

Test Outline
1
Slide 1
Content line 1
Content line 2
Content line 3
2
Slide 2
Content
Content
Content
3

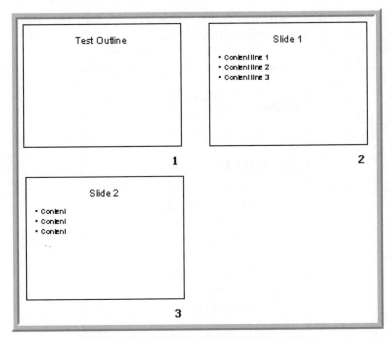

Figure 2-2: Notepad Outline in PPT

Creating An Outline In Word

Using Word to create an outline is simpler because of a feature that integrates the two applications.

Open Word and go to the Outline view (View→Outline). PowerPoint uses the names of the heading styles as the indicators for placement of text. As long as less than five outline levels are used in the presentation, text typed in Word in Outline mode should transfer directly over to PowerPoint slides, in the same manner as the Notepad file.

Keep in mind formatting done on the Word side will not transfer to the PowerPoint file. It may look like some formatting transfers, but this is purely a coincidence. Any settings on the master slides will override any formatting sent from Word. (Master slides are explained in Chapter 17, the template chapter.)

When you are done creating the outline, save the file (so a backup is created) and then go to File→Send to and select PowerPoint from the list. PowerPoint launches and a new document is created with your slides.

An outline created in Word looks something like this:

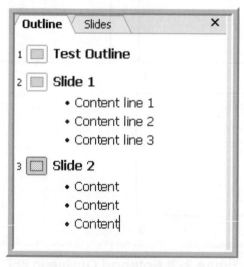

Figure 2-3: Word Outline

This file creates three slides that look like this when viewed with PowerPoint's Slide Sorter view:

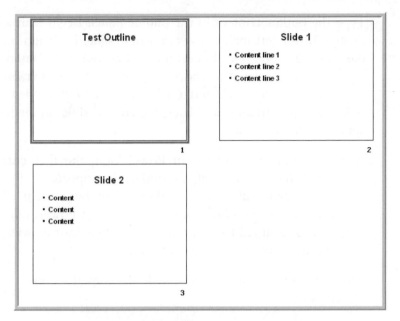

Figure 2-4: Word Outline in PPT

They look a lot like the slides created from Notepad, don't they? There are some differences. And, because Word is designed for working with text, you can use its built-in tools to verify correct spelling, grammar and style usage.

In addition, you can add text between outline entries by viewing the Word document using Word's Normal view. This text is not transferred to PowerPoint, so it can be used for editorial notes, speaker notes and reminders. These notes can be edited at any time.

Creating An Outline In PowerPoint

Creating outlines directly in PowerPoint saves time and energy because you can see the slides being created as you type the outline content.

Outline content is created in Outline view. In PowerPoint 2000 and earlier, this view is shown by going to View→Outline. In PowerPoint 2002 and later, Outline view is on the left-hand side of your screen at all times. To work with the text outline, select the Outline tab (the first one on the outline panel).

Type the outline content in the outline panel. Begin with a line flush with the left margin to start a new slide. Each tab moves the text inward one bullet level. Because the outline is immediately translated to slides, the format of the text can be seen by switching back and forth between Outline view and Normal view. (In 2002 and later, the created slides immediately appear in the main pane.)

When an outline is created in PowerPoint, the first entry is handled differently than if an outline is imported. For an imported outline, all slides are assumed to be content slides. However, when an outline is created natively in PowerPoint, the first slide is assumed to be a title slide. All slides following the first one are assumed to be content slides.

An outline created in PowerPoint looks something like this in Outline view:

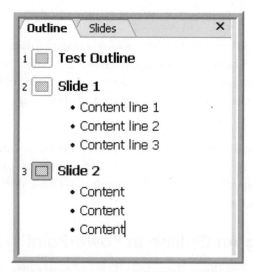

Figure 2-5: PowerPoint Outline

The three slides look like this when viewed in PowerPoint's Slide Sorter view:

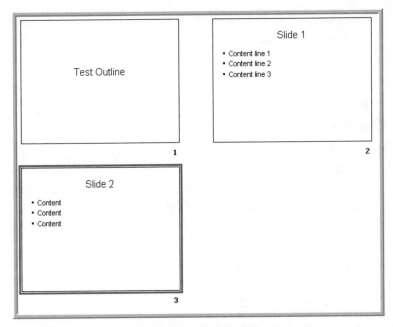

Figure 2-6: PPT Outline

Tip 6: **Turn on the Outlining Toolbar**	Would you like to see your outline formatted? Turn on the Outlining toolbar by right-clicking in any toolbar and clicking on the word Outlining. The toolbar appears down the left side of the screen and: • Quickly promotes and demotes bullets • Creates a summary slide • Sees the outline as formatted text, rather than just as the default Arial text

Now, Generate The Outline

Now that you know what tool you are going to use to create the outline, grab your messages table and start typing.

Note: If the table was created in Excel or Word, cut and paste of the messages into the outline to save yourself additional work.

Start with the most general presentation. Make a slide for each main message. Place the details for that slide underneath the message. If a message needs more than one slide, make the message a title slide with a summary of the information. Then, follow the title slide with one slide for each element in the summary.

Tip 7: Create a Summary Slide	This button, active only in Outline view, creates a new slide listing the title of each slide in the file.
	If PowerPoint encounters a slide without a title while creating the summary slide, it stops processing. If you have a slide with a title you don't want to show, drag the title placeholder off the visible area of the slide.

Content Limitations

Speaker-led presentations

For speaker-led presentations, use no more than five lines of content (six if you count the slide title) on each slide.

Each line of content should have few enough words to be read at a glance by the participants from any corner of the room. Keeping the text for each slide short keeps the audience focused on the information and instead of squinting to read the slide.

Kiosk or self-running presentations

Presentations without a speaker can have more content per slide. If the presentation is going to be fully automated, keep reading speed in mind when determining animation and transition times.

Text-heavy presentations are okay for these presentations, but be careful the presentation is not so text heavy it becomes a challenge for the participant to stay focused. You want them to concentrate on the messages, not the medium.

If you are generating presentations with large amounts of text, generate the outline in Word where spelling, grammar and language tools are available. Use of the word count and reading level tools help keep the content appropriate for the intended audience.

Don't Forget The Graphics And Multimedia

When building the outline, don't forget to leave placeholder slides for non-text slides. For these slides, create a slide title, and then use the bullets to sketch out the purpose, type and message of the slide content.

- Graphs: Describe the type of graph, the data to be presented and any animation to do. Detail what message you want the participants to get from the data presented.

- Movies: Describe the message and the style of the movie, as well as the length of the piece. It is also a good idea to decide if the piece exists already or needs to be created.

- Picture slides: Describe the type of shots, the number of shots to be used and any animation effects to use.

- Clip art slides: Describe the same things as for picture slides but also mention the style of artwork you want.

While creating the outline, the details for the non-text slides are probably not yet known. That is fine. Use the placeholder slides to document what is known and add the rest as it becomes clear.

Alternatives To Outlines

If you don't like working with purely text outlines, there are two alternatives you may want to investigate:

- Storyboarding

- OneNote

Storyboarding

Some presentations do not lend themselves to text outlines very well. In addition, some designers do not think in text, but rather in pictures and content flow. In these cases, *storyboarding,* an alternative to outlining, should be used.

Storyboarding involves developing a series of draft pictures or slide summaries show the messages and information for each slide. Connections between slides can be shown with arrows and numbering schemes. Content may not be as detailed as with an outline and the wording of points is temporarily ignored. Instead, the flow of the content and the presentation's messages are highlighted.

When a presentation relies strongly on visual slides to get its messages across, layered storyboarding can help ensure the presentation flows and the multi-media elements added to the presentation are necessary and complete. Layered storyboarding involves creating an overview storyboard for the main presentation, with sub-storyboards created to detail the movies, pictures or graphics used within the presentation.

Storyboarding is also a good solution when the main messages are known, but brainstorming is needed to flush out the delivery mechanisms. Because of the visual nature of the storyboard, some presentation designers find it a more free-flowing method for presentation design.

OneNote

OneNote is a new product released at the same time as Office System 2003. This product lets you create electronic "notebooks" for keeping track of your ideas. These notebooks are made up of sections relating to topics you create. In addition, each section is made up of a series of pages. Each page can also be named according to what you have included on the page.

OneNote pages can contain text, graphics, chunks of handwriting, data tables, graphics, to-do lists and more. Notes are created by clicking your cursor anywhere on a page and typing, drawing or pasting content.

OneNote creates formatted and ordered text outlines, free-flowing storyboards or any combination of the two. Once the outlines have been saved, the note page can be dragged across to PowerPoint and used as the basis of your presentation.

If any of the content you are using in your outline comes from a web page, drag it to OneNote before you put it in PowerPoint. OneNote automatically annotates the reference with the URL for the site. You can then add that information to the slides as direct content or to the notes as additional information.

Using OneNote for outline development allows you to move between graphical information design and textual information design. If your presentation contains both (and what good presentation doesn't), you may find learning this tool worth the time.

This page left intentionally blank.

3. Developing The PowerPoint File

- ➢ Before You Start
- ➢ Creating a Text Presentation from a Template and an Outline
- ➢ Placeholders
- ➢ Adding Pictures
- ➢ Auto Shapes
- ➢ Adding Sounds
- ➢ Simple Animation
- ➢ Slide Transitions
- ➢ Setting Up a Show to Run
- ➢ Hidden Slides
- ➢ Custom Shows

By following the advice in Chapter 2, Jane was able to develop an outline for her informational, speaker-led presentation. She built the outline in Word and sent it to PowerPoint.

As preparation for using PowerPoint, I gave her *10 Things to Do Before Doing Anything in PowerPoint.*

Before You Start

I recommend adjusting a few default settings before creating the PowerPoint file. These are things that should always be checked when working on a new installation of PowerPoint, regardless of the version.

1. Turn off the Fast Saves feature

2. Turn on the AutoRecover feature

3. Verify the default save location

4. Install drivers for a local printer

5. Adjust your Most Recently Used files list

6. Verify the size of WAV files to be included in your files

7. Adjust the number of undos

8. Turn off Background Printing

9. Verify Macro Security Level

10. Adjust automatic layout options

One thing Jane learned is to check these things any time you change to a new computer. These settings go with the computer, not the presentation. Since Jane was developing her presentations at the office and at home, she needed to make the adjustments on two PCs.

Turn Off Fast Saves

Fast saves sounds like something everyone would want, right? The idea behind this option is to allow only the changed parts of the file to be saved, therefore shortening the time to save the file. Only one problem: historically, fast saves has caused more corrupted presentation files than any other culprit.

When PowerPoint does a fast save, it guesses what has changed. It can mess with file structure, place actual changes at the end of the file and adjusts pointers inside the file to record what was changed. When PowerPoint is closed, the various edits are pulled together into the main body of the file.

Because PowerPoint is trying to keep track of every action taken, the file size grows exponentially. The tradeoff originally became the time between a fast save while editing and the disk space it used. While the feature worked properly, it came with the side effect that the chances of the file corruption are now increased exponentially.

Instead, I recommend turning off fast saves and doing regular saves. This way, every time the save button is pressed, the full file is saved as a straight PowerPoint file and no interpretation is needed upon re-open, which in turn requires less disk space.

Tip 8: Sequential Saves	In addition to turning off Fast Saves, I strongly recommend you get Microsoft PowerPoint MVP Shyam Pillai's Sequential Save add-in. This add-in is available from his site for free. It adds a button to your toolbar you use instead of the regular Save button.
	Once the add-in has been set up for a file, it automatically saves your file under a new name each time you click the button. No more lost presentations!
	The URL for the add-in is:
	www.mvps.org/skp/seqsave.htm

To turn off Fast Saves, select Tools → Options. Select the Save tab and remove the checkmark from Allow Fast Saves.

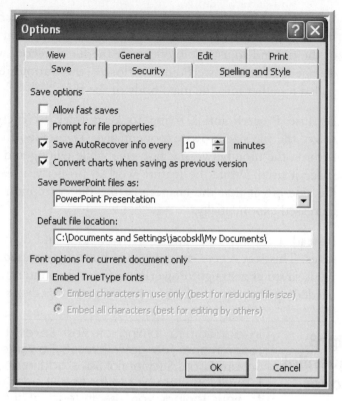

Figure 3-1: Save Options

Turn On Autorecover

Unlike Fast Saves, AutoRecover is a useful option. This option creates snapshots of your file and stores the snapshot in a temporary file. The name of this file is created by taking the first two characters of the filename and replacing them with "~$".

Setting AutoRecover causes less data and work to be lost if PowerPoint or the computer crashes. Unless saving files every ten or fifteen minutes is an unbreakable habit, this option can save you quite a bit of re-work.

Make the time setting long enough to not interfere with or slow down work, but short enough to prevent loss of large amounts of work.

As shown in Figure 3-1, 10 minutes is a good, round choice. Make sure the checkbox is checked to turn the option on.

Verify Default Save Location

Default File Location (shown in Figure 3-1) defines the location where PowerPoint looks for files to open and where it saves your files by default. By setting up your own save location, you ensure the files are stored where you want them, instead of where PowerPoint thinks you want them.

The default for the save location is My Documents. If you use My Documents, then you don't need to change the setting. However, if you store the documents elsewhere on the hard drive, change the directory name and save some time and mouse clicks when you open or save files.

Install Drivers For A Local Printer

In order for PowerPoint to run correctly, a local printer must be defined. PowerPoint uses this local printer definition to determine available fonts, default page setup information and several other options. If you don't have a local printer defined, PowerPoint may run, but in a very limited manner. It won't be able to find the fonts on your system or do a print preview.

Even if your computer uses a network printer all the time, install a local set of print drivers. In general, the process to add a printer is to bring up the Control Panel and select Printers. Select to add a printer and work through the wizard.

Adjust Your Recently Used File List

While it is not required the number of files in the recently used list be adjusted, the default value of 4 is generally too low. The maximum allowed value is 9, but I recommend 6. To change the number, click to the General tab on the Options window (see Figure 3-2). Adjust the number up to as far as desired and ensure the checkbox is selected.

Verify The Size Of WAV Files To Be Included In Your Files

Multimedia files other than WAV files are not included in the PowerPoint file, but are linked to the file. WAV files are only included if your sound file is smaller than the value indicated on the General Tab.

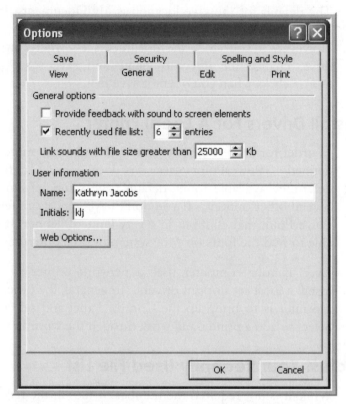

Figure 3-2: General Options

PowerPoint defaults to a value too low for realistic usage. If you create presentations that include WAV files, set the size to any number up to 50000 Kb (that's 50 MB). To make it easy on myself, I set the number to the maximum value and leave it.

The only time I set this number lower is when I am working with a presentation in which I don't want the sounds ever included in the PowerPoint file. Then, I set the value to a very low number so all sounds are linked.

Adjust Number Of Undos

PowerPoint allows a maximum of 150 actions to remain on the undo list. Don't do it. The more actions on your undo list, the more space and memory PowerPoint needs to store the information.

Similar to fast saves, keeping track of this many actions can cause PowerPoint to become lost. This results in program crashes and file corruption.

As can be seen in Figure 3-3, 20 (the default) is a good, round number. It is high enough to allow you to change your mind about actions, but low enough to avoid document corruption. So why mention it? Because there are times when you may want to have your value higher or lower than the default. If you are trying out different fonts, styles or pictures in a presentation, you may want to set the number of undos to a higher number temporarily, allowing you to play around with changes, but still go back to the original set up.

If you are low on disk and/or temporary space, set this number to a very low number. The lower the number, the less temporary information PowerPoint keeps around and the less space it needs for a file.

If working on a number of presentations at once, do the same: Set the undo number lower so each presentation has more memory with which to work.

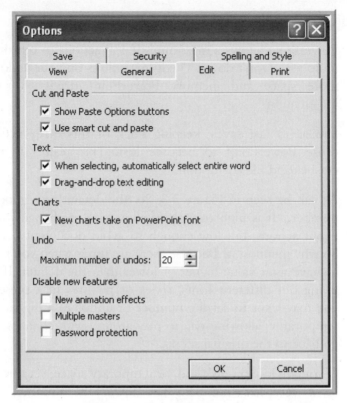

Figure 3-3: Edit Options

Turn Off Background Printing

Background printing allows PowerPoint to print the document while you continue to work on it. The side effect is the computer may slow down. Your ability to edit and move around in the document may be impaired while the presentation prints.

PowerPoint is enough of a resource hog that turning this option on can be hazardous to the performance of a computer. It won't cause crashes, but it usually slows down the entire computer, limiting what you can work on until it is finished printing.

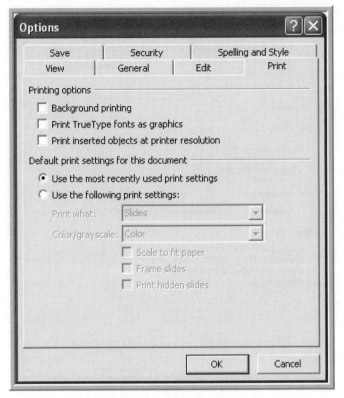

Figure 3-4: Print Options

In general, keep background printing turned off, as shown in Figure 3-4. If you need to background print, turn it back on by checking the box on the Print tab of the Options window.

Verify Macro Security Level

Your security level setting determines which macros can be run from within PowerPoint, if any. To get to the Macro Security information, go to the Security tab of the Options window (see Figure 3-5).

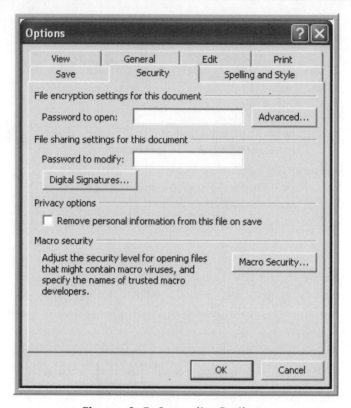

Figure 3-5: Security Options

Click the Macro Security button to choose the level of macro security you wish to use (see Figure 3-6). The Security window sets up both the security level and the trusted sources for the macros. Trusted sources relate to digitally signed macros. Digitally signed macros can generally be trusted to be virus free. You shouldn't need to worry about the trusted sources tab, but you should set the security level as you expect to need it.

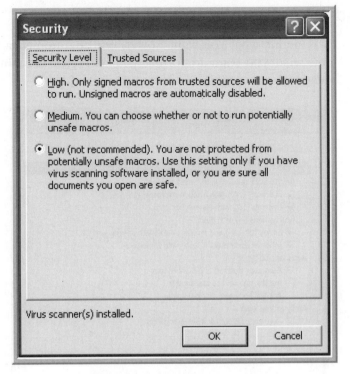

Figure 3-6: Security Levels

If you don't expect to run macros, the security level can be left at the default level of High. This turns off all macro functions.

If you don't know whether macros will be run regularly, select medium security. This option allows the user to decide on a case-by-case basis whether to enable macros to run.

If you expect macros will be developed and used frequently on a machine, set the macro security level to low. This will prevent annoying security messages from coming up. Be aware this allows all macros to be run. If you open a PowerPoint File with a macro virus in it, you will not be protected from the virus.

You are done with the Options window for now. Close it and move to the Tools→AutoCorrect Options.

Adjust Automatic Layout Options

You define what you want PowerPoint to automatically format and what you want to format yourself from the AutoCorrect window.

Figure 3-7: AutoFormat Options

Unless you want PowerPoint to define a lot of the formatting on the slides, turn off the bottom three options. Leaving them on allows PowerPoint to adjust cut and paste items to fit into the placeholders or objects.

The two AutoFit options ignore any formatting done via the slide master (the template) or on the slide itself. Having these options on changes the size of the text so it all fits in the placeholder. This means if you put in a lot of text, the font may become smaller than defined by the master and if you put in a small amount of text the font may become larger than defined by the master. Automatic layout for inserted objects changes your slide layout if you add certain shapes or items. Since it is likely that you want to make these decisions, remove the checks from these boxes and move on.

Creating A Text Presentation From A Template And An Outline

Now that Jane has her computer set up, it is time to take the outline she created and turn it into a presentation. The first step is to select a template for the presentation. Once that is done, we apply the template to the real presentation and verify it looks great.

What Is A Template?

A PowerPoint template is a PowerPoint file with the extension "pot." The template contains master slides and other elements to create and apply changes to the presentation quickly and consistently. It determines the look and feel of the presentation. PowerPoint comes with a fairly large selection of pre-created templates. In addition, many other template sources can be found in the resources area of Appendix A.

Basic template files consist of a *slide master*, a special type of PowerPoint slide containing no content, only formatting. Templates define the format of the text, the background of the slide, the format of the bullets and other features of a slide. All content slides in the presentation inherit the formatting defined by the master slide.

Most template files also have a title master slide defined. This master slide contains formatting applied automatically to any title slide. When a title slide is added, it takes all of its formatting from the current title slide master.

Tip 9: **Multiple Masters**	In PowerPoint 2000 and earlier, only one master slide and one title slide are allowed in a presentation. In PowerPoint 2002 and later, multiple master and title slides are allowed.
	Multiple masters can be very useful for presentations where some of the content needs to be visibly set apart from the main presentation.

Template files may also include a handout master and a notes page master. The final part of a template is the color scheme. Color schemes are easy ways to change the basic colors used in the presentation. Color schemes are discussed in Chapter 5.

Which Templates Come With PowerPoint?

The templates installed with PowerPoint depend on the version as well as the type of installation performed (complete, custom or typical). For PowerPoint 2002, over 40 templates are installed with a complete install. Each installed template contains a background, text formatting and a series of pre-defined color schemes.

To see the templates installed on a specific computer, perform the following steps:

In PowerPoint 2000 And Earlier, Do One Of The Following:

- Right click on a slide and select Apply Design Template from the menu.
- From the main menu, select Format→Apply Design Template.

The Apply Design Template window lists each template available with a template preview shown in the right-hand pane.

In PowerPoint 2002 And Later, Do One Of The Following:

- Right click on a slide and select Slide Design from the menu. A taskbar containing thumbnail pictures of each of the templates installed on the machine appears on the right side of the screen.

- Select Format→Slide Design. A taskbar containing thumbnail pictures of each of the templates installed on the machine appears on the right side of the screen.

- Select File→New. The New Presentation taskbar appears on the right of the screen. Click on General Templates, the Templates window opens.

Tip 10: Microsoft Template Packs	With the release of Office 2003, Microsoft developed three template packages available from their website. These three downloads contain the complete set of Microsoft templates available from PowerPoint 4.0 and upward. The templates in each pack are in alphabetical order however, the packs were not created in alphabetical order. The first pack contains templates with names starting with letters between A and E; the second pack, Q to Z; the third pack, F to P.

Select And Apply A Template

Now that we know templates are available on the machine, it is time to play around a little and check out which templates you like. I have created a short presentation I use to check out templates when I get them. I adapted this presentation for use in this chapter. I recommend that, rather than playing with the actual outline, create your own temporary presentation and use it for these next few steps.

PowerPoint's default template formats your text in a standard font, with black lettering on a white background. This template is called Blank Presentation.pot in PowerPoint 2000 and earlier versions; Blank.pot in PowerPoint 2002 and later.

Opening my test outline with the default template gives a slide that looks like this:

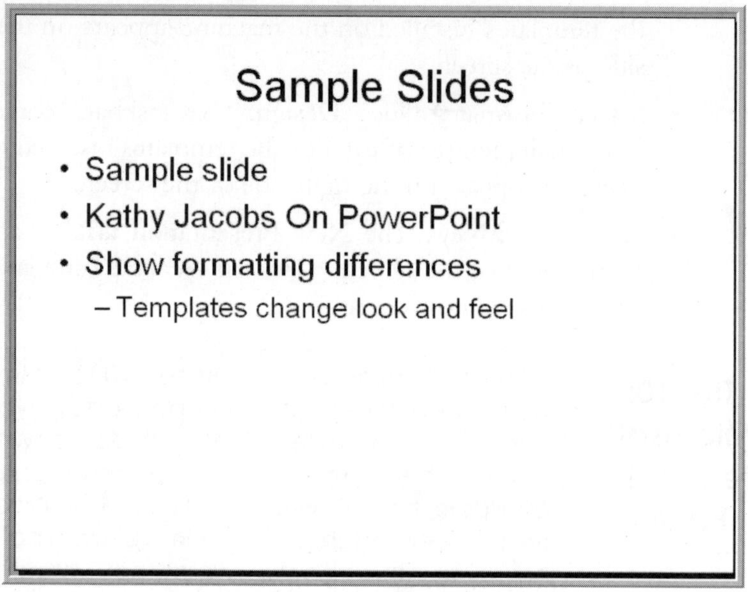

Sample Slides

- Sample slide
- Kathy Jacobs On PowerPoint
- Show formatting differences
  - Templates change look and feel

Figure 3-8: Default Template

The entire look and feel of the presentation changes when a template is applied. Templates are usually designed to help emphasize a message or to unify a presentation's look and feel.

Application of different templates can make the same content convey different messages. Template changes can make content more formal or less formal, change where the emphasis goes or change the background so the presentation can be viewed in different environments and lighting situations.

Look at Figure 3-9, 16, 17, 18. Each picture shows the text used in my sample slide with a different template applied. Think about the audience to which the template is aimed. Think about how the template changes the message of the text.

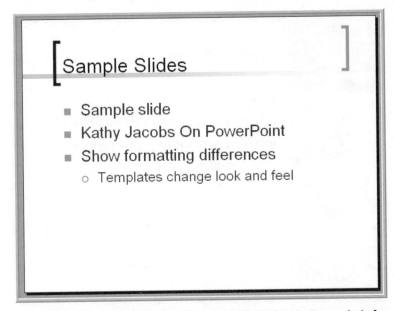

Figure 3-9: PowerPoint Sample Slide (Axis Template)

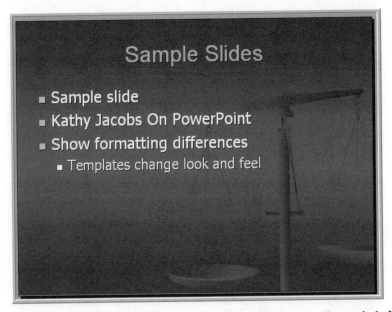

Figure 3-10: PowerPoint Sample Slide (Balance Template)

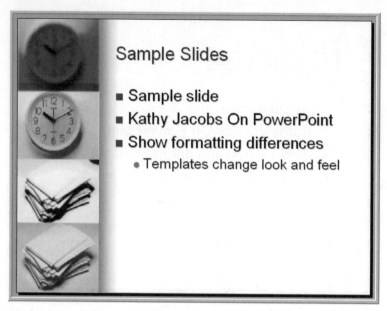

Figure 3-11: PowerPoint Sample Slide (Proposal Template)

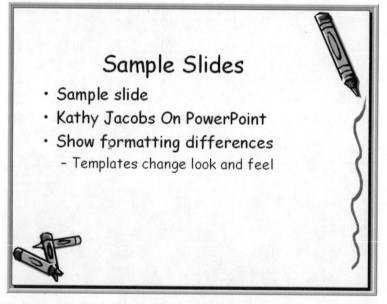

Figure 3-12: PowerPoint Sample Slide (Crayons Template)

Now, take a few minutes and play around with your test presentation. Look at how the templates change the text when applied to the presentation.

Verify And Save Your Presentation

When you have found a template that matches the message emphasis and audience for the presentation, open the outline and apply the template to it, just as you did on the test outline. Whenever applying a template to an outline or existing presentation, page through the slides to make sure everything still fits within the slides. You may find the font changes and the layout changes have made the text too long, pushing it below the bottom edge of the slides. You need to decide whether to shorten the text or split the slide.

Save the presentation to the hard drive under a new name. The text outline has now been converted to a basic PowerPoint presentation. It is now ready to be enhanced into a full-fledged, full-featured PowerPoint presentation.

Jane chose a template called "Maple." It is a simple template with maple leaves on the background and clean fonts. She felt this background would fit well with the yard work project.

Placeholders

Did you notice the text from the outline was placed in specific areas on the slides? These areas are called *Placeholders*. Placeholders are special-use holders for slide elements such as text, graphs, graphics, multimedia items, etc.

All versions of PowerPoint recognize the same placeholders. With the exception of text placeholders, there can be only one of each type per slide. For text placeholders, there can be only two placeholders on any given slide. You will be able to have more than one of each element on a given slide, but only the first one(s) can be in placeholders. None of them have to be in placeholders, but not using placeholders makes formatting changes harder to do.

The content from the outline went into title, sub-title or text placeholders. Since you need to work with all of the placeholder types, let's review each type:

- Title placeholders contain the title of the slide. Besides being a good focal point for a slide, this placeholder helps presenters know their location in the show. Even if you do not plan to show a title on a given slide, you should always make a title for each slide. If you do not want the title to show, drag it off the slide.

- Sub-titles are special-case text placeholders. They contain regular text instead of bulleted text. They only appear on title slides. They show up in the outline as text without a bullet.

- Text placeholders contain bulleted list text. Text in this place holder can be indented up to five levels.

Tip 11: What text animates?	In PowerPoint 2000 and earlier versions, only placeholder text can be animated to enter a slide one line at a time.
	In PowerPoint 2002 and later, this restriction has been removed.

- Clip art placeholders allow a graphic from the clip gallery to be inserted onto the slide. Inserted graphics may be photographs, clip art or other graphics.

- Chart placeholders contain the data and chart for information inserted via MS Graph. See Chapter 10 for more on MS Graph.

- Media clip placeholders allow an animated graphic, movie clip or sound effect to be selected from the clip gallery and inserted onto the slide.

- Table placeholders allow a PowerPoint table to be inserted. These tables should be used for layout purposes only. They do not have any additional functionality, such as totaling columns, etc. In PowerPoint 97, the tables were actually Word tables.

- Diagram or Organization Chart placeholders allow a variety of diagrams using PowerPoint's diagramming tool to be inserted. PowerPoint 2000 and earlier versions only allow Organization Charts to be built and inserted, while PowerPoint 2002 and later versions allow a variety of diagrams to be built. See Chapter 10 for more information on these two tools.

You can format placeholders by hand. Since they inherit any formatting done on the master slide, it makes more sense to do the formatting on the master and limit slide-by-slide adjustments to a minimum. Using masters to do the formatting increases your productivity and the consistency of the look and feel of the slides.

Adding Content With Placeholders

Add content to placeholders by clicking in the placeholder. For text or title placeholders, single click the placeholder to add text. For other placeholders, a double-click adds the appropriate item.

Multipurpose Placeholders – A Special Case

In PowerPoint 2002, the Content placeholder was added. These placeholders allow the user to add a variety of content types with a single placeholder. It can contain a table, chart, piece of clip art, picture, diagram, organization chart or media clip.

 Content placeholders have a multi-use icon in the center. To use multipurpose placeholders, double-click on the icon representing the object type you want to add.

Selecting Slide Designs

Use the Slide Layout options to determine which placeholders will show on any single slide. Access the layout choices in one of two ways:

- Right-Click → Slide Layout
- Format → Slide Layout

The steps to access the layouts are the same from version to version, but the information is presented differently.

In PowerPoint 2000 and earlier versions, the slide layouts are presented in a scrollable message window. The layouts are listed sequentially, with no sub-sections.

There are two screens of slide layouts available:

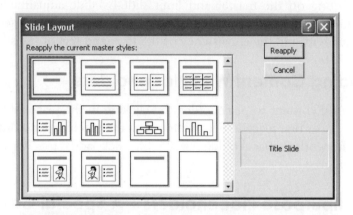

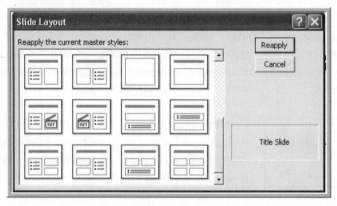

Figure 3-13: PPT 2000 and earlier Slide Layouts

In PowerPoint 2002 and later versions, the slide layouts are in a scrolling task pane. The layouts split into four sub-sections.

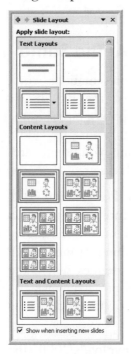 

Figure 3-14: PPT 2002 and later Slide Layouts

Note: If you use PowerPoint for very long, you may want to add new placeholders to the presentations. Unfortunately, no existing PowerPoint version allows you to do it.

Adding Pictures

Now that you have chosen a template, the basic text and formatting are done. It is time to add some pictures and other graphics.

Pictures are added one at a time to any given slide using any of the content or clip art placeholders. To do this, set the layout for the slide to either the clipart or the multi-purpose placeholder. Double-click the placeholder, browse to the picture and insert it.

Pictures can also be added one at a time via the Insert→ Picture menu. This inserts graphics of almost any kind either via direct creation or from a file.

Adding Multiple Pictures At The Same Time

Jane knew one of her future presentations would be a status report on the project. One of the big drawbacks of that presentation is the section of photographs from the first few cleanup projects. She didn't want to add each photo individually. Lucky for her, and you, there are two add-ins available to make this task much easier.

- Photo Album – New in PowerPoint 2002, this add-in makes a shape for each picture and sets the background for the shape to the picture. To use this feature, use Insert→ Picture → New Photo Album. Once the Photo Album window appears, the user defines where the pictures are going and what the album layout will look like. A PowerPoint 2000 version of the add-in is available from Microsoft at URL:

    office.microsoft.com/Downloads/2000/album.aspx

- Image Importer – Developed by Shyam Pillai, this commercial add-in picks up where the photo album add-in lets off. In addition to the ability to pick where pictures come from and how they look when inserted, this add-in also allows the user to set up captions, sequential ordering, automatic linking and many other useful options. It is available for download from here:

    www.mvps.org/skp/iiw.htm

Auto Shapes

While text and pictures are the backbone of any presentation, there are times when you need to add content that is visual, but for which the appropriate graphic is not already created. AutoShapes allow standard shapes to be easily turned into great graphics.

What Shapes Are Available?

The shapes have been categorized into nine basic categories. Each category of shape has several different optional shapes to choose from.

- Lines: 6 types of straight and curved lines, with and without arrows on the ends.

- Connectors: 9 mechanisms for connecting shapes and lines to each other

- Basic shapes: 32 shapes, including squares, circles, faces, etc.

- Block Arrows: 28 different wide arrows, including curved, straight and corner arrows.

- Flowchart Symbols: 28 useful symbols for charting process and code flows.

- Stars and Banners: 8 different stars and 8 different banners for adding emphasis to text

- Callouts: 4 thought balloons and 16 different boxes for marking information on a chart or diagram

- Action Buttons: 8 basic buttons used on web pages

- More AutoShapes: Customizable list of clip art items that can be used like autoshapes (see page 66 for more details)

How Are Shapes Added?

When viewing slides in edit mode, there is an AutoShapes button in the bottom left corner of the screen. This button provides a selection of basic shapes. Once the shape is created, it can be customized as desired.

To insert a shape, click and hold the AutoShape button. Slide up to the category you want and then to the specific shape. Release the mouse button. Now, either click on the slide or click and drag on the slide to insert your shape. Clicking inserts the default sized shape. Clicking and dragging inserts a shape of any size desired.

In one area of Jane's presentation, she wants to show a person thinking about the project and trying to decide whether to participate. She already has a picture of a woman, but she wants to add a thought balloon. First, she needs to select the callout autoshape that looks like a thought balloon. When she clicks on her slide with the shape selected, she gets a thought balloon, but the balloon isn't quite what Jane wants. Jane knows she can change almost everything about the shape, including its size and orientation, text, background color and edge color. She now is going to combine these options to make the woman in the image "think."

Changing The Shape

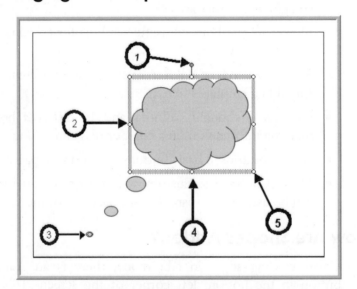

Figure 3-15: Modifying an AutoShape

See Jane's thought balloon in Figure 3-15. Notice it is surrounded by a gray box with eight small white boxes imbedded in it. These boxes are *handles*. They allow the size and orientation of the shape to be adjusted. Each item on the selected shape changes something different.

1. The green dot at the top of the autoshape only appears in PowerPoint 2002 and later. It allows the autoshape to be rotated.

2. The white boxes on the left and right side of shape change the size of the shape vertically.

3. The yellow diamond changes the orientation of shape. It appears on each AutoShape. In the case of the thought balloon, it allows the balloon to be connected directly to the head of a character, showing what the character is thinking.

4. The white boxes on the top and bottom of the shape change the size of the shape horizontally.

5. The handles on the corners do a proportional change both vertically and horizontally.

Figure 3-16: Add Text to an AutoShape

Now we need to know what the person is thinking. One way to do this is to add text to the thought balloon.

To add text, right click inside the thought balloon and select Edit Text. You can now type text directly into the autoshape. The text appears in the default text format for the presentation. The look of the text can be changed by selecting the text and choosing Format→Font. In PowerPoint 97, you can double click a shape to add text. In the newer versions, this only works with textboxes.

Did the balloon change its size as text was typed? This happens when auto-resize is turned on. To prevent this from happening, right-click on the shape and select Format AutoShape. From the Text Box tab, clear the Resize AutoShape to fit text checkbox. Notice there are other options here as well. For example, the start location of the text can be changed from the top of the shape to the bottom or middle of the shape.

Change The Color And Edge Of The Shape

Now the basic shape has been established, we need to change what is inside the thought balloon, behind the text. There are more fill and line options in PowerPoint than we have space to cover here, so let's cover some of the more useful ones.

To change the background of the autoshape, right-click and select Format, AutoShape and click on the Colors and Lines tab. Examples of what can be done:

1. Colored background, no line – Set the fill to a color other than white and set the line color to none.

2. White background, colored line – Set the fill color to white and the line color to blue.

3. Turtle Clip - Set the fill color to a piece of clip art and the line to a blue, one-point line. On the dropdown box for color, select Fill Effects. From the Picture, select a picture or graphic. PowerPoint fills the balloon with the picture. Another picture effect can be achieved by selecting the Pattern tab and selecting the picture or graphic for the pattern.

4. Gradient with fine line - Set the fill color to a gradient and the line to a burgundy, two-point line. On the dropdown box for color, select Fill Effects. From the Gradient tab, choose a preset gradient or create one.

5. Background with a line - Set the fill color to none and the line to a blue, one-point line. This allows content behind the shape to show through. In this case, it shows the background.

6. Background fill with a line - Set the fill color to the background and the line to a blue, one-point line. To accomplish this, select background from the color dropdown box. This takes the background color or design and uses it to fill the shape. If the background is changed, the shape background changes as well. The difference between this and the previous choice is the background is centered in the shape here, where the other shape shows the section of the background the shape is over.

After setting everything up, Jane's final slide looks like this:

Figure 3-17: The File Slide

To Set Default Shape Properties

There are many times when you know the settings for a shape are going to be used over and over during your presentation. PowerPoint simplifies this by saving the shape properties as the default for new shapes.

Go to the properties for the shape to be duplicated (Format →
AutoShape). At the bottom of the Color and Lines tab, there is a check box labeled Default for new objects. Check this box and all future shapes default to the setting on this tab. Shapes can still be customized, but they start out being formatted more closely to the desired result.

What More Can I Do?

Remember the More AutoShapes option I mentioned earlier? Well, that option takes the autoshape functionality and applies it to basic clip art pieces, which gives the option of changing the background color or the line style of all clips. In addition, on simple clips, you can even change the color of the shapes themselves

Adding Sounds

Now that Jane has created all of her slides, she wants to add some sounds and a narration file. She knows sound files in a presentation can be a great addition or a great distraction. She also has learned all sounds must be tied to the message of the slide or they really don't serve their purpose.

PowerPoint sounds break down into a number of categories:

- Sound effects – Short clips attached to a specific action. These clips are generally only a few seconds long and are used as a trigger for the participants.

- Music clips and Background sounds – Used to add interest to a presentation, especially graphics presentations and photo albums. These clips are longer than sound effects and are used to sustain interest across a section of a presentation.

- Narration – Verbal additions to the presentation used to explain the slide content. These sounds are used for kiosks presentations or self-running presentations.

Presentation sounds of all types can either be included in the presentation file or linked from another location. The only sound files included in presentation files are WAV files and narration. All other presentation sounds are linked. Linking of sounds will be covered in Chapter 9.

Adding Sounds And Narration

Basic sounds are added via the Insert → Movies and Sounds menu. You can add sounds from the Clip Organizer, a file or a

CD-Rom. Narrations are either recorded directly into the slide or linked in from pre-created sound files.

Basic Sounds

Sounds are represented on the slide by a megaphone icon, which indicates a sound file, or by a CD icon, which indicates the sound file came from a CD.

When adding sounds from a CD, the Movies and Sound Options window appears (Figure 3-18). This window determines which tracks are played and gives the ability to loop the sound continuously. If you don't set the sound to loop until stopped, it plays only once.

Figure 3-18: Movie and Sound Options

Basic Narration

Narration is added via Slide Show → Record Narration. The Record Narration window (Figure 3-19) customizes the development of your narration.

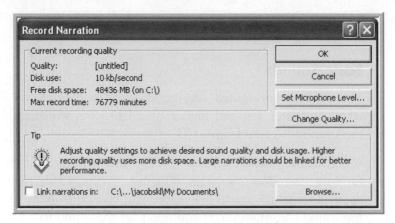

Figure 3-19: Record Narration

When recording narrations, you can only adjust quality levels at the start of narration. Later adjustments must be done outside of PowerPoint. Keep in mind the trade-off between the quality of the sound and the size of the file. The better the sound quality, the bigger the PowerPoint file will be. The bigger the file, the more stress PowerPoint puts on a computer when running the presentation.

When a sound is inserted, the presentation creator chooses whether to start the sound automatically or to require the sound icon be clicked. No matter which option is taken, the decision can be changed later from the animation options.

Tip 12: Get the rights!	If the presentation contains music, you must get publication rights to use the file from any performers, the author of any lyrics and the composer of the music before distributing the presentation. In general, all these rights come together as a package deal.

Don't Want The Icon To Show?

If a sound or piece of narration is set to start automatically, it is usually better to hide the icon on the slide. However, for purposes of slide editing, you'll still want to know which slides have sounds on them. Click once on the sound icon and drag it off the slide, if desired. The sound still plays at the specified time and for the specified interval, but the icon is not visible on the screen.

Playing Sounds For Large Audiences

When you play a presentation with sounds in front of a large audience, test out the sounds in the actual space before the audience gets there. To be sure everyone can hear the sounds, hook into the sound system for the room. If this isn't possible, use regular external speakers so sounds are loud enough for everyone to hear.

Simple Animation

The next step in creating the basic presentation is to decide when and where animation will be used and add it to the slides. The use of animation, like the use of sound, is something that should be considered carefully and planned out before it is implemented.

Think about the presentations you have watched. When there were animations, did they add to the content and messages of the presentation, or did they distract you? If you found yourself watching for the animations, you likely were watching a presentation with too much animation. On the other hand, if there is no animation, the presentation can become boring.

So how do you know when to use animation? Having all the text enter a slide at one time can be useful if you keep the slide content short and focused. However, if you have extensive textual content, or if setting up a kiosk, you want to be able to keep the audience's attention on what you are saying and not on what you will be saying next. You can do this with simple animation effects.

To prevent audience boredom, add some simple animations to the slide contents, without overwhelming the content. A presentation with no effects would be very boring to watch.

Tip 13: Consistent Animation	When adding animation to a presentation, it can be very tempting to use as much animation as possible, in as many different ways as possible. This is not a good thing!
	To keep presentations looking professional, decide ahead of time what will be animated and how each item will be animated. Use similar animation settings on similar objects and text, and the animation itself becomes a trigger for the participants.
	It is even helpful to create a storyboard for the animations if you have a lot of different settings on a single slide.

Accessing The Animation Options

In all versions of PowerPoint, animations can be accessed via either the Slide Show → Custom Animation menu item or via the Custom Animation menu item on the right-click menu. In order to access these options via the right-click menu, you must first left-click to select an object to be animated.

In PowerPoint 2000 and earlier versions, these actions bring up the Custom Animation window. In PowerPoint 2002 and later versions, they bring up the Custom Animation Taskbar.

Because animation of elements changed drastically between PowerPoint 2000 and PowerPoint 2002, the later version makes a big difference in how you animate the objects. We cover the PowerPoint 2000 animation process first, then present PowerPoint 2002 And Later on page 74.

PowerPoint 2000 And Earlier Versions

Figure 3-20 shows the Custom Animation window used in 2000 and earlier. Animations in these versions are straightforward entrance and emphasis effects. Timed effects follow a simple timeline. One effect is done at a time, with gaps of 0 seconds or greater between animations. Effects are initiated by either the click of a mouse or by the passage of time.

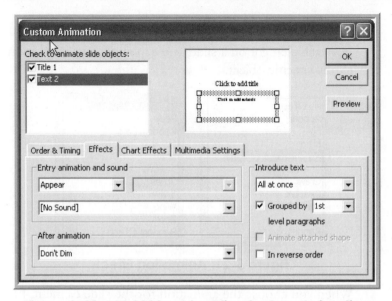

Figure 3-20: PPT 2000 and earlier Custom Animation

Each element on the slide can be animated by checking the box next to the element name. To apply animations, click on the Effects tab. Click on the Order & Timing tab to change the timing and order of element animations. Charts and multimedia elements each have tabs for the options related to animating those items. Chart animation options are covered in Chapter 10. Multimedia settings are covered on page 85.

Unless the template used for the presentation has animations on its master, the default animation for each item is No effect. Setting an effect is the first step to animation.

The Effects Tab

For each element on a slide, you can apply one of 18 animations to any specific object.

Figure 3-21: Animation Effects

When you choose the animation for the slide element, the other options on the tab become available and the tab changes to look like Figure 3-22:

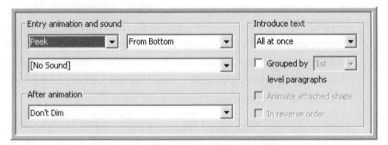

Figure 3-22: Animation Options

Now, you can customize the animation to your specific needs. First, set how the object appears on the slide during the presentation. For Peek, the options are from top, bottom, left or right. For Flash, the options determine how quickly the object will flash. Several animations do not allow any customization, so this box remains grayed out.

Next, decide if you want an entrance sound. If you do, keep it very short. Be careful when using entrance sounds; the sound plays every time the animation is played. If overused, entrance sounds can be very annoying for audience members.

The After animation options allow the user to change the look of the shape or text after the animation occurs. Options available include changing the shape to a different color, hiding the object after animation, hiding the object on the next mouse click or leaving the object as it started out.

The right side of this box decides how much of the text is introduced at once: an entire bullet at once, one word at a time or one character at a time. You can also choose whether to animate the attached shape and whether to bring in the text from the top or the bottom of the list.

For placeholder text, you can modify how much of the placeholder text to enter at one time: all of it or grouped by paragraph levels. If you are going to bring in the placeholder text by paragraph levels, it is best to set the grouping to be equal to or one level higher than the number of bullet levels on the slide.

Animate attached shapes is only available when text is in an autoshape has an animation predefined. For example, if using an animated gif, decide whether to animate it along with the text. When set, it allows the autoshape animation to play during entrance of text. This is another option to use cautiously, as it can sometimes be more distracting than useful.

In reverse order sets the text to enter and be animated from bottom to top. Think of this as a way to create top ten lists, where the least important elements are at the bottom of the list but should be revealed first. This option is only available if the grouped by box is checked.

The Order & Timing Tab

Once elements have animations defined, decide when each animation will occur and how each animation will start.

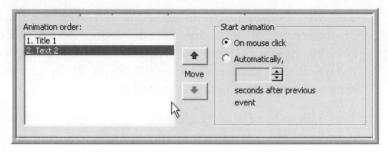

Figure 3-23: Animation Timing

The default order is the order in which the objects were created. The default start method is On mouse click. Very seldom will you find either the order or the start method has defaulted to what you actually want to do.

To change the order, click on an item in the list and move it up or down using the arrows in the center of the tab. Choose the start method by clicking on the appropriate radio button. For automatic animations, a time delay needs to be set for each animation. The default is zero seconds. The maximum delay is 59 minutes and 59 seconds.

When finished setting up the animations, click the preview button to see how they flow together. If they don't flow the way you want, make changes and preview it again. Once you are satisfied with the flow, click OK to save the changes. Repeat the process with each slide.

Tip 14: **Master** **Animation**	To start with the same base animation for each slide, put your animations on the master slide. Each slide in the presentation inherits the settings. You can then adapt your individual slides as needed.

PowerPoint 2002 And Later Versions

Animations in 2002 can be much more complex then in earlier versions. PowerPoint 2002 added exit animations, enhanced the entrance and emphasis animations, and added many other options to the animation pallet. Because the animations are organized along a more complex animation timeline, these versions also let you set up multiple animations to occur at the same time.

Combining several of the more extensive animation options with the new types of effects added in PowerPoint 2002 gives presentation developers a much wider range of animation options. Details on using the more complex animation options available in PowerPoint 2002 and later are provided in Chapter 6. For now, we'll focus on creating basic entrance and emphasis animations.

To work with its animation properties, right-click on the object. The Animation Pane appears on the right side of the PowerPoint desktop. An empty animation pane looks like this:

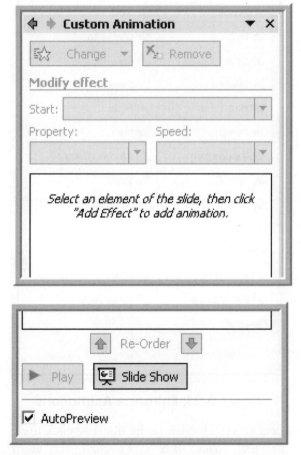

Figure 3-24: PPT 2002 and later Animation

To animate an object on a slide, bring up the Animation Pane as discussed on page 70. Select the object and the entrance effect you want to use.

Basic Entrance Animations

To select the entrance effect desired, click on the dropdown box next to the words Add Effect. Slide down to the Entrance Effects entry, then over to either the effect desired or the More Effects menu entry.

Figure 3-25: Entrance Animations

To select an effect, click on its title and click the OK button. If the Preview Effect box is checked, the animation will be performed as the effect is selected.

Tip 15: What do the icons mean?	There is a star-based icon in front of each animation name. These icons show how the animation is executed. Options include: • Animations that happen to an object statically (such as appear or flash once) • Animations that cause an object to change while animating (such as diamond, circle or box) • Animations that take an object along a simple path (such as fly in or crawl in) • Animations that affect the size of the object while animating (such as expand) • Animations that affect the appearance of the object during animation (such as color changing animations)

Next, tell PowerPoint when to start the effect. When you add an effect to an object, it defaults to the on click start method In many cases, you will want to change to one of the other start methods. There are three basic ways an animation can be started:

- On Click – Occurs when the object is clicked during the presentation
- With Previous – Occurs as the previous animation completes
- After Previous – Occurs a set number of seconds after the previous animation completes

To set up when you want the animation to start, click the Start dropdown arrow and select the option to use.

For many of the entrance effects, there are two other effect options that need to be set. These options are Direction and Speed. If the AutoPreview box is selected, option changes are previewed on the screen as they change.

For emphasis, Jane wants the title on the main slide to appear in a checkerboard pattern. She wants the checkerboard to run from top to bottom at a medium speed when the mouse is clicked. After setting up her animation, the top portion of the Animation Pane changes to look like this:

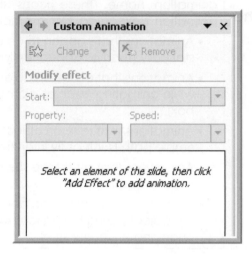

Figure 3-26: Custom Animation

When animations are applied to slide elements with multiple lines of text, the center panel looks something like this:

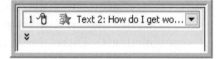

The double arrow indicates only a summary of the effects is being shown. Clicking the arrow reveals the complete animation for this element. In this case, the arrow click reveals one line for each line on the slide, as shown below:

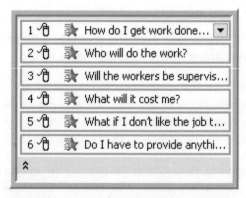

Figure 3-27: An Animation Listing

When you need to make detailed changes to the slide animation, click on the animation in the list and then click the animation's dropdown arrow to bring up an option list. Clicking either Effect Options or Timing from this list brings the three-tabbed window with a title that matches the name of the animation being affected.

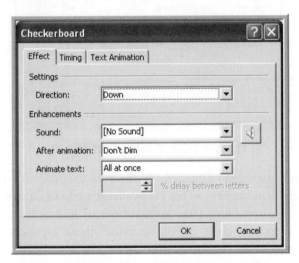

Figure 3-28: Customizing an Animation

Effect Options Tab

This tab changes the direction of the current animation effect and make enhancements to the effect.

Choosing the direction can be done on the direction dropdown on the main animation pane. In fact, this value always matches the value on the animation pane.

Sounds inserted via this tab should be short sounds. Be cautious about adding sounds to the animations, as the sound plays every time the animation plays. If you overuse this option, the audience may get annoyed or they may pay attention to the sound effects instead of the presentation messages.

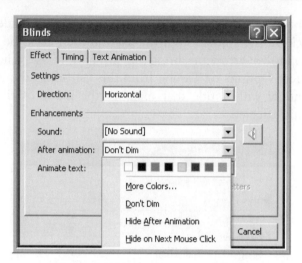

Figure 3-29: Animation Effect

After animation changes the look of the shape or text after the animation occurs. Options available include changing the color, hiding the object after animation and hiding the object on the next mouse click. You can use these options as a simple alternative to emphasis animations.

These options are especially useful when used in combination with the Animate text options and with the options on the Text Animation tab.

Animate text allows text to be brought onto the screen all at once, one word at a time or one character at a time. The name of this option is confusing, since it is so close to the name of the Text Animation tab. They both refer to how much and how fast text appears on the slide. However, the Animate text option sets a more defined entrance pattern. This is another option to be careful using, since overuse can be annoying to the audience.

Timing Options Tab

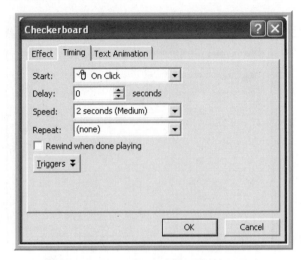

Figure 3-30: Animation Timing

This tab allows more precise timing for animations. These settings are refinements of the timing set in the custom animation pane.

The start and speed options are the same as on the animation pane. They set the trigger for the effect and the speed at which the effect occurs. Like the direction option on the effect tab, the values always match between this tab and the custom animation pane.

The delay option adds a delay to the start of the animation.

The repeat option determines how many times the effect runs before stopping. Effects can be: repeated a certain number of times, until the next mouse click or until the end of the slide.

The rewind option sets the animation back to its start when the presentation transitions to another slide.

Triggers allow effects to be started out of sequence. This is an advanced option and is covered in Chapter 6.

Text Animation Options Tab

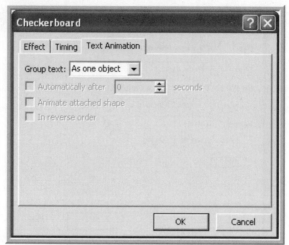

Figure 3-31: Animation Text

This tab determines how many lines of text appear at one time. While the name of the tab is the same as the option on the Effect tab, the entries here refer to text bullet levels instead of text characters or words.

Group text defines how much of the text is brought in at once. Options include: all text at once, by paragraph or by paragraph level. When using this option, it is best to set the grouping to be equal to or one level higher than the number of bullet levels on your slide.

If grouping option is set, the Automatically after option becomes available. This determines how long of a time gap to allow between text group entrances. Use this option when creating self-running presentations. Be sure the amount of time between text entrances is sufficient for the participant to read the entire text before the next chunk is brought in.

Animation of attached shapes only is applicable when text is in an autoshape with an animation predefined. When set, it allows the autoshape animation to play during entrance of text. This is another option to use cautiously, as it can be more distracting than useful.

The option of having items enter in reverse order is also available. With this option set, the text animates from bottom to top. Think of this as a way to create top ten lists, where the least important elements are at the bottom of the list, but should be revealed first.

Emphasis Effects

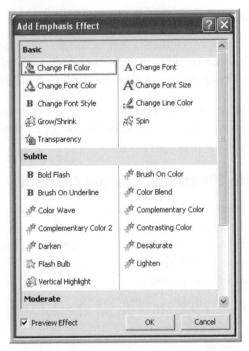

Figure 3-32: Emphasis Effects

Adding an emphasis effect allows the audience's attention to be focused on a specific slide element while other items are on the screen. For example, an emphasis effect might be used when displaying a chart of data. Since it is useful to have all the data on the screen while individual elements are discussed, entrance effects for the elements are not useful.

Instead, the various data elements would have an emphasis effect added to ensure participant attention is focused where desired.

Emphasis effects are accessed and customized using the same process as entrance effects. However, since emphasis effects generally revolve around changing the element in some way, the available modifications on the task pane and on the Effect tab of the Effect Options window are different for each effect.

We cover using emphasis effects in detail in Chapter 6.

Multiple Effects On A Single Slide

When multiple elements on a single slide are animated, an additional set of adjustments becomes available: the Re-Order arrows. These arrows change the order of the effects.

Once the animations for each individual element are set up on a slide, you may need to change the order of the animations. Use the re-order buttons to do this.

Multiple Effects On A Single Element

In all versions from PowerPoint 2002 on, more than one animation effect can be performed on any given slide element. The details on this process are discussed in Chapter 6. For now, it is important to know elements can have both entrance and emphasis effects applied.

To add a second effect to an element that already has one effect:

- Click off the element to be changed
- Click back on the element to be changed
- On the Add Effect dropdown, select Emphasis and the desired effect and effect options

Note: If the only animation options available are to delete or change the existing animation, the animation is selected instead of the object. Click off the object and back on again.

What About Animating Sounds?

Sounds are animated the same way as any other object. The sound icon is selected and the animation process for the PowerPoint version is followed.

To continue a sound across multiple slides, the animation effect options must be set. These options tell PowerPoint when to start the sound and how long to play the sound.

In PowerPoint 2000 and earlier versions, this is done with the Multimedia Settings tab of the Custom Animation window.

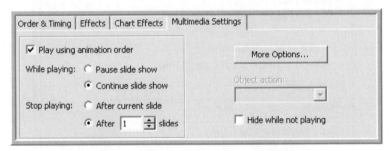

Figure 3-33: Multimedia Settings

The Play using animation order box defaults to the setting chosen when you inserted the sound. If you decide to play the sound using the animation order, checking this box sets up whether to pause the show until the sound completes or continue the show while the sound plays through a pre-determined number of slides.

In PowerPoint 2002 and later, sound animations are shown in the animation task pane. A 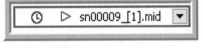 selected sound element looks something like this:

You access the effect options for sounds in the same way as any other PowerPoint 2002 animations. However, the effect tab changes from the effect option tab shown earlier in this section to Figure 3-34:

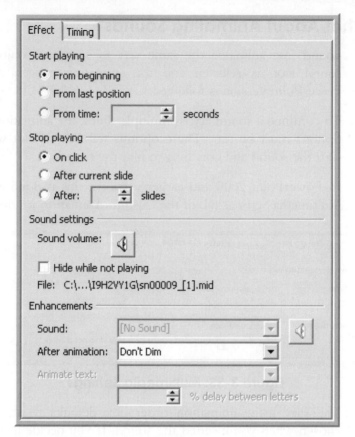

Figure 3-34: PPT 2002 and later Animation Effects

Notice in PowerPoint 2002, there are many more options for sounds than in the previous versions. You can define when to start playing, when to stop, the volume of the sound and whether the sound icon is hidden on-screen when it is not playing.

Multiple Slide Sounds? Be Careful Of This Gotcha!

There is a small gotcha in the number of slides sound plays through before stopping. This number is the total number of slides played, not the sequential number of slides in the file. For example: If the presentation is 12 slides long and you insert sound on slide three set to play for nine slides, that sound plays through the next nine slides. Sounds simple enough, right?

However, if during the presentation a question comes up on slide 6 requiring the presenter to go back to slides 1 and 2, the sound continues to play. However, the sound now stops playing on slide 7, as 9 slides have been presented.

Slide Transitions

Jane's presentation is looking better and better all the time. However, she has now noticed the transition from one slide to another has very little impact. Since there are places she really wants the slide transitions to grab the audience's attention, she needs to work out which slide transitions she is going to use in her presentation.

Slide transitions can be applied to individual slides or to a group of slides. Individual slide transitions are set by viewing the slide and going to the Slide Transition menu or task pane. Transitions are applied to multiple slides by changing to the Slide Sorter View, selecting the slides and doing the same thing.

In all versions of PowerPoint, slide transitions can be accessed via either Slide Show→ Slide Transition menu item or the Slide Transition menu item on the right-click menu. In PowerPoint versions 2000 and earlier, these actions bring up the Slide Transition window (Figure 3-35). In 2002 and later, they bring up the Slide Transition Taskbar (Figure 3-36).

Figure 3-35: PPT 2000 and earlier Transitions

Figure 3-36: PPT 2002 and later Transitions

Using Slide Transitions

Transitions are applied by selecting the specific transition to be used, setting its speed and sound, and determining whether the transition occurs automatically or on mouse click.

Like animations, too many different transitions can be confusing to the audience and make the presentation look unprofessional. While PowerPoint allows a different transition for each slide, doing so is not a good idea.

It is better to pick a simple transition and use it for all content slides throughout the entire presentation. A separate transition can be used for title slides than for content slides; however, be sure the two transitions do not conflict visually with each other. Following these rules allows the more emphatic transitions to be used as needed to focus attention on major points within a presentation.

The options available for transitions are very similar to those for animation effects. You can:

- Set the speed for most transitions to fast, medium or slow
- Select a sound to be played during the transition between slides
- Set how to advance to the next slide (by mouse click, after a certain amount of time or both)
- Set whether the transition is to be applied to the selected slides or to all slides

As with animation sounds, transition sounds can become annoying to the audience. Use them sparingly or the audience may revolt!

Learn From My Mistake

There is a Microsoft template, High Voltage, which comes with PowerPoint 2000 and earlier. Early on in my PowerPoint career, I used this template for a training presentation. I had put the presentation together on a machine without speakers, so I was unaware this template sets up every transition with a moving electronics-type sound.

When the presentation started, the sound was interesting and got the participants attention. However, after three or four slides, everyone in the room was ready to break the speakers. This was not a good way to learn about transition sounds, believe me!

If you are going to use a transition sound on more than one slide, be sure to play the presentation on a system with sound before releasing it. You will likely find that, unless the sound is very simple, it quickly becomes annoying.

Tip 16: **Avoid these three transitions!**	Random Transitions: This option takes design control away and hands it to a random number generator.
	Fade Through Black: While greatly improved in PowerPoint 2002, this transition is very CPU intensive. Because of the amount of processing power needed to run the transition, it seldom looks good.
	Dissolve: Dissolve is better than Fade Through Black, but is still not a smooth effect. It appears as a fine checkerboard transition rather than a true dissolve.

Setting Up The Show To Run

Now that Jane has finished with her presentation, it is time to set it up to be self-running. Jane knows that she needs to set up presenter-led, self-running, and kiosk presentations, so she decides to investigate the options under the Slide Show → Set Up Show menu.

Because she needs to know both the older and newer ways to set up shows, we cover PowerPoint 2000 and earlier versions first, and then go over the added functionality for PowerPoint 2002 and later versions.

PowerPoint 2000 And Earlier

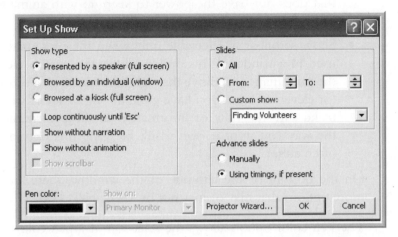

Figure 3-37: PPT 2000 and earlier Set Up Show Window

To select the presentation type, click one of the three radio buttons on the top left of the window. This decision was made during presentation design.

When creating a kiosk, provide clickable navigation buttons as any key press and general mouse clicks are ignored for all keys except the escape key. We cover how to add these navigation elements in Chapter 9.

Underneath this set of options are four options regarding how the presentation will play.

- Loop continuously until 'Esc' returns the presentation to the beginning of the show when it ends. Because this is a built-in feature of kiosk presentations, this option can't be selected when a kiosk presentation is selected.

- Show without narration plays a presentation with recorded narration without the narration. This switch is useful for speaker-led presentations are also used as automatic presentations. For example, Jane sets up this option when she completes her initial project and has recorded the narration for it.

- Show without animation allows the flow of the presentation to be checked without animating each slide. It is also useful if running the presentation on a computer that does not have the power to keep up with animations. You probably won't use this option very often.

- Show scrollbar is selectable only when the presentation is used in a window. This option allows the person viewing the presentation to move through the slides with a scrollbar (or elevator). Since you have gone through a lot of work to make sure the flow of information in the presentation is the way you want it, you won't be using this option very often either.

On the bottom of the left side of the window, there are two more options that may or may not be selectable.

The Pen color option allows the selection of a pen color other than black. Pen colors can only be selected for speaker-led presentations. It is useful for those situations when the pen color would not otherwise be visible on the slide background. You can also change the pen color when running a presentation by right clicking and selecting a new pen color.

The Show on option is only accessible if the computer being used has the hardware installed to run two monitors. If this hardware is installed, the presentation can be shown on either the primary or secondary monitor.

Tip 17: The presentation doesn't show!	If the presentation doesn't show when set to run, the Show On option may well be the culprit. If the presentation is set up to run on a secondary monitor and then moved to a machine without a secondary monitor, PowerPoint still tries to run it on the second monitor.

That finishes the left side of the window. The right side is a little more interesting. The first option is which slides to show when the presentation starts. There are three options: all slides, a consecutive subset of slides or a custom show. Custom shows are covered on page 99.

Move through slides by pressing a key, clicking the mouse button or set them to move themselves after a set amount of time. These two radio buttons define whether the presentation is controlled manually by keyboard action or by mouse click, or controlled using timings to move (if timings exist). Even if timings have been set, the presentation moves to the next animation or slide on a mouse click or key press if the presentation is not in kiosk mode.

Finally, the Projector Wizard button runs a wizard that helps the presenter ensure the projector is communicating with the computer and displaying the presentation correctly. This wizard was useful when laptops and projectors used different resolutions. With projection equipment made in the last five years, resolution problems are less frequent. You probably won't use this wizard much.

PowerPoint 2002 And Later

That takes care of PowerPoint 2000 and earlier version setups. In PowerPoint 2002, several new features were added. The new window looks something like this:

Figure 3-38: PPT 2002 and later Set Up Show Window

The new Set Up Show window contains much of the same information as the old window, but some of the information has moved. The changes are:

- The Show scrollbar checkbox has been moved to a more logical location under the browsed by window option. Since this is the only type of presentation that can have scrollbars, the newer location makes more sense.

- A new section, Multiple monitors, has been added. This section selects which monitor to use to view the presentation. It also contains the new option Show Presenter View. Presenter view shows the presentation on one screen with the notes visible and on another screen without the notes visible. If you click this box when a second monitor is not installed, PowerPoint automatically invites you to set one up.

- A second new section, Performance, has also been added. This section turns off graphics acceleration for the show. It also determines a precise monitor resolution for displaying PowerPoint shows. These two options provide easy debugging of one of the most common problems in PowerPoint usage: the appearance of monitor problems when viewing a show. Clicking the Tips button brings up the Microsoft Help page, which offers hints on how to use these options to the best of the computer's abilities. This is one of the most useful help pages available in PowerPoint.

- The Projector Wizard has been removed from the Set Up Show window. With the newer technologies in projection equipment, this wizard is no longer needed.

One Last Note About Setting Up Shows...

Most of the show options are saved with the presentation file and only affect that file. However, the performance settings in PowerPoint 2002 and later versions are machine-specific options. Once changed on a specific computer, they affect any presentation run or edited on that computer. If you move the presentation to a new machine, verify the settings there are what you need.

Save That Presentation!

Done? Nope, not yet! We need to save the presentation first. There are many options available for saving presentation files. Different formats can be selected, different extensions can be used and presentations can even be packaged for sharing with other users. The details of all these different options are covered in various places in the rest of this book. For now, we need to cover a few quick pointers about saving PowerPoint files:

- Turn off fast saves! Yes, this was already covered in this chapter, but that was many pages ago. Go check it was done.

- Save frequently. Losing presentations happens all the time. The more you save, the less likely you'll lose yours.

- Always keep a backup copy of your file. If it is too tempting to make a backup regularly, get Shyam Pillai's free *Sequential Save* add-in for PowerPoint from his site at www.mvps.org/skp/seqsave.htm. This add-in sets up a naming sequence so the file gets a new name every time it is saved.

Now That The Presentation Is Saved...

...we'll continue on with the regularly scheduled portion of this book. Next up are two somewhat hidden but useful tools for organizing the presentation content.

Hidden Slides

Hidden slides are useful when information in the presentation may not be presented every time. By creating hidden slides, this information is available if needed, but can easily be skipped.

Hidden slides show in the slide outline, in the slide sorter view and in the individual slide list during edit. However, the slide is skipped when the slide show is running. If the information is needed, the slide can be accessed via the right-click menu or via the slide number.

Slides are hidden by selecting the slide and then going to Slide Show → Hide Slide. Multiple slides can be hidden at once by using the Slide Sorter view and either Shift+Click to select multiple sequential slides or Ctrl+Click to select multiple non-sequential slides, and then setting them to be hidden.

In PowerPoint 2000 and earlier, there are two indications (during editing) a slide is hidden:

- When viewing the Slide Show menu, the slide icon to the left of the words Hide Slide has a diagonal line through it.

- When viewing the slides in Slide Sorter view, the slide number has a box around it and a diagonal line through the box and the number.

In PowerPoint 2002 and later versions, a more useful indicator has been added to the list. When viewing the slide in Normal view, the slide number on the slide list in the left pane has the same box and line as the slide number in Slide Sorter view. Unfortunately, this extra indicator was not carried over to outline view.

Hidden Slide Example: FAQ Slides

One great use for hidden slides is to add informational slides and frequently asked question slides to the end of the presentation. To implement the FAQ slides, create each slide as a simple question and answer slide, based on questions likely to come up during the presentation. Make sure the question is in the title placeholder.

Store these slides either at the end of the presentation or in a separate presentation. If the slides are stored in a separate presentation, be sure to use the same template as the main presentation so the movement to the hidden slides is as seamless as possible.

Next, create a summary slide of the FAQ slides. The easiest way to do this is with the summary slide option built into PowerPoint. This option creates a single slide with the title of each of the other slides in the presentation as its content, like a table of contents. Edit the text of this slide so only the FAQ slides are listed. Next, select each line of text and hyperlink it to the corresponding slide. Move this summary slide to the end of your main presentation.

The FAQs are now ready to be used. How to use them depends on whether this is a presenter driven presentation or a presentation without a presenter.

When the questions come up during the presenter driven presentation, have the presenter note the slide number of the current slide, then go to the keyboard and type the number 999 followed by the enter key. This set of actions takes you to the last slide in the presentation. Mouse to the presentation containing the answer (probably while saying something to the effect of "That's a great question, in fact, it's right here on the FAQ slide").

Tip 18: **Keep track** **of your slide** **numbers**	Don't know how to tell what the number of the current slide is? Keep an index card next to the computer with the titles and slide numbers listed!

For an even slicker method of going to the FAQ slide, make a button on the master slide with no fill or edges, and memorize where it's placed it. Do a quick mouse move and click, and the FAQ slide appears like magic.

When with the slide, ask the group if that answered the question, then type the slide number of the original slide followed by the enter key. This returns focus to the slide where the question was asked, so the presentation can be continued seamlessly.

For a presentation without a presenter, put a "Questions Answered Here" button on each slide. Do this quickly by putting it on the master slide. Link that button to the FAQ title summary slide. Then the user can find the question on the page and click to go there. In this case, it is a good idea to put the FAQ title summary slide and the answer slides in a separate presentation. Then, place a note on each slide, again via the master, that says "Press escape to return to the presentation." When the user presses escape, the FAQ presentation closes and the original presentation appears.

FAQ slides for PowerPoint presentations can also be created thru the use of Custom Shows. Custom Shows are subsets of the slides in a single PowerPoint file that can be used as stand-alone presentations or linked to from within the current presentation.

Custom Shows

Content within a single presentation often needs to be presented to a number of different audiences. Think about Jane's final message table. She has some messages everyone involved in the project needs to hear, so it makes sense to put them in a single file. There are also some messages only certain audiences need. The slides for these messages should be in the same file as the main presentation, but Jane only wants to show them to some of the audiences.

Jane's solution is to create one file with all of the content, but several Custom Shows. A custom show is a subset of the slides in the file, which can be re-ordered and re-used as desired for multiple purposes.

Let's look at an actual example from Jane's main presentation. She has created a series of slides to cover the message "Where are the volunteers coming from?". The following slides have been created:

- Title Slide
- 3 content slides discussing organizations helping to acquire volunteers
- 3 content slides discussing a media campaign to find volunteers from the general community
- 3 content slides discussing a campaign with the school district to target high school students who need community service hours

Jane isn't going to show all 10 slides in all presentations, but she wants the information to be available if questions are raised. Jane could put the slides in the middle of the presentation as hidden slides.

However, she found out there is an easier way: Place the slides at the end of the presentation, create a custom show containing only these slides, and link to the custom show.

Create A Custom Show

Custom shows are created using Slide Show → Custom Show. Accessing this menu brings up a blank Custom Shows window. Click the New button to bring up the Define Custom Show window (Figure 3-39).

The default name for any custom show is Custom Show followed by a number. Since this is not a very descriptive way to identify the shows, it is always a good idea to change this name. In this case, Jane changes it to "Finding Volunteers."

Down the left side of the window, there is a list of the titles for each slide in the presentation. For a slide to be in the custom show, its title must show in the right side of the window. To add it to the show, either double-click on the name or highlight the name and click the Add >> button. You can multi-select slides by using the shift key or the control key while clicking on slides.

Figure 3-39: Define Custom Show Window

If a slide is accidentally moved to the custom show list, it can be removed by highlighting the title in the right column and clicking the Remove button.

Now that Jane's basic list for a custom show has been created, click OK to save the show. This returns focus to the Custom Shows window, but now the created custom show appears in the list.

Notice there are now two active buttons at the bottom of the window instead of one. In addition to the Close button, there is now a Show button. This new button allows the user to run the custom show. This is a useful feature when testing out more complex custom shows.

Accessing The Custom Show

Custom shows can be run in many ways. The file containing the show can run directly from the Custom Show window. It can be set up to run when the main file is running by setting the Set Up Show options. Finally, the custom show can be accessed via a link from within either the file that contains it or another file.

The simplest way to run a custom show is to open the file, go to Slide Show → Custom Show, select the show and click the Show button. The show runs and returns to the normal view when complete.

If this custom show is always used when the file is run, it is better to set up the show to always run this custom show. To do this, go to Slide Show → Custom Show. Click the radio button for Custom show. The first custom show created appears as the default show. If this is not the desired show, use the dropdown to find the correct one.

Most often, custom shows are set up to be accessed thru a hyperlink or action setting from within the file or from another file. The basic process for creating a hyperlink to a custom show is to select the item to be clicked and link it to the show. The details for creating hyperlinks are covered in Chapter 9.

Tip 19: Access custom shows seamlessly	To access your custom show smoothly, set up a hyperlink or action setting to the show. When you select the custom show for hyperlinking, be sure to check the box Show and return. This closes the custom show when it is complete and returns focus automatically to the main presentation.

Other Uses For Custom Shows

There are many other uses for custom shows. Three you will find yourself using most frequently are:

- Use a custom show to hide detail slides when presenting summary information. The information is still available for access via the right-click menu, but can be easily skipped if not required.

- Insert the same slide into the show multiple times. Because custom shows do not actually move slides around, but instead link to copies of the slide, the same slide can be shown multiple times. This is especially useful if you need to refer back to information during a presentation.

- To make accessing hidden slides easier, create custom shows with the hidden content and link to the custom show instead of to the first hidden slide.

What's Next?

Jane's first presentation is complete. She has taken everything she has learned up to this point and quickly creates the presentations she needs for the project. She knows there is still a lot to learn about PowerPoint. Since she has a good grasp of the basics, we will say goodbye to her.

Before you move on to the rest of the book, take a break and play with the skills and ideas covered to this point. Practicing these basic items now makes learning the rest of PowerPoint much easier.

4. Presentation Fonts

➢ Font Basics

➢ Text Size on Slides

➢ The Best Fonts

➢ The Worst Fonts

➢ Replace Fonts

Denny leads a training group within a large computer firm. He regularly works with other members of his organization to improve the presentations are given to other employees, corporate partners and corporate clients. One problem he regularly runs into is helping others understand what fonts to use and why.

I am working with several divisions to create slides for our new product launch. Each division has its own standard for fonts, none of which really look good on screen. Can you provide some tips on picking the right fonts?

I am also going to need to quickly change the fonts on several of the presentations from the current fonts to fonts that work better for our various audiences. Is there any way I can go through a presentation quickly and make the changes?

Denny has discovered a universal truth in the world of PowerPoint users: Fonts are fun! Unfortunately, if you don't know how to choose and use the right fonts, they can also be fatal to your messages.

Fonts that are too small make it difficult for the audience to even see what you are saying. Fonts that are too large limit how much can put on a slide. The latter isn't usually a problem, but if you go to extremes, it can be.

Another thing presenters need to keep in mind is the audience for the presentation. The more formal the audience, the simpler the fonts used on the slides should be. Fun, funky, artistic fonts are fine for emphasis, but not as the main font in the presentation.

Let's look at a couple of the slides Denny received from the various departments as examples. He received slides from four departments, including his own. They are:

- Interface
- Data Warehouse
- Marketing
- Training

Interface is responsible for creating the interface to the new product. They created this slide listing the benefits of the interface:

Figure 4-1: Interface Department Slide

Data Warehouse is responsible for importation of data from other programs. They created this slide listing the various types of data that could be imported:

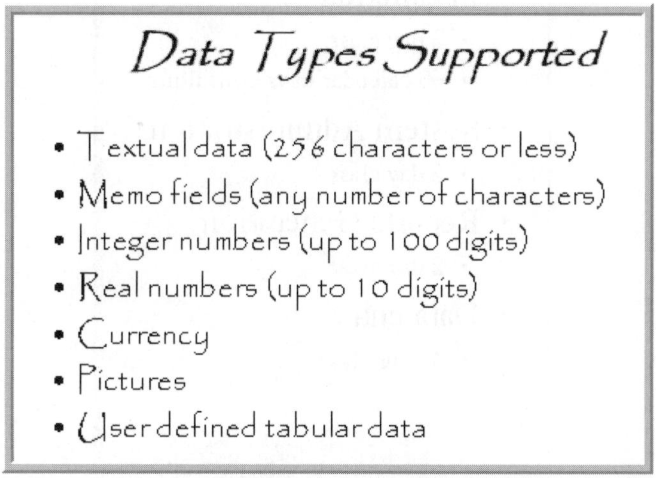

Data Types Supported

- Textual data (256 characters or less)
- Memo fields (any number of characters)
- Integer numbers (up to 100 digits)
- Real numbers (up to 10 digits)
- Currency
- Pictures
- User defined tabular data

Figure 4-2: Data Warehouse Slide

Marketing is responsible for the PR for the product. They sent this slide listing the prices and packaging of the product.

PRICING

- Main Program: $15,000 per server
- System Administrators: $500 per seat
- Data Input Users: $120 per seat
- Report Generation: $120 per seat

Figure 4-3: Marketing Department Slide

Meanwhile, Denny himself created this slide, which details the training available for clients:

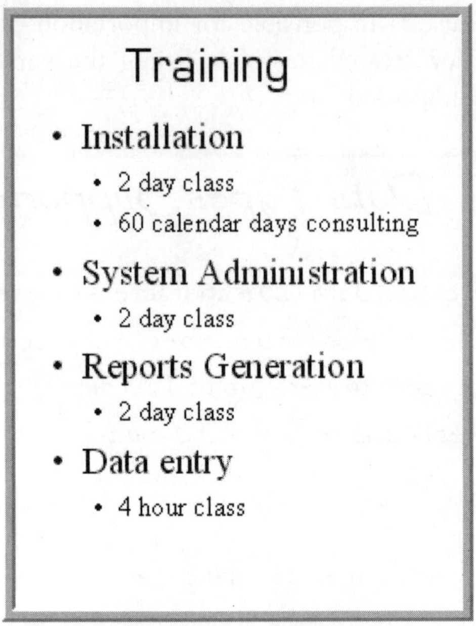

Figure 4-4: Training Slide

Ask yourself:

- Which of these slides are easiest to read?
- Which of these slides have more power and impact?
- Which of these are the most and least formal?

So, how does Denny get the presenters started on the path to correct font usage? He needs to start by explaining the basic ways fonts are grouped, what the various font types are called and what they mean.

Font Basics

Fonts are designed as mono-spaced or proportionally spaced fonts. Mono-spaced fonts, such as Courier, use the same amount of space for each character in the character set. Proportionally spaced fonts, such as Arial, adjust the amount of space needed to the specific character(s) being used.

This means some fonts have different sized spaces for different letters. Most of this book is done in proportionally spaced fonts. Let's look at a sample paragraph in our main font:

Lorem ipsum dolor sit amet, consectetuer adipiscing elit, sed diam nonummy nibh euismod tincidunt ut laoreet dolore magna aliquam erat volutpat.

What if this were in a mono-spaced font, such as Courier? It would look like this:

```
Lorem ipsum dolor sit amet, consectetuer
adipiscing elit, sed diam nonummy nibh
euismod tincidunt ut laoreet dolore magna
aliquam erat volutpat.
```

See how much more space the second paragraph uses than the first one? This is because the letters are not compressed to take up the optimum space for each character. You also probably found the second paragraph harder to read than the first. This is because your eye expects the spaces for letters to change. Keeping each letter the same size breaks the flow of the characters and makes your eye work harder to transmit the information to the brain.

Fonts also are designed as either *serif* or *sans serif*. In the font world, serif is commonly used to mean "foot". Serif fonts have little feet on each character. Sans serif (literally, "without feet") fonts have no feet. The majority of the text for this book is in Garamond, a serif font. However, the chapter and section headings are in Century Gothic, a sans serif font, as shown:

Lorem ipsum dolor sit amet, consectetuer adipiscing elit, sed diam nonummy nibh euismod tincidunt ut laoreet dolore magna aliquam erat volutpat.

Fonts are measured in points (12, 14, etc.). However, not all font sizes are created equal. Look at our sample paragraphs again. They seem to be different sizes, don't they? While the fonts for each paragraph are different, each is in the 12-point size for the font.

Fonts also have attributes. Attributes tell the font how each character should appear. The most common attributes are bold, italics, underline, superscript and subscript. Again, each font designer determines how the attributes are interpreted. Let's take our sample paragraph one more time and look at it in Garamond with some of the various attributes turned on:

Lorem ipsum dolor sit amet, consectetuer adipiscing elit, sed *diam nonummy nibh euismod tincidunt ut laoreet* <u>dolore magna aliquam</u> ***erat volutpat.***

Bolding the text changed the weight of each letter as well as the heaviness of the ink for each letter. Some fonts look better bolded, some are unreadable when bolded. Play around with the fonts on your system to determine which ones you like and which ones you don't.

Italics can be a real nightmare when used with certain fonts. Notice the difference between the letters only italicized in the sample paragraph and the characters italicized and bolded. Is one easier to read than the other?

Because italics fonts tend to be more compressed than regular fonts, the busier the font is, the harder it is to read in italics. Some people do not like having any text in italics. Since each person has an opinion about which fonts look okay in italics, play around with sample text and decide for yourself. I like italics on larger fonts, but only if the font stays clean and easy to read. My husband does not like italicizing any fonts. While reviewing this chapter, he wanted me to recommend to NEVER use italics!

Most font designers specify how the font looks in bold, italics, underline and the basic combinations of these three. However, some fonts do not have a bold version; others do not have an italicized version. Some fonts only come in uppercase. Even if there is a version defined for a given font, it may not be installed on the computer in use.

PowerPoint adjusts the attributes of any text, as long as the font used has the attribute defined. In some cases, PowerPoint offers a software-generated version of the font when the official versions are not installed.

Tip 20: Strikethrough	While PowerPoint lets you change the attributes of any piece of text on a slide or in the notes, it does not let you automatically create text with lines through it. In order to create the illusion of strikethrough text, you need to create a drawn line and lay it over the appropriate text.

What About Kerning?

Kerning is the automated ability to change the spacing between specific sets of side-by-side letters. It allows the eye to move over the letters more easily and provides a more professional looking text appearance. Unfortunately, no version of PowerPoint supports kerning at this time. Basic character spacing is supported, but kerning is not.

How Do I Change Fonts?

Fonts in individual placeholders, textboxes and autoshapes are changed by selecting the object or the text and then using Format → Font or the font list on the formatting toolbar. To change the fonts on an entire presentation, change the master or use the Replace Fonts option, which is discussed on page 117. Because different fonts are different sizes, changing the font may change the word wrapping within the placeholders.

Text Size On Slides

Remember Marketing's slide? It had text so small it became too hard to read here in a printed book. Imagine trying to read the slide when it is projected fifteen feet away!

Let's Get This Out Of The Way....

Just because there is more content than will fit on a slide, do not make the fonts so small the participants can't see them. If there is too much content to allow an adequate font size, then split the slide into two slides!

So What Is The Right Font Size?

The right size is large enough so all participants can read the text from a reasonable distance. Because the distance depends on the type of presentation being created, let's look at the two basic types of presentations separately.

Speaker-Led Presentations

Text on a speaker-led presentation should never be smaller than 24 point. In addition, most text on speaker-led presentations should be at least 36 points, which allows the font to be visible from a reasonable distance when projected.

Text in PowerPoint title placeholders should be 54 to 72 points in size. This is not always possible because it makes the number of characters per line too short, so the smallest title text should be is 12 points larger than the other text on the slide.

If text is to be animated, test the font and size combinations on a projection screen before making any final size decisions.

A general rule of thumb for speaker-led presentations is to have no more than ten lines of text on any slide, including the slide's title. Besides ensuring the text is large enough to be visible to all participants, this rule ensures content on any given slide is cohesive and connected.

Animated Or Kiosk Presentations

Because animated and kiosk presentations are generally developed for one viewer at a time, the font sizes can be smaller. General text can be as small as 14 point, title text can be as small as 26.

Just because a smaller font is being used does not mean an overload of information ought to be presented on a single slide. Be sure someone views sample slides for readability before finalizing the presentation design.

Anything Else About Font Sizes?

Because different fonts interpret the point sizes differently, be sure sample slides are created and tested before font choices are finalized. Remember the best test for font choices is really participant comprehension. If the text is hard for participants to read and interpret, then they are too small.

The Best Fonts

While font decisions are dependent on the way the presentation is used, Denny came up with these basic rules for choosing fonts:

- Fonts should make presentation pieces easy to read
- Presentations that are shared should use common fonts
- If a non-standard font is used, it should be embedded
- Pick three or four coordinated fonts and don't add any others

Make It Easy To Read The Presentation

The simpler the font, the easier it is to read. Curly Q's and fancy edges are nice for graphics and emphasis, but they become tiring to read after a while. This means more work for the eyes, which in turn limits the amount of information the audience can absorb.

For large amounts of text, use serif fonts. They are easier to read, as the feet help the eye move from one letter to the next.

For headlines and quick text, use sans serif fonts. The lack of feet makes the eye concentrate on the words, increasing the impact of each word.

Use Common Fonts When Sharing Presentations

If the presentation is going to be shared with another user or computer, the presentation fonts should be limited to the fonts delivered with the basic operating systems and the basic Microsoft Office versions. To see the current list of fonts for each operating system and Office versions, check out this PPT FAQ entry: www.rdpslides.com/pptfaq/FAQ00256.htm

Embed Non-Standard Fonts

For fonts that may not be available on other systems, PowerPoint offers the option to embed the fonts into the presentation file. This option is useful, but has some limitations.

First off, the presentation developer must ensure the font is able to be embedded. Many fonts are sold for use on a specific machine only and, therefore, not able to be embedded without breaking copyright rules.

Next, only TrueType fonts are able to be embedded and they will only embed if they are of the right type. To determine if a font is a TrueType font, look at the font dropdown list. TrueType fonts have a TT to the left of their name. If the font name has a printer icon, it is not able to be embedded.

The next criterion is the level of embedding allowed by the font designer. The most restrictive fonts can't be embedded at all. The other three font levels are previewable/printable, editable and installable.

PowerPoint treats editable and installable fonts the same. If they are set up as Type 1 fonts, they can be embedded and used fully on the receiving system. Previewable/printable fonts can be embedded only for viewing and printing. If the text is changed, the font is not used.

Font embedding does have its drawbacks. Beyond needing to know if the font is able to be embedded, the rough size of the font file should be known. Since the actual font file itself is included with the presentation, embedding fonts can greatly increase the file size. If a single presentation has multiple embedded fonts, the file size quickly gets too large to move from system to system in any manner other than via CD-ROM.

Tip 21: More on font embedding	One of the best summaries of font embedding information was written by Trina Roberts and can be found in this PPT FAQ entry: www.rdpslides.com/pptfaq/FAQ00076.htm

Coordinate Your Fonts

There is a real temptation by all PowerPoint users (myself included) to use a font because it is there. For example, while testing a presentation you decide a segment needs to be highlighted for some reason.

You start to think: All those fonts on my system and on the internet must have been developed and offered for me to use all together, right?

Next thing you know, you are using a whole new font for the highlighting. This distracts the audience from the flow of the presentation and counteracts design work already done. Using too many fonts in the same presentation leads to seriously ugly slides. Too much variety in the fonts on a slide can distract the participants and make them work too hard to interpret the content.

Use one font for headings and one font for the bulk of the text. Then, select a single font for the emphasis font. Don't have more than three or four fonts on any one slide.

When choosing fonts, be sure they go together in style, formality and size.

The Worst Fonts

Some fonts should never be used in a PowerPoint presentation. These are the fonts that do not scale well, too decorative to read, too light and don't have fully defined character sets. Let's look at some examples for each.

Fonts That Don't Scale Well

Some fonts don't look as good in small sizes as they do in larger sizes. Other fonts look quite nice when used in smaller sizes, such as for on-screen use, but do not display well via a projector or large-screen monitor. Two fonts that show this quite well are Vivaldi and Blackadder ITC:

Vivaldi	Font Size
Our numbers are up this quarter	14
Our numbers are up this	26
Our numbers	48
numbers	72

Vivaldi is a font that looks better as it grows larger. Notice that as the size of the characters grow, the characters get darker, more defined and easier to read. While the same level of detail is in each character, the larger size makes it easier to read, instead of harder.

Blackadder	Font Size
Our numbers are up this quarter	14
Our numbers are up this	26
Our numbers	48
numbers	72

Blackadder looks nice when printed using small to medium character sizes. However, the larger this font gets, the more the jagged edges show. If you have this font on your system, type in a few lines of text using the font. Notice the spacing on the lines is greater and greater as the font size grows, but not in proportion with the size of the letters.

Overly Decorative Fonts

Fancy fonts are harder to read than simple fonts. They are great to use for emphasis and punch, but should never be used for the main text of a presentation.

Test it out. Which of the following two fonts are easier to read?

- This text, which is in Arial

- Or this text, which is in Jokerman?

Now, take that example even further. Imagine the participants' frustration level after trying to read the titles of 50 slides in each of those fonts.

Fonts That Are Too Light

Some fonts are lighter than others. The lighter ones do not project as well, making it harder for participants to read. This also impacts how the font looks on a non-white background.

While all of the examples here have been black text on a white page, the problems with lightweight fonts can be seen even more drastically when viewed as colored text on a dark background. Try it and see.

Fonts With Incomplete Character Sets

Most fonts created and sold today have a full complement of small letters, capital letters, numbers and special characters. However, there are still a significant number of fonts are missing some of the lesser used characters.

When missing characters are typed, an empty box or random character shows instead of the character expected. For example, when the following Arial text is converted to PipeDream, some of the characters are replaced:

The Quick Black Fox Jumped Over The Lazy Dog.

T☐☐ Q☐☐☐☐ B☐☐☐☐ F☐☐ J☐☐☐☐☐ ☐☐☐☐ T☐☐ L☐☐☐ ☐☐☐.

[THE QUICK BLACK FOX JUMPED OVER THE LAZY DOG.]

This happens most drastically with display fonts and special character fonts. However, it can also happen with font sets that only have capital or small letters defined.

In the case of PipeDream, the only defined characters are uppercase letters, numbers and basic punctuation. Lowercase letters and special characters were not defined by the font designer.

Fonts That Don't Travel Well

Some fonts on your system may not be installed on other systems. Beware that embedded fonts can be harder and slower to print. If the target printer needs to download the font from information in the presentation, it may take longer to print.

So What Fonts Should Denny Use?

After learning all he needed to know about fonts, Denny decided he didn't like the fonts the different Divisions were using, and he didn't like the fonts he had originally selected either. All of the font sets were too difficult to read for various reasons.

Denny decided to go with a very standard set of fonts. He chose Bookman Old Style for main text font, Trebuchet for title text and Lucinda and Impact for specialty fonts. After making these choices, he needed to quickly change all of the fonts on the slides for each division.

Denny knew he could change the text in the placeholders by changing and re-applying the corporate template. However, he still needed to update all the text boxes and the autoshape text in the presentations. His answer: Replace Fonts.

Replace Fonts

While the Replace Fonts tool is useful in a number of different ways, we are only going to look at the two most common uses: changing the look of an entire presentation with just a few clicks (like Denny needs to do) and discovering and correcting missing fonts.

Basic Usage

Font replacement is easy. Access it via Format → Replace Fonts. This brings up a two-line window:

Figure 4-5: Replace Font Window

The first line contains the name of one of the fonts used. Use the dropdown to set this to the font to replace. The fonts are displayed in alphabetical order. The second line is the font to use instead. Once both the old and new fonts are selected, click the Replace button and all instances of the first font are changed to the new font.

After the replacement is complete, the font in the replace field changes to the next font in the list and the original font is no longer in the top list. Since the Replace Font window remains open, multiple font changes can be done in quick succession.

If the entire look and feel of a presentation is being changed, each font in the list can be replaced with a new font.

The most useful application of this tool is to change how a presentation appears. This is useful if the same presentation is going to be used for multiple audiences, but the audiences are of drastically different formality, etc.

The most recently used fonts are placed at the top of the list. The other installed fonts are listed in alphabetical order. The font currently shown in the Replace field does not appear in the With field.

Unavailable Fonts

The second most useful application of this tool is to find which fonts are used within the current presentation but are not installed on the current system.

To find these fonts, click on the dropdown arrow for the Replace field. Any font in the list starting with ??? (three question marks), was used in the presentation but not installed on the current computer nor embedded in the presentation.

To rectify the situation, select the missing font from the Replace list and choose an available font from the With list, then click the Replace button.

Warning!

After the replace fonts tool has been used, glide through the presentation to check for unexpected changes. These changes can include:

- Text no longer fits in the space provided
- Text is no longer appropriately formatted
- Unexpected changes such as those within autoshapes you didn't intend to change

Text within graphics created outside of PowerPoint are not changed by replace fonts. However, fonts in grouped items are changed.

Single-Byte And Double-Byte Fonts

At some point, while using the Replace Fonts tool, PowerPoint may pop up with this message:

Figure 4-6: Double-Byte Replacement Error Message

Perfectly understandable message, huh? Let's clarify.

Single-Byte Vs. Double-Byte

In general, fonts are designed in such a manner that each character uses one byte of computer space. This works fine for languages with small character sets. Examples of such languages include English, French and Spanish. However, certain languages have so many characters they need two bytes to store the character set definitions. These languages are mainly the pictographic languages; character sets include glyphs for each word instead of each character. Examples of such languages are Japanese, Chinese, or Korean, or the extended languages such as Hebrew, Arabic or Cyrillic.

While it would seem double-byte fonts would only impact users in certain areas of the world, the truth is it is fairly easy to end up with double-byte fonts in a presentation by mistake.

Problems....

Double-byte languages cause three main problems for PowerPoint designers. First, because they are larger, they increase the file size. Second, text in a double-byte font cannot obviously or easily be changed back to a single-byte font. Finally, once a double-byte font has been used in a presentation, it remains attached to that presentation, even if the characters using it have been removed.

Resolutions....

All hope is not lost. There are a couple of ways to remove double-byte fonts are no longer needed.

The Long Way

Click each object in the presentation. Find the ones in a double-byte font. Re-create each from scratch. Do not copy and paste the items, they will retain the double-byte attribute.

The Short Cut

The first step is to make sure Arial Unicode is installed on the system. If it isn't there, find it at Microsoft's website and add it to the machine. Once it is installed, use Replace Fonts to change the unreadable fonts to Arial Unicode. The file still contains a double-byte font, but it is one that looks nicer and is slightly smaller.

Go A Step Further

Change the double-byte fonts to Arial Unicode. Save the PowerPoint file as HTML. Open each of the HTML files in Notepad (or equivalent). Find and replace Arial Unicode with Arial or another single-byte font. Save changes and close. Repeat with each HTML file generated.

Now comes the fun part. Return to PowerPoint and open the webpage. It comes in as a PowerPoint file with the fonts changed to single-byte fonts. Save the file under a new name (as a PowerPoint file).

So, What Did Denny End Up With?

After changing the template, applying it to each presentation and using Replace Fonts, the four presentations looked much more consistent, professional and impressive. See for yourself...

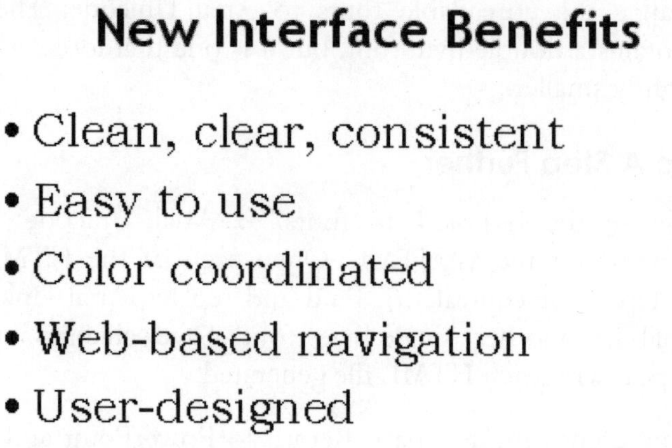

New Interface Benefits

- Clean, clear, consistent
- Easy to use
- Color coordinated
- Web-based navigation
- User-designed

Figure 4-7: New Interface Department Slide

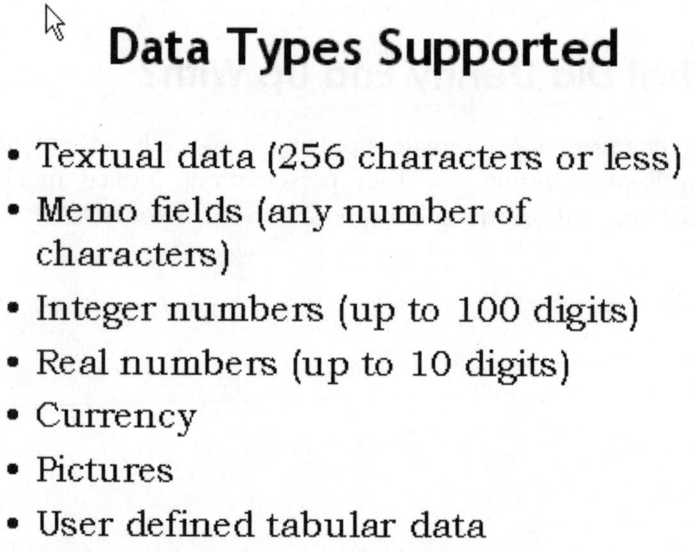

Data Types Supported

- Textual data (256 characters or less)
- Memo fields (any number of characters)
- Integer numbers (up to 100 digits)
- Real numbers (up to 10 digits)
- Currency
- Pictures
- User defined tabular data

Figure 4-8: New Data Warehouse Slide

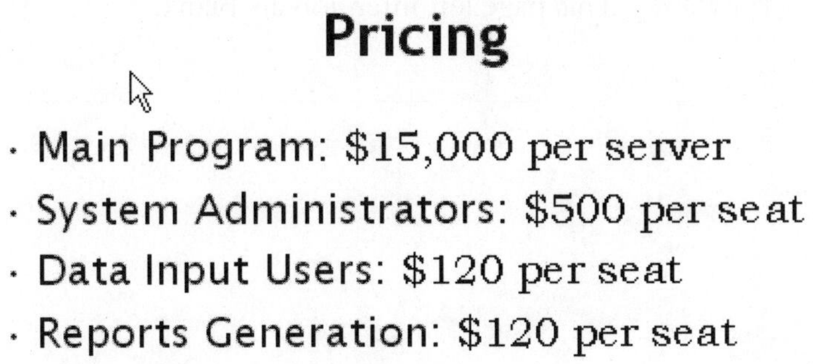

Pricing

· Main Program: $15,000 per server
· System Administrators: $500 per seat
· Data Input Users: $120 per seat
· Reports Generation: $120 per seat

Figure 4-9: New Marketing Department Slide

Training

- Installation
  - 2 day class
  - 60 calendar days consulting
- System Administration
  - 2 day class
- Reports Generation
  - 2 day class
- Data entry
  - 4 hour class

Figure 4-10: New Training Slide

This page left intentionally blank.

5. Colors And Color Schemes

- ➢ Picking the Right Colors for the Presentation

- ➢ Color Scheming

- ➢ Gradients

- ➢ Color Gotchas

George is creating a presentation describing a new endeavor for his company. He emailed me looking for help with the colors for his presentation.

I have to create a presentation to introduce and get funding for a new line of business for my company. Entering this new area will cost the company money; however, estimated return on the investment is full payback within the first nine months.

I think I need some help with the colors for the presentation. My slides currently have a green background, with pink and orange text and objects.

I picked these colors because the corporate logo is a light orange. I chose the green background because I think it represents growth. However, when I placed the logo on the page, I realized the colors weren't going to work out.

Can we schedule some time to get together and fix this mess?

Picking The Right Colors For The Presentation

As with many of my clients, the first item of business is a discussion of my "Rules for Colors"

1. Presentation colors should work together, not fight with each other. Stick with colors based on two of the three primary colors on a single slide.

2. Match the background color to the presentation environment.

3. Text and title colors should coordinate, not clash.

4. Presentation colors should reflect the messages of the presentation, not work against them.

5. Always have someone else check the color combinations before the presentation is finalized.

Rule 1: Pick Colors That Work Together

In general, if the background color is consists of two of the primary colors, the titles and text should use shades of those colors instead of a third color.

To test this, let's experiment.

1. Start a new, blank presentation

2. Insert a single slide with a title and some text

3. Right-click on a blank area of the slide and select a background

4. Click the dropdown box and select More Colors

5. Set the background to grass green

6. Save the change and return to the slide

7. Right-click in the title placeholder and select Font

8. In the Font window, click the dropdown for the font color

9. Select the More Colors option

10. Set the font color to orange and click ok

11. Type some text in the title placeholder

12. Repeat steps 7 through 10 to set the text color in the text placeholder

13. Click off the placeholder so nothing is selected

These colors don't look so good together, do they? Do you know why? The background color is made up of blue and yellow. The text colors are made up of red and yellow colors. Putting these colors together breaks the first rule of color.

To fix this, we need to do one of the following: Change the background to a red-based color or a yellow-based color, or change the text colors to yellow-based colors or blue-based colors.

Let's play with the background first. Set the background color to red and then to yellow. Look at each closely enough to decide how they look. Then, set the background color to a light orange. Do any of these color combinations look good to you?

Okay, try changing the font colors instead. First, undo the text color changes so it is back to the green background with the orange title and the pink text. Now, change the text color to navy blue and the title color to a yellow. How does that look? Better or worse?

The colors go together better, but the yellow may look somewhat washed out, depending on which green is used. Play some more with all three colors (background, font and title) until there is a combination you like. I like yellows on blues, as they go together well and are easy on the eyes.

For more practice and examples of good and bad color combinations, check out these websites:

- Color Schemer Online – Click on a color in the color choices or enter the RGB color number and this tool determines a color scheme based off that color. www.colorschemer.com/online.html

- VisiBone's Online Color Wheel – Shows the impact various colors have on each other. Click on each color in a scheme and see them stacked next to each other. www.visibone.com/colorlab

- WebWhirlers' Colour Wizard – Give this online tool the RBG values for a color and it returns a page of color relationships based purely on mathematical evaluation. www.webwhirlers.com/colors/wizard.asp

- Colormaker – Unique tool showing exactly how text looks on colored backgrounds. The interface isn't as nice as the others, but the resulting color combinations are good. www.bagism.com/colormaker

Rule 2: Base Background On Environment

This presentation uses combinations of yellows and blues. Since reds can be hard to read for some people, avoid them. For now, we'll play around with green backgrounds to see how the blues and yellows contrast.

Having decided which of the primary colors we are going to use, we need to decide which hues of these colors work best for the presentation. To make that decision, look at the presentation location and the size of the group.

Dark, deep hues work well for backgrounds for a dark room, and brighter, lighter backgrounds work well for well-lit rooms. This has a lot to do with how the human eye works in different light situations.

In George's case, he is presenting to a large group, turning off the lights and using a projection system. He needs a dark color background.

Change the color of the background several times to various shades of dark green. Stop when you have one that looks dark enough to project well and contrasts with the text and title colors. To find a color that works well, stick to the outside of the color wheel. Blue-green colors also work well.

If George were going to email his presentation to each person, he would probably want a color that draws a little more attention to the slide. To see some good selections for this setup, play around with the greens closer to the center of the wheel. (The font colors won't look as nice on the lighter green because they blend in more. For individual presentations, deepen the font colors so they retain the contrast with the background.)

Now, undo any changes made and set the background color to a deep forest green. I like the greens just to the right and left of the darkest greens on the color wheel.

Rule 3: Coordinate Your Text And Title Colors

Next, cleanup the font colors so they work as well together as they do with the background color.

Title and text colors should coordinate together, but contrast with the background. The color wheel helps accomplish this. Colors on the same ring go well together, but may not contrast enough. Colors on the same spoke contrast well, but may not always coordinate. Furthermore, the primary color most prevalent in the background is easier to coordinate than the less prevalent one. In this case, the blue is more dominant than the yellow in the green, so it will be easier finding blues to match than yellows.

Start by changing the mustard yellow to a brighter yellow. Try one of the yellows close to the center of the color wheel for the best results. Once you have a color you like, change the blue color. The blues that will probably look best are the navy blues and the bright blues.

Rule 4: Choose Colors That Reflect The Message

When selecting colors, think about the messages the colors suggest. In George's case, he has selected a green background because green, to George, means growth. To many people, green means money. Because he really wants financial support for the new project, he would probably do better with a different background.

Think about the presentation from management's viewpoint. Every time the green color comes up on the screen, management is likely to think about money, while George wants them to think about the return on the investment.

If George's cause already had colors attached to it, such as red, white and blue, he could change his background colors to one of those and make the audience think less about the money and more about the cause. However, because his company has orange as its corporate color, he does not want to do this. Why? Orange is a hard color for new designers to work with, since it is hard to match.

I recommend blue as the best choice for the background. It melds well with other colors. George wanted to use white, but I discouraged this idea because the glare of a pure white causes eyestrain, which makes the slides hard to look at for long periods. Avoid true red as a background color, since it is hard to coordinate. In addition, red could be a constant reminder of the possible debt might come from the additional funding.

Since we are changing the background color to blue, the text and title colors need to be changed as well. As an exercise, change the background to a blue that works for projector use and set the fonts appropriately.

Tip 22: Learn more about color meanings	Want to learn more about the meanings people tend to attach to various colors? Check out these sites: www.color-wheel-pro.com/color-meaning.html www.factmonster.com/ipka/A0769383.html graphicdesign.about.com/library/weekly/aa062703a.htm

Rule 5: Have Someone Else Look At The Colors

Always verify the color scheme with someone. Have a member of the target audience check the colors. You don't want to be like George and pick a color that means something you haven't thought about.

Rule 5 – B: Color For The Color Deficient

Because about 8% of all adult males in the U.S. have color vision problems be sure the presentation is set up to minimize problems caused by color vision. (Want details on what percentage have which kind of color loss? Check out webexhibits.org/causesofcolor/2C.html)

People with color deficiencies generally do have some color vision; they can tell differences between colors, but they do not see colors the same as people with full color vision.

One of the common forms of color vision problems is the inability to differentiate between some greens and some reds. If using different shades of red and green to indicate positive and negative comments in a presentation, you run the risk of not presenting the message to portions of the audience, since they may see the opposite of what you expect them to see.

Another example is a presentation with light red or pink text elements on a brown background. A color-deficient audience member may not see some of the text, depending on the specific color combinations used.

A third common color vision problem comes into play with those who do not see shading. A common color vision problem is the inability to tell blue shades from one another and from purple shades. In this case, blue-on-blue presentation elements fade together and may not be visible.

One other common problem for people with color deficiencies is light levels. Darker areas will greatly change the amount and strength of the colors they can see. Rooms with scattered brightly lit areas will also make it hard for those with color vision problems.

What Can The Presentation Developer Do?

Educate yourself. Learn about colors that work well together from the perspective of the audience. If you know someone who has color problems and is willing to work with you on color combinations, ask for help. No matter what, test out the color combinations in the actual lighting environment.

There are many great web resources available to educate yourself and check presentations. I have found these sites to be the most useful.

- VisiCheck (www.vischeck.com) This site has great information and links regarding how colors are seen by people. They have a program that can be run either from the web or from a computer that does a simulation of how images and web pages look to persons with color vision problems. How does this help the PowerPoint developer? You can either save the presentation as a web page and run the color checker on a site or save the presentation as JPEGs and run the image checker on the files on disk. If using the checker several times, it is worthwhile to download the tool. Instructions for doing so are at the site.

- WebExhibit's Causes of Color articles (webexhibits.org/causesofcolor/index.html). This site contains several articles describing how the eye sees colors, how color vision problems affect colors and what percentage of the population is affected by the different color vision problems.

Color Scheming

Now that George has a good grip on which colors work well in which situation, he is ready to take the idea even further...

Now that I know how to set up my presentation with my own set of colors, is there an easy way to save the color schemes? Since I don't know whether I will be presenting my plan to the whole group at once or via email to each member, I would really like to set up the presentation so I can switch between the two.

What George needs to set up are PowerPoint's Color Schemes. With Color Schemes, you can have several different schemes for each presentation created. What's more, after the schemes are created, the colors for a whole presentation can be changed.

Every presentation created in PowerPoint has one or more color schemes associated with it. These schemes can be viewed by right clicking on a slide and selecting Slide Color Scheme in PowerPoint 2000 and earlier versions. This opens the Color Scheme window, which has two tabs. The Standard tab shows miniature slides with the various color schemes already set for the current design. The

Custom tab shows the color categories and the current scheme color for each category.

In PowerPoint 2002, the color schemes are accessed by right clicking on a slide and selecting Slide Design. A new pane appears on the right side of the screen. At the top of the pane are three options. Color Schemes brings up the available color schemes for this design. At the bottom of the pane is a link to Edit Color Schemes. Clicking this brings up the Edit Color Scheme box, which offers the same basic options as the same as the Color Scheme window described above.

Each color element in the color scheme defines the color for a number of elements within the PowerPoint presentation, as shown in the following table.

Color Category	Base or Default Application
Background	• Base background color for a slide. However, if a background fill or image has been applied to the slide, you probably won't see this color • Background color for charts and graphs
Text and Lines	• All text entered in placeholders, autoshapes and text boxes • Borders on autoshapes • Text and lines on charts and graphs
Shadows	• Autoshape shadows • Selected text • Fifth series on charts and graphs
Title Text	• All title text on slides, charts and graphs • Sixth series on charts and graphs
Fills	• Fill used for autoshapes • Fill for first series on charts or graphs
Accent	• Fill for second series on charts or graphs • Unfollowed hyperlinks • Third series on charts or graphs
Accent	• Followed hyperlinks • Fill for fourth series on charts or graphs

To change a color scheme item, click on the color swatch and press change color. It brings up a color picker window. Once the new color is chosen, click Preview to check the look. When satisfied, click either Apply to change only the current slide or Apply All to change the entire presentation. Clicking either option saves this scheme with the template/presentation. A maximum of 16 different color schemes are saved with any single PowerPoint file.

What if the slide background is not just a single color? If automatic is selected for the chart background, the chart is created with the background color, not with the background picture or fill. If the actual background is expected to show through the chart, select a chart background of None.

Besides providing quick and easy access to groupings of colors, color schemes have another use. If a presentation is going to be changed into a template, the users of the template may not want to use the colors originally defined. By offering several color schemes with the template, the users are provided options for their use. Good options to build into a group of color schemes include schemes for viewing in a lighted room, schemes for viewing in a darkened room and a white background scheme for printing.

When bringing up any screen providing default color choices, the colors used in the color scheme will show up as the first eight choices. The color choices are grouped as follows:

- Automatic
- A large block of color swatches
- A row of eight swatches matching the color scheme
- A row of the last eight color swatches used that were not in the color scheme

Choosing Automatic leaves the background of the chart the same as the background color in the color scheme. If Automatic is chosen and the color scheme changes, the background color for the chart changes. If using anything other than Automatic, the fill color will remain the same when the color scheme is changed.

When a different color scheme is chosen, the color choices in the next to the last row change, but items already colored do not change. If custom color has been selected for any object, the new color replaces a color in the last row, but objects that have already had the replaced color applied do not change colors.

Tip 23: The black and white color scheme	If the presentation has a bright colors and graphics and is being printing to a black and white printer, the results may not be as expected. In this case, set up and use a white background scheme specifically for printing. When ready to print the presentation, change to the black and white color scheme and verify all automatic items will show when the presentation is printed. In PowerPoint 2000 and earlier, use View→ Black and White to do the verification. In PowerPoint 2002 and later, use View→ Color/Grayscale and choose pure black and white or grayscale.

How To Delete A Color Scheme

If there is a color scheme to which others should not have access to, or if there is a color scheme you decide you really don't like, it can be deleted.

- Bring up the Standard tab of the Color Scheme window
- Click once on the scheme to be deleted
- Click once on the Delete Scheme button at the bottom of the window

Color Gotchas

Besides the possible color problems we have already addressed, there are three very common problems with colors and color schemes you need to understand how to handle.

Color Numbers: CMYK, RBG, Etc.

In the graphic design world, there are several different color models. The most popular are CMYK, Pantone (PMS), HSB and RBG.

- CMYK – Abbreviation for Cyan, Magenta, Yellow and Key (Black). These are the four colors of ink from which all other printed colors are created. Each color within this model is given a number indicateing how much of each of these main colors are used to create the target color. CMYK colors can be approximated on monitors, but are designed for use on four-color offset printers.

- Pantone (PMS) – Model where each color is defined by a single number. That number corresponds to a color in the Pantone Matching System color definition book. This book provides the ink setup for the color. While monitors can approximate all colors in the set, the actual color is only defined for printing.

- HSB – Abbreviation for Hue, Saturation and Brightness. The colors are based off how much black or white is mixed with the original hue to make the end color brighter or darker. These colors are used in a variety of ways, but are not as formally defined as the other systems.

- RBG – Abbreviation for Red, Blue and Green. The colors in this system are represented by three numbers. The first number is the amount of red in the color, the second the amount of blue and the third is the amount of green. RBG numbers are based off the three guns originally used to "shoot" colors at monitors and television sets. These numbers are designed for on-screen use such as viewing material on monitors, TV screens and projectors.

Tip 24: RBG Color Numbers	RBG color numbers can be either decimal numbers or hexadecimal numbers. Hexadecimal numbers are *base 16* numbers. Instead of using 0-9 for digits, they use 0-9 plus A-F for digits.
	If you look at the color definitions on a web page, they are RBG numbers in hexadecimal. If you look at the RBG numbers in PowerPoint, they are in decimal. You need to convert the numbers from one system to the other in order to check the colors. Some online number conversion tools are:
 • www.cerebuswebmaster.com/ onsite/rgbhex.php
 • www.two4u.com/color/dec-hex.html
 • www.afineride.com/dechex.html
  The first site does the number conversion and displays a swatch of the color. The other two sites just do the conversion.
  Numbers for each of the three colors range between 00 (none of the color) to FF or 256(all of that color).

Why should the PowerPoint developer care about color numbers? Graphic designers tend to work in CMYK or PMS. PowerPoint only works with RBG. So, if the graphics were created in PhotoShop or another high-powered graphics tool, they were likely saved with a color scheme PowerPoint can't duplicate. Instead, it approximates the colors and translates them to the closest RBG color available.

While this is fine for most work, your company may have a corporate color defined and that color is likely to have been designed for printed materials. When PowerPoint gets its hands on that color, it changes the color to RBG. The translation may not be as close as you would like. You may or may not notice the difference on the screen, but when the slides are printed you most likely will.

What can you do about it? Not much. If you are taking graphics defined for the print world and using them in PowerPoint, the best bet is to see if the graphics can be saved with RBG colors. This way, you have a better interpretation of the colors, and the graphics look better when printed.

My Text Keeps Disappearing

Ever had text disappear when selecting it for editing? This is the fault of an improper color scheme.

The person developing the color scheme inserted a graphic as the background, but did not check the setting of the background color. Because of this, the designer didn't know the background color was set to the same color as the text color.

When selecting text, PowerPoint automatically sets the text color to something contrasting with what the color scheme has as the background color. However, since the graphic inserted as a background is a different color, it will seem as if the text disappears.

Another common problem is followed hyperlinks. If the followed hyperlink color contrasts with the original background, but not the actual background, the followed hyperlink can disappear while the presentation is run.

How to get around this gotcha? Simple: Test out the color schemes any time the background is changed. Be sure each of the eight default color swatches still show on the new background.

Wall Color

When projecting a presentation, it is always best to use a white or off-white projection surface. If the surface is colored, be sure to test the background before the audience gets there. Orange walls, green walls, even blue walls change the color of the background and you may not like the results.

If presenting on a dark wall, brighten the colors considerably to compensate for the light absorption of the wall. If the presentation will be displayed on a colored surface, set up a color scheme ahead of time can compensate for the surface color.

Gradients

Now that George knows how to set up good color combinations for presentations, it is time to discuss the other color combination tool in PowerPoint: Gradients.

Gradients are combinations of two or more colors or shades fused together to form a pattern. Colors in gradients flow together to create an even, but varying, background.

Gradients work well as backgrounds or as colors for individual elements. However, don't use gradients for text colors.

Gradients are defined on the Gradient tab of the Fill Effects window. There are three types of gradients PowerPoint can define (Figure 5-1):

- One color: Based on a single color, which PowerPoint changes to create the pattern

- Two colors: Based on two colors or shades, which PowerPoint then merges to create the pattern

- Preset: Pre-defined mixes of a series of colors, which are used in the pattern you choose

For each style of gradient, choose the style of the gradient and the specific variant of that style to use. If working with a shape or other element, define its level of transparency (how well you can see through the gradient to the items behind it). Transparency on backgrounds cannot be set, as they are always the bottom layer of any slide.

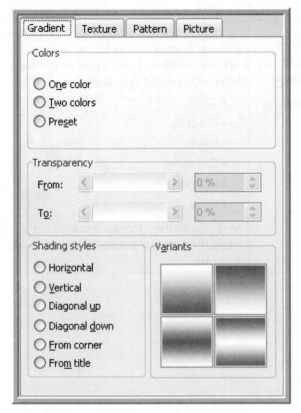

Figure 5-1: Fill Effects Gradient Window

The only way to have a PowerPoint gradient use more than two colors is to use one of the 24 preset gradients. While most of these gradients are too bright to use as backgrounds, adjusting their transparency makes them very useful as overlays to change the look of a particular slide.

Tip 25: Add a rainbow	For an attention grabbing effect on a black slide, create a box to appear over the text. Define the box to have a fill effect of either of the rainbow gradients. Change the transparency to allow more or less of the black to show through. This effect gives a high tech look. Don't use this in a presentation to be projected – the effect doesn't work as well.

Tip 26: Add a metallic sheen	To add a shine to an object or slide background, create a shape the same size as the area. Bring up the fill effects window and select one of the following preset gradients:
	• Gold
	• Gold II
	• Brass
	• Chrome
	• Chrome II
	• Silver
	Next, set the transparency fairly high for the object and make sure the line for the object is set to none.

6. Make It Move

➢ Animations in PowerPoint 2000 and earlier versions

➢ 2002 and up: Even Better!

➢ Timing

➢ Motion Paths

Alicia is an elementary school teacher. Every year, her class has a session on whales and their migration. About three years ago, Alicia developed a series of PowerPoint presentations centering on the life and migration of a whale she called the "mythic whale." Two years later, she emailed looking for help with animating her presentation.

A couple of years ago, I decided to create a presentation to help me teach my students about animal migration. I am now ready to take that presentation to the next level, but really don't understand PowerPoint animation. Can you help me out?

Currently, the presentation is slides of bulleted text, including a definitions slide, a slide with a picture of a whale's anatomy, a map with the migration pattern on it and some other informational slides.

The presentation as it exists is boring. I have tried to play with PowerPoint's animations, but I don't know what I am doing. Can you help me make the presentation a little more worth sitting through?

In all versions of PowerPoint, you can choose a variety of ways to make an object:

- Become visible

- Move across the screen

- Change or disappear or change in a number of different ways.

In PowerPoint 2000 and earlier versions, the animation options are very limited. Each object can have at most one animation applied to it. Objects can only be moved on the screen after they become visible. Once an object is visible on the slide, the only built-in way to make it invisible is to make it change on the next mouse click or animation. All animations in these versions occur on the entrance of an object. The animation timeline for a slide is fixed. To have an action occur outside of the fixed timeline, other slides must be used to fake the effects.

In PowerPoint 2002 and later versions, all this changed. Objects can have three types of effects: entrance effects, emphasis effects and exit effects. Each object can have multiple animation effects applied to it, including multiple passes through the entrance and exit sequence. The addition of motion paths allow objects to move from one point on the screen to another along a predefined or user-drawn path. Animations can now occur in a non-linear manner through both animation ordering and animation triggering.

Animations In PowerPoint 2000 And Earlier

Alicia's original slides were quite boring. For example, her definition slides looked like this:

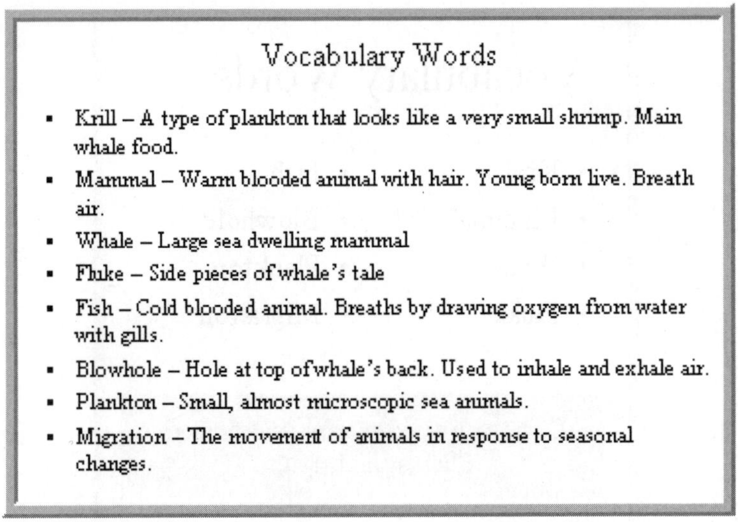

Vocabulary Words

- Krill – A type of plankton that looks like a very small shrimp. Main whale food.
- Mammal – Warm blooded animal with hair. Young born live. Breath air.
- Whale – Large sea dwelling mammal
- Fluke – Side pieces of whale's tale
- Fish – Cold blooded animal. Breaths by drawing oxygen from water with gills.
- Blowhole – Hole at top of whale's back. Used to inhale and exhale air.
- Plankton – Small, almost microscopic sea animals.
- Migration – The movement of animals in response to seasonal changes.

Figure 6-1: Initial Vocabulary Words Slide

The first thing to do is to change the slide so it only contains the words to be defined. Because we are adding action to this slide, we are also going to tell the students how to access the additional information.

To explain how PowerPoint actually animates objects, we change this slide to make it less text intensive. Because it would also be useful to be able to click on any of the words and have the definition for the word appear and then disappear, we use the process of creating this effect to demonstrate how PowerPoint actually animates objects.

PowerPoint 2000 only allows objects to appear and disappear in a set order. To make PowerPoint do what we want, we need to fool the students into seeing what we want them to see.

The new slide looks like this:

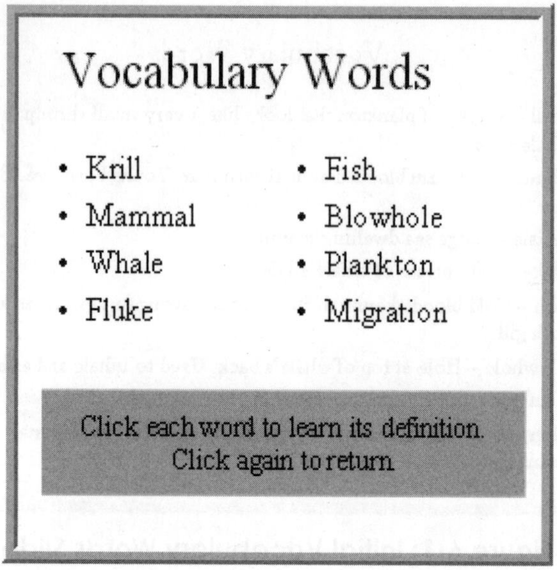

Vocabulary Words

- Krill
- Mammal
- Whale
- Fluke

- Fish
- Blowhole
- Plankton
- Migration

Click each word to learn its definition.
Click again to return

Figure 6-2: Redesigned Vocabulary Words Slide

This main slide is linked to a series of other, almost identical slides that show each individual definition on the screen. By linking each slide to a word, clicking any word appears to make a box with its definition appear. Clicking a second time returns to the word list. Using this process, the students are fooled into believing the definitions appear and disappear, no matter what order the words are clicked.

What we are going to do is to make it impossible to tell we have changed slides. PowerPoint animation works much like an old-fashioned child's flipbook. As long as the background stays the same, making small changes in slide objects allows the viewer to see movement.

In this case, we are going to move from the slide in Figure 6-2 to a slide containing the definition of the word krill.

When we click on the word, the definition box appears. When done with the animation, we click again. This returns us to the word list slide. The effect is the box disappears. Since the animation of the definition for krill is now on a separate slide, we can do things outside of a linear timeline and make it appear everything is happening on the same slide.

Example: Create The Slides

Let's create a sample definition slide so you can see exactly how this is going to work. First, create a presentation containing the word list shown above. Next, use Insert → Duplicate Slide to create a copy of the slide.

On the first duplicate slide, add an autoshape box or circle and enter the definition for the first term (krill). Since we want the words to zoom out on the slide, make the autoshape into a 3-D shape. The final slide looks something like this:

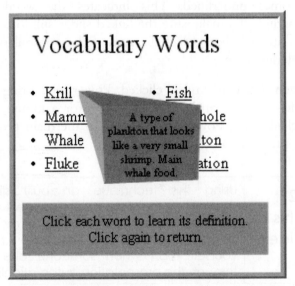

Figure 6-3: Defining Words using Linked Slides

We are now ready to make the box and the graphic appear. Go to the Custom Animation window and set up the definition shape and the graphic to appear after no delay, using the Zoom from center effect. This causes both items to enter as soon as the slide comes up. Test the slide to make sure it works.

Once the slide is working, create a custom show containing just this slide (see Custom Shows in Chapter 3). Once the custom show is created, hide each of the definition slides so they do not play when the presentation is run.

Finally, we need to be sure everyone knows there is more information available on the word krill. To do this, select the word and create a hyperlink to the custom show containing the new slide. When creating the hyperlink, be sure the Play and Return box is checked. Then, the word krill might look like this:

- # Krill

After creating the link, the word Krill changes color and becomes underlined. This indicates the word contains a hyperlink. To make sure the linked slides still look the same as the original slide, select the rest of the vocabulary words and underline them.

When the word krill is clicked, PowerPoint bring up the new slide, runs the animation and waits for a mouse click. When clicked again, PowerPoint returns to the main presentation so the presentation can continue on.

Tip 27: Apply this to built slides	Using this technique on built slides? After duplicating the slide, delete any text not showing on the screen. This situation is more likely to appear when presenting the presentation yourself than when someone else is working through the presentation automatically.

One Slide, Many Tips?

Create a link, a custom show and a hidden slide for each tip. In our case, after creating all the links the main slide would look like this:

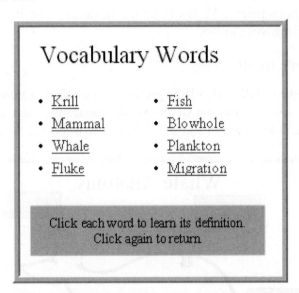

Figure 6-4: Completed Linked Vocabulary Words Slide

Making Things Appear And Disappear In Order

To set up several pictures to appear and disappear on the same slide, use the Hide on Mouse Click options on the custom animation pane. Animate each picture to appear in order with the animation desired and the hide option set. When someone is viewing the presentation, clicking on a picture makes it disappear and makes the next one reappear.

Want this to happen automatically? Instead of setting the animations to happen on mouse click, set each one to happen after a set time has passed.

Create A Review With Animation

The same technique can be used to make the whale's anatomy slide into a review instead of just a presentation of the information. This slide lets the students know if the answer they provide is the right one or the wrong one.

To do the review, Alicia displays the main slide. When she points to a box, the students call out an answer. By clicking in various places, Alicia can let the students know if they gave the right answer or not.

Let's Try It!

Make a slide with a large picture of a whale. Create callouts next to several elements of the whale's anatomy, such as the teeth, the flukes, the tail and so forth. Figure 6-5 is the base slide.

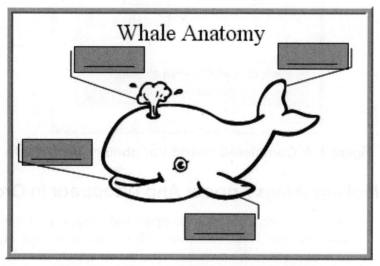

Figure 6-5: Base Whale Anatomy Slide

For each callout, make another slide brings up the right answer. For the fluke, this slide would look like Figure 6-6:

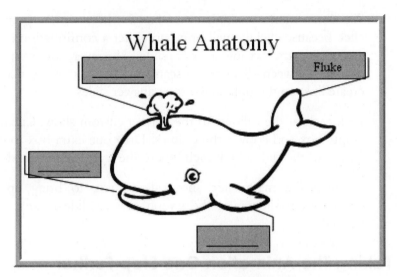

Figure 6-6: Correct Answer Slide

In addition, create a slide with the whale with a graphic over it that says "Wrong answer." This slide would look like Figure 6-7:

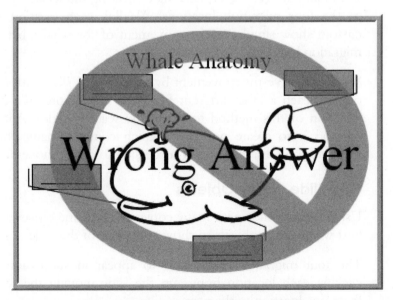

Figure 6-7: Incorrect Answer Slide

Create a custom show for each of these slides and then hide them.

We don't want the students to know where we are going to click because clicking will bring up either a confirmation of the answer or the wrong answer slide. However, we want the transfer between slides to be seamless. To do this, we need to create links to the right and wrong answer slides.

Link each of the callouts to the correct custom show. Create an empty box and copy it three times. Drag one extra box to each corner of the slide. Link each box to the wrong answer slide.

Running the main slide show allows you to bring up the confirmation slides and the wrong answer slide in any order desired.

Taking The Animation One Step Further

Alicia's definitions now work much better. It is time to move on to the slide with the migration path of the whales.

To achieve the look Alicia wants, we combine the two techniques above. We create a slide showing the whales at each of the four migration locations. We link each location to a custom show simulating the movement of the whales between migration locations.

We can achieve the movement by creating one slide with many objects, each a little different from the one before. We use a variation of this method to create the seasons slide. Another method is to create one slide, which contains many objects appearing and disappearing in succession to depict movement.

One Slide, Many Objects

Using a single slide with many copies of the same object works best when all the objects to show at the end of the slide.

The four migration paths need to appear in succession and clicking each location brings up the slide moving the whales from one location to the next.

Place the whales and season names at the appropriate locations along as shown in Figure 6-8:

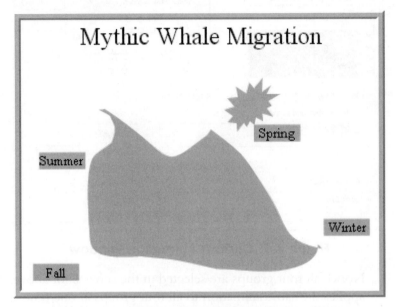

Figure 6-8: Preliminary Whale Migration Slide

Because we want the whale and the season to appear at the same time, group each pair together.

Set up the custom animation to make each group appear in succession. Open the custom animation window and set each group to appear automatically after 2 seconds. Set the order of the animations to go around the circle. The animation window should look about like Figure 6-9:

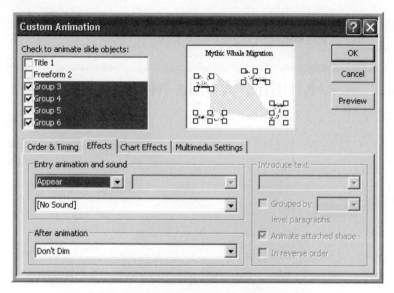

Figure 6-9: Custom Animation Window

Notice all four groups are selected in the screenshot above. This applies the same animation to all four groups at one time.

Many Slides, One Object

Using one slide for each movement works best when you want only one object on the slide at any time. This technique makes it easier to select and work with the correct item for animation.

Use Insert → Duplicate slide from the migration slide to create the base slide for each show. Set each slide to transition automatically after zero seconds to the next slide. Hide each of these four slides. Do the following process for each season:

- On the first slide, delete all whales and seasons except the word Spring and its whale. This is the starting point for the whale animation.

- Duplicate this slide. Ungroup the whale and the word. Move the whale one-half of its width along the path to the summer location. The slide will look something like Figure 6-10:

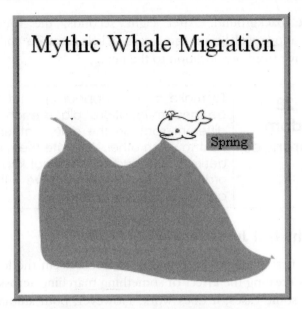

Figure 6-10: Simulating Motion Using Duplicate Slide

- Repeat the previous step several times, moving the whale small amounts each time. Because you are using duplicate slides, the animation settings and the transition settings should remain as you want them.

- When satisfied with the number of whale movements, hide each of these slides. Now move to the second of the four slides you created at the start of this process. On this slide, delete all whales and seasons except the word Summer and its whale. This is the ending point for the animation.

- Create a custom show containing the spring slide, the in-between slides and the summer slide. Call this show SpringToSummer.

- Go back to the slide containing all four seasons. Select the word Spring and its whale. Create a hyperlink from them to the show SpringToSummer. Be sure to click the Show and return box.

Verify the slides work as intended, then repeat the process for each of the other three season changes.

After completing the creation of all four custom shows, test out the slide show. Entering the migration slide should bring up just the background. After eight seconds, the four migration locations will be on the screen. Click a season and the whales move from one location to the next.

Tip 28: Random appearances	To make objects appear in what appears to be random locations, place each object in a different spot on the slides, rather than right next to each other. Animate them in the order desired. The audience will not know what the order is and will believe the object appearances are random.

Why Not Just Use "Fly" Or "Crawl?"

At first glance these two effects would seem the logical choice for creating the effect of something marching across the screen. In some cases, it does work. However, both animation effects have the limitation that the timing cannot be controlled. Fly is always very fast, crawl is always very slow. If these are the right speeds, use them.

2002 And Up: Even Better!

Now that Alicia understands how to do her animations in PowerPoint 2000, it's time to move to PowerPoint 2002. This version revolutionized the way animation works for objects on slides. There are now three different classifications of animations:

- Entrance animations are covered in Chapter 3.

- Exit animations allow objects on a slide to disappear in a wide variety of ways. They can subtly fade out, they can explode and they can do many amazing things.

- Emphasis animations give focus to objects on the screen by having the object move or change. These include changing size, shape and color.

Another addition is the animation timeline. Instead of object animation being limited to a single linear timeline, animations and effects can now happen in a non-linear manner. Multiple animation streams can occur at once. Single objects can have more than one animation effect applied.

Oh, and did I mention speed can now be controlled on a much finer basis? Each effect has a more detailed set of timing options. For example, you can more finely adjust the speed at which effects occur, including the fly and crawl speeds.

Sound confusing? It isn't. Let's work through the whale examples and see how much easier they are to create with the new animations.

First Step: Create The Graphics

To demonstrate the new animation effects, we are going to create a slide showing how the change of seasons impacts the krill in each area. As in previous versions, you need objects to animate. Our object is a shape representing the krill population. Before animating the population, it is a blob next to the spring migration location, as shown in Figure 6-11:

Figure 6-11: Preliminary Krill Animation

We are only going to work through the spring krill arrival. If you wish, do the others for practice.

Second Step: Make The Krill Appear

Click on the krill star. Open the custom animation pane, either via the Slide Show menu or the right-click menu.

Under Add Effect, select Entrance → More Effects. From the Moderate list, select Stretch. Set the stretch to occur From

Bottom and Slow. On the options, ensure the effect starts on-click.

At this point, the effects list should look like Figure 6-12:

Figure 6-12: Animation Effects Window for Krill Appearance

The star on the slide has a 1 in a gray box next to it. The 1 indicates this shape has an animation attached and it will animate first in the sequence of slide actions. From here on, every time an animation is set up on an object to be activated with a click, the object is assigned a number. These numbers make it much easier to find and follow the order of the animations.

Third Step: Make The Krill React To The Temperature Change

Select the star again. We want it to darken. To add the darken effect, click anywhere in the animation pane (but not on one of the listed animations). This leaves the star selected, but no animations selected. Now add an emphasis effect of Change Fill Color. This effect is under the Basic effects list of Emphasis → More effects. Use the drop-down for the fill color option to select the new color. Set this animation to occur after the previous animation.

Now, the effects list should look like Figure 6-13:

Figure 6-13: Changing the Animation Fill Color

Fourth Step: Make The Krill Disappear

Select the star one more time to add an exit effect. The star will exit by contracting slowly after the previous effect has finished. After adding the exit effect, the effects list should look like Figure 6-14:

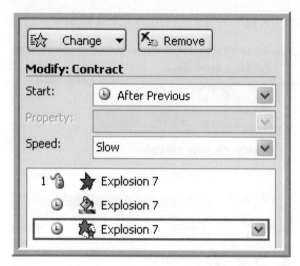

Figure 6-14: Making the Krill Disappear

To have multiple polls of krill, copy the star after applying the animations and paste it wherever else the krill will appear. The animations are copied along with the object. To make them appear at different times, change the timing and start options to the desired setup.

Timing

At the start of this chapter, we created a page of word terms to be defined. The user clicked on a word term and another slide appeared containing the definition. This can be quite tedious as the presentation design gets more complex.

The animations we have done up to this point in PowerPoint 2002 and later are easier to set up because things can appear and disappear on the same slide. However, all of these are still part of a sequence of either timed animations or click-initiated animations. The ultimate way to set up a definition page would be for the animations to occur outside of a preset timeline, with a click. *Triggers*, which were added in PowerPoint 2002, allow these types of animation sequences to be created quickly and easily.

What Is A Trigger?

A trigger is a click that initiates a series of animations and effects. Triggers are set up via the Timing tab of the Effect Options window.

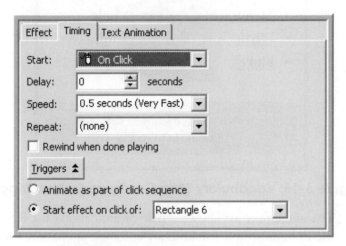

Figure 6-15: Timing Effects Window

The trigger information only shows when the Triggers button has been clicked. To set up the trigger for an animation, click the Start effect on click of radio button. To change the animation back to a regular animation, click the Animate as part of click sequence radio button.

Triggers are clicks on objects on the screen, including placeholders. Unfortunately, triggers cannot set on a word of text within a placeholder; triggers can only be set on objects.

Setting Up A Trigger

The first step to creating a triggered animation is to create the slide and the elements that should appear when the trigger is clicked. In our case, start with the definitions slide.

Add the definition boxes that appear when a word is clicked. Then, set up the animation for the boxes. Each definition should be set to zoom in when clicked and disappear when clicked a second time. After adding the definition box for krill, the slide looks like Figure 6-16:

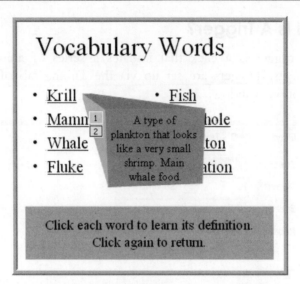

Figure 6-16: Vocabulary Slide Configured with a Trigger

The animation list shows a pair of animations for Rectangle 5, the definition box for krill: an entrance animation and an exit animation. The next step is to make them triggered animations.

We cannot click on the words to start the animation sequences, because they are all part of the same object/placeholder. Because triggers must be set to unique objects on the slide, we create an empty box slightly larger than the word krill, place it over the word and set the trigger on the box.

Now, we determine the name of the empty box. To do this, add an animation to the empty box. You see a new entry at the end of the animations list, which should look like Figure 6-17

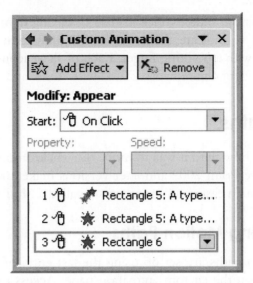

Figure 6-17: Custom Animation Window for Triggered Words

Note the new element is called Rectangle 6. Click on the animation and delete it. You do not want to delete the shape, only the animation.

To set up the trigger:

- Right-click on the entrance animation for the definition and select effect options.
- Bring up the timing tab and click Triggers.
- Click the radio button for Start effect.
- From the drop-down list, select Rectangle 6.
- Click OK. The triggered animation moves to the bottom of the list.

Repeat these steps for the exit animation of the krill definition. At the end, the animation list should look like Figure 6-18:

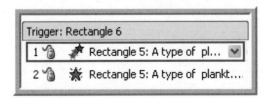

Figure 6-18: Trigger Animation

Look at the slide. Notice instead of having numbers next to the shapes to indicate the order of the animation, there are now hands with a pointing finger. Each of these icons indicates there is a trigger animation associated with this shape.

Motion Paths

Remember how hard it was to move the whale around the migration circle? PowerPoint 2002 and later versions make implementation of that slide much easier via a mechanism called a Motion Path.

Accessing Motion Paths

Motion paths are set up using the last entry of the Add Effect menu on the custom animation pane. Access the More Effects option of this menu; there is a selection of pre-defined motion paths, including basic shapes, lines, curves and special paths. If you can't find the path you want to use among the pre-defined paths, use the Draw Custom Path option to create freeform shapes and lines.

Making The Whale Migrate (A Simple Animation)

As an exercise, take the whale and move him along the migration path from Spring to Summer.

Start with the slide showing the island, the names of all four seasons and the four pictures of the whale. Ungroup each of the whale/season pairs. Animate each whale so it appears when the appropriate season is clicked. The animation list should look like Figure 6-19:

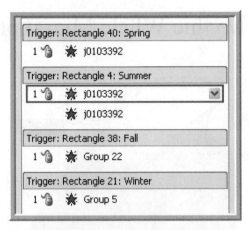

Figure 6-19: Spring to Summer Animation List

Click on the spring whale. Add a motion path curving up and over to summer. Notice the motion path shows on the slide as a dotted line with a green arrow, the starting point, at one end and a red arrow, the ending point, on the other end. An order indicator appears above the object.

Suppose the motion path curves in the opposite direction. Just right-click on the path and select Reverse Path Direction.

The default length of the curved path is probably not long enough to reach from spring to summer. To adjust the length of the path, click on the red arrow and drag it up or down. To adjust the location of either the start or end point, click on the appropriate arrow and drag it to the desired location.

Move the motion path animation down in the list so it follows the appearance of the spring whale. Set the motion path animation to start after the previous effect.

After adding the curved path and adjusting its length, the migration slide now looks something like Figure 6-20:

Mythic Whale Migration

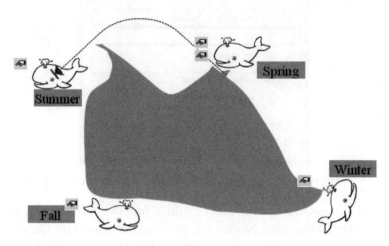

Figure 6-20: Spring to Summer Motion Path

Playing this slide moves the whale from Spring to Summer. The only thing left to do with this whale is make it disappear when we start the summer whale on its path. To do that, create an exit animation for the spring whale and set it to trigger when the word Summer is clicked. Rearrange the order of the animations so the spring whale disappears as the summer whale appears. At this point, the animation list should look like Figure 6-21:

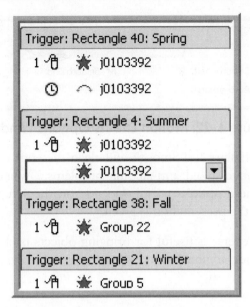

Figure 6-21: Motion Path Animation List

To complete the slide, add the same animation to the summer, fall and winter whales.

Path Properties And Options

There are three path properties to be aware of:

- Unlock: The path ends, locations and length move when the associated object is moved. You will usually want this option selected.

- Lock: Prevents the path ends, locations and length to be changed when the associated object is moved. Using this option is a good idea if building complicated slides. The paths for each object can be built then the object moved itself out of the way.

- Reverse: Path Direction: Flips the path so the end becomes the beginning and vice-versa. This can have a weird effect during the presentation because the object starts at the end. If the object is on the screen before the path is started, the object jumps to the start point before executing the path.

For a motion path, the effects tab of the Effect Option window has four path options (Figure 6-22):

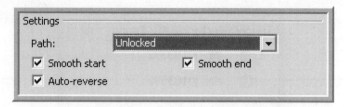

Figure 6-22: Motion Effects Options Window

Smooth start and Smooth end clean the ends of the path as an attempt to avoid anti-aliasing problems. Whether or not you find these options useful depends on the setup of the system where the presentation is given.

Auto-reverse is useful for bringing objects back along the same path they originally traveled.

7. Adding Movies

> ➤ Working with Movies

> ➤ Movie Gotchas

> ➤ What is a CODEC?

> ➤ What about Flash?

Daniel teaches high school biology to gifted students. Every year, he assigns his class members to create a presentation. After several years of working with the students by himself to improve how the presentations looked, he brought me in to help the students create their presentations.

Each student needs to create a PowerPoint presentation of at least 15 minutes that shows the lifecycle of one of the plants or animals we have studied this year. Each presentation must contain static and animated elements, as well as a movie showing the lifecycle of the plant or animal.

Originally, everyone used the same computer to create their movies. However, as technology has moved into the home environment, more and more of our students are creating their movies outside the classroom. This is causing problems when it comes time to play the presentations for the rest of the class because the movies won't always play on the school computer, even though they play on the students' computers.

I would love it if you could do a session or two with the class members on movies and PowerPoint. I think it would help them considerably.

Working With Movies

The first thing Daniel's class needed to learn was what a movie is and isn't. PowerPoint considers any file with the following extensions to be a movie:

- AVI : Audio Video Interleave
- MPG: Motion Picture Experts Group
- MOV: QuickTime
- QT: QuickTime
- ASF: Microsoft Streaming Format

The programs that create and run movie files have changed over the years. For us, that means we have to watch out for not only the file extension, but the type of file the extension represents. For example, there are four versions of QuickTime movies. PowerPoint supports only QuickTime versions one and two.

In general, the best movie formats for PowerPoint use are AVI and MPG. While other formats work, they are more likely to have compatibility problems from one computer to the next. There are other movie file types in use today, but I do not recommend using them with PowerPoint. If you have movie files other than the ones listed above, it is a good idea to convert them to AVI or MPG.

Notice animated gifs are not on the list. While they do move, they are not movies; they are graphics and PowerPoint treats them as such.

Tip 29: The best places to get movie help	There is someone who knows everything about using movies in PowerPoint: Austin Myers. Austin shares his knowledge readily in the PowerPoint newsgroup. In addition, he has developed a great series of FAQ entries known as the *Myers Multimedia FAQ*. You can find these articles at: • The PowerPoint FAQ site (www.pptfaq.com) under *Myers Multimedia FAQ* • On Sonia Coleman's site at www.soniacoleman.com/Tutorials/PowerPoint /multimedia.htm

Inserting Movies

The insertion process starts before opening PowerPoint. Just as with most sound files, movie files are linked, not embedded. The first step in adding a movie to a presentation is to put a copy of the movie in the same folder as the presentation. This way, the link to the movie is a relative link. Moving the folder from one computer to another does not affect PowerPoint's ability to find the file.

Next, open the presentation and go to the slide where the movie is to play. Insert → Movies and Sounds → From File. The window opens up to navigate to the presentation directory and open the movie.

You are asked if you want the movie to start automatically. If yes, it starts when it appears on the screen. If no, the movie must be clicked to start it.

What you see after the movie is inserted depends on which version of PowerPoint is running. If PowerPoint 2000 or earlier versions, a blue megaphone icon appears. If 2002 or later, a still shot of the first frame of the movie appears on the slide.

Another way to add a movie to a slide is to create a hyperlink to it either directly or via an action setting. This gives more control over how the slide looks. This method of movie access is good if the first frame of the movie isn't exactly what you want people to see just before the movie plays.

For example, one of Daniel's students created a movie for the lifecycle of a rose. When he inserted this movie, instead of getting his title, he got a plain pink square. I had him link the movie to a jpeg of a rose instead of just inserting it. This allowed him to adjust the slide look as he wanted.

How Does PowerPoint Run My Movies?

Contrary to popular belief, PowerPoint does not use the Windows Media Player to run movies. Instead, it uses a program called the MCI player (mplkay32.exe). This player is built into the operating system. Other programs use this player as well.

Unfortunately, some programs replace parts of the MCI player with their own code., which can make the program unusable for PowerPoint movies. Example: when another media player is installed, the new program may change the default file associations.

If movies stop working, or if transferred to another machine and they don't work, verify MCI is still handling the file type used. To do this, adjust some system file settings. I usually re-read Austin's tutorial before I do anything with these settings. I suggest you do the same.

When Does PowerPoint Run Movies?

If movies are set to play automatically, it plays as soon as it enters the slide or as soon as the slide has focus. It continues to play until it is over. The presentation can be set to continue while the movie is playing by setting the animation effects option for the movie.

Where Does PowerPoint Run Movies?

PowerPoint runs all movies in the *top layer*. That means the playing movie covers everything else on the screen while it is playing. To show text on top of a movie, use a movie editor to add the text to the actual movie frames where you want to see it; this is not a feature in PowerPoint.

This also means if the movie is set up to show in a large window and is set it to continue the show while playing, it should not put it on the master slide. It will cover up all other action on all slides until the movie is over. It should not be placed in the center of the screen on any slide, because it will cover up actions on following slides until it ends.

Movie Gotchas

The vast majority of the problems reported with movies and PowerPoint can be linked to one of the following:

- The presentation and the movie were moved from the original folder and the link between them broken.
- The machine in use has a corrupt or outdated copy of DirectX.
- The multimedia settings on the machine are incorrect.
- The movies won't display on a projection screen.
- CODEC compatibility problems

Moved One Of The Files

Happens all the time. You go to show the presentation and find the links are broken. One of the files was moved and you didn't notice, or the files weren't in the same folder before you linked them.

Guess what? If you don't want to do all the re-creation of the links beforehand, there are two automated solutions.

- *FixLinksPro*, from Steve Rindsberg - The demo version is free. The demo won't fix the movie links, only tell which links are broken. The full product will actually fix the links.
- *PowerLink*, from Sonia Coleman and Aladat – The demo version is free. PowerLink checks all links within a presentation, fixes broken ones, moves the files to a new folder and tells which links it fixed. The program runs free for two presentations then costs to register.

To fix the links by hand, copy each file to the directory with the presentation, delete the old link, create the new link and reset any animations.

Directx Problems

DirectX is one of the pickiest pieces of software I have ever used. Because it relies on common Windows components to work, it breaks when any other program breaks one of those components. In addition, Microsoft frequently puts out new versions of DirectX. So what can you do?

Regularly check the DirectX site for newer versions. If I even suspect there is a problem with running my movies, I download the latest version.

- DirectX home page:

  www.microsoft.com/windows/directx/default.aspx

- DirectX download page:

  www.microsoft.com/windows/directx/default.aspx?url=
  /windows/directx/downloads/default.htm

Incorrect Multimedia Settings

Much like the problems other programs cause for DirectX, other programs on a computer can affect the multimedia settings.

The most common problem is some other media player has taken over for or corrupted mplay32.exe, the MCI player PowerPoint uses. The best way to find out if this is what is happening is to search for mplay32.exe and see if it has been changed more recently than the other files in its folder. If so, you probably want to restore it to a real copy by bringing it back in from backup.

Another common cause is conflicts with RealPlayer software. If using any kind of multimedia in PowerPoint, do not install RealPlayer, if avoidable. RealPlayer and PowerPoint do not get along well.

Movies Won't Show On Projection Screens

This problem often occurs on laptops due to their video capacity. Some laptops do not have the computing power to allow movies to be displayed in more than one place at a time. Things may need to be set up so the presentation is only showing on the projection screen and not on the laptop display.

Another fix is to go to the display settings and look for the ability to change which monitor is in use, either Primary or Secondary monitor. The appearance of the controls are dependent on the drivers installed for the monitor, so everyone's can be different.

If monitors are switched via the display properties, the audience can watch the movies on the projection screen while you are running the presentation and you will see an empty black box on the laptop screen.

Side Note: What If My Presentation Doesn't Show At All?

You have used the PowerPoint multiple monitor setup to have the presentation run on the secondary screen. You run the presentation for the audience and it works great. Now, you go back to your desk and bring the presentation up to do some more work with it. It works fine until test it. You hit play and the presentation disappears.

What happened was that you forgot to change the presentation back to be viewed from the primary monitor instead of the secondary. Escape out of the presentation, go back to the multiple monitor setup and change to Primary. When you run the presentation again, it will show on your screen.

What Is A CODEC?

CODEC stands for Coder/Decoder. It is the software used to turn movies from static frames into digital data that software can display. It compacts the data so the files don't take up as much space on a hard drive and so they are easier to transfer from one machine to another.

Such a simple concept, yet it causes so many problems for those of us in the PowerPoint world. There are literally hundreds of different CODECs in use. Each video device company has developed their own CODECs and so have several software companies.

Tip 30: Looking for a specific CODEC?	Dave Wilson maintains The Almost Definitive FOURCC Definition List - Video Codec List. This list contains information on the history of data conversion and compression for the video world. His site can be found at www.fourcc.org/indexcod.htm
	SigGraph.org also has a list of CODECs at www.siggraph.org/education/materials/ HyperGraph/video/codecs/Default.htm

Remember the problems Daniel's class was having with movies that would play on some computers but not on others? The problem was the movies had been encoded using different CODECs, and not all the CODECs were available on the school's computers.

There are two ways to fix CODEC problems: Move the CODEC with the presentation or use a standard CODEC.

Moving and installing the right CODEC with the movie seems to me like a gigantic hassle. Thanks to an ingenious group on the web, there is a place to download all of the most popular CODECs at once. The site contains links to a full CODEC version and a light version containing only the most popular of the popular CODECs. The URL is www.divx-digest.com/software/ nimo_pack.html.

Converting the movies to a standard CODEC is an extra step, but can eliminate problems for users of the presentation, if run on multiple machines. The most standard ones are DIV-X CODECs and AVI CODECs.

There was a time when there were only two DIV-X CODECS, the CODECs for MPEG-4 and newer MPEG versions. Unfortunately, now there are many DIV-X CODECs and more are developed all the time. Because of this, a company named Stoik has developed a free program that converts many of the non-standard CODECs to a standard AVI CODEC. The program can be found near the bottom of www.stoik.com/downloads/downloads_frm.htm.

Another good source of consistently useful, correct and up-to-date CODECs compatible with PowerPoint is Microsoft. Go to the Microsoft site and search for "CODEC download." You are provided with a list of the pages on the site containing the most current CODECs for Windows machines.

What About Flash Movies?

All versions of PowerPoint 2000 and later support Flash movies. Flash movies are created using a standardized format developed by MacroMedia. Instead of using the movie interface to run Flash movies, PowerPoint uses ActiveX components. This is good because Flash movies do not depend on system configurations to run. However, the computer running the Flash movie must have the Flash Player installed. Download it from the Macromedia site at www.macromedia.com/shockwave/download/download.cgi?P1_Pr od_Version=ShockwaveFlash.

There are two great sources for information on Flash and PowerPoint. Both sites talk about both using Flash movies in PowerPoint and converting PowerPoint presentations to Flash movies.

The first site is Rick Turoczy's Flash Geek site. It can be found at: www.flashgeek.com. This is THE resource for all Flash and PowerPoint issues and information. This site contains tutorials on everything including how to link to the files and have them run, how to rewind the files and how to make the Flash files show on the projector.

The second site is Geetesh Bajah's Indezine. Geetesh has written many articles about PowerPoint and Flash. The list of articles can be found at www.indezine.com/articles/index.html. As you skim through the list of articles, you will find many on the Flash/PowerPoint topic. All are good reading.

8. Timing

➢ It Isn't Going to be Exact

➢ Faking Time Criticalness

➢ Running a Continuous Loop

For years, Wayne's church has used PowerPoint to display the words to the hymns and other songs during services. One year, he decided to expand that usage to teach the music for a series of special musical services held during the holiday season.

He needed to teach three new songs to the adult choir and five new songs to the children's choir. He didn't have much time to spend with the groups, so he started looking for a way to create presentations to help him out.

For this year's holiday music services, I am teaching many new songs. I want to use PowerPoint to create a series of presentations that can help me teach the music quickly and easily, and which the choir members can use from home for review.

I tried synchronizing the music to the slides directly. When I changed from my home machine to the church's machine, the timing was off. How can I use PowerPoint and still keep the timing in sync?

It Isn't Going To Be Exact

The quick answer to Wayne's problem is "You can't." One of PowerPoint's biggest limitations is it doesn't run presentations consistently from one computer to the next or even from one showing to the next. PowerPoint depends on system resources to run. Since different machines have different processor speeds and different background tasks, the timing of a presentation on different computers can vary widely. To minimize these problems, try the following:

Build On The Slowest Machine

Always build the presentation on the slowest machine running the presentation. PowerPoint will not speed up a presentation if more resources are available then needed, but it will slow down if fewer resources are available than needed.

By building the presentation on the slowest system, the timing is set using the worst resource. PowerPoint will not change that timing if more resources are available, so the timing should stay as set.

Pre-Run Presentations

The first time a presentation is run, PowerPoint goes through a preload process. That is, it sets up the next slide while it displays the current slide. The preload can use up valuable resources. The preload runs each time PowerPoint is closed and reopened, and run a particular presentation. After that, the presentation can be run as much as wanted without having to preload as long as PowerPoint is not shutdown.

When showing a presentation for the first time, do a dry run on the machine to be used for the presentation. This will force the presentation to preload before being done for real. Simply click through the slides. PowerPoint will do the pre-loading and continue on. Now, when presentation is run, it will not be working against another PowerPoint process.

Pre-running the presentation will lessen the need for the extra work during the presentation, but will not eliminate it.

Run From A Local, Hard Drive Copy

Running a presentation from a network drive, a web site or a CD slows down the presentation because it take longer to access the presentation itself. The less work PowerPoint has to do to access the presentation, the more resources it has to run the presentation. For optimal performance, always run the presentation from a copy placed on a local hard drive

Turn Off Background Programs

Any program running in the background of the computer is going to steal resources from the presentation. Examples of these programs include:

- Anti-virus software
- Email checkers
- Instant messenger programs
- Browser sessions

For optimal timing, turn these programs off while running the presentation. It is safe to turn off the anti-virus software after all programs with access to external files have been shutdown. Remember to enable or turn on the programs when done running the presentation.

Improve Your System Performance

In addition to turning off the background programs, also look at improving the overall system performance. The better the system is running, the better PowerPoint can run the presentation. Here are some simple tasks to improve performance.

Clean Up Temp Space

Every program run on a computer uses space on the hard drive. Many of the programs leave temporary files behind on the hard drive to make it easier for them to start up next time. These files can and should be deleted.

Every time you visit a website, the browser stores that site and its cookies in temporary space. These files can be deleted, as they will be recreated on the next visit the site.

If Windows 2000 or XP is the operating system, clean up disk space by right clicking on the disk and selecting Properties. Towards the bottom of the first tab you will see the Disk Cleanup button. Use it to remove temporary files.

If running one of the older Windows operating systems, you will need to clean up temporary files by hand. Linda Johnson has a great tutorial on her site about cleaning up temporary files by hand. The URL is www.personal-computer-tutor.com/deletingtempfiles.htm Another good tutorial can be found on The Office Experts website at www.theofficeexperts.com/cleanyourpc.htm

Turn Off Fastfind Indexer

When Windows was installed, the operating system started a process of indexing every file on the hard drive. This process makes it easier to find files by content, but it can really slow down a computer.

I never leave this turned on and have never had a problem searching for and finding files I need. When I first turned it off, I noticed a 10% increase in my computer's processing speed. That doesn't sound like much, but it can greatly impact PowerPoint's abilities to keep to a pre-defined timeline.

To turn off the indexer, remove the program from the StartUp folder. Open Windows Explorer and find all folders named StartUp. There will be one per user on the computer, plus one for All Users. Check each folder for a program called "Microsoft Office FindFast Indexer". Drag the icon to the desktop. Make sure to remove it from each startup folder where found.

To turn the indexer back on, drag the icon from the desktop back to the StartUp folder. It will start back up on the next computer reboot.

Another way to prevent StartUp items from running is to temporarily disable them. From the Start menu, select Run. Type msconfig and hit enter. Uncheck the Load startup items, and restart the computer. After presenting, run msconfig again, recheck Load startup items and restart the PC. While Windows 2000 does not come with msconfig, the executable, msconfig.exe, can be copied from a Windows XP machine, or downloaded from the internet.

Do Regular Disk Maintenance

Remove unneeded programs. Clean out the mail folder. Empty the trash. Defragment the hard drive regularly. Each of these items is one more step toward making a computer run smoother and free up resources for PowerPoint.

Hard drive fragmentation happens when files are deleted and added to a hard drive. Files are packaged into chunks by the operating system. These chunks are then spread across the hard drive. The smaller the available spaces on the hard drive, the more pieces the files are broken into. Each file must be put back together in order to be run.

Estimated disk usage before defragmentation:

Figure 8-1: Sample Fragmentation Window

When you run defrag on a hard drive, the picture will be color-coded. The codes are explained on the defragmentation screen. Figure 8-1 shows a disk badly in need of defragmentation. Notice there are many small stripes showing. These stripes represent used and unused areas on the disk.

Click the View Report button to view a text report summarizing the fragmentation of the hard drive. Note the Volume and File fragmentation sections. They look something like Figure 8-2:

```
Volume fragmentation
    Total fragmentation                       = 15 %
    File fragmentation                        = 31 %
    Free space fragmentation                  = 0 %

File fragmentation
    Total files                               = 12,434
    Average file size                         = 170 KB
    Total fragmented files                    = 1,012
    Total excess fragments                    = 10,230
    Average fragments per file                = 1.82
```

Figure 8-2: Sample Defragmentation Report

If All Else Fails...

Get more memory and/or a faster processor for the PC. The more power available, the better PowerPoint runs. If distributing the presentation for use on other machines, you probably won't be able to affect the setup of those machines.

Another Option: Manual Advance

Another option is to run the music outside of PowerPoint and use clicks to advance the animations and slide transitions on the correct beats or measure starts.

For example, during services, each slide Wayne displays shows one verse of the current song. At the proper point in the music, he moves either forward to the next verse or back to a previous verse. The congregation never gets lost in the music and the transitions are timed exactly as Wayne wants them.

This works well if the PowerPoint user is familiar with the music. Unfortunately, since Wayne's choirs are just learning the music, this is not an option for his holiday music.

Wayne did make as many of the system changes as he could, cleaned up the PC's temp space and things ran better. It still wasn't what he wanted, but it was closer.

So, is Wayne out of luck? No, he isn't and neither are you. You can fake time-criticalness. Before we do that, consider whether PowerPoint is the right application for what you are trying to do.

Are You Using The Right Application?

PowerPoint is designed with the intention there be some human intervention in the presentation. Either someone is running the presentation or someone is interacting with the presentation. If you don't want either of those to occur, think about an alternative solution:

- Create the presentation in PowerPoint and record it with a screen capture program.
- Create a movie instead of a presentation.
- Convert the presentation to a Flash movie.

In many cases, people use PowerPoint to create displays that really should be movies or streaming video. They use PowerPoint because they know it or because they cannot afford additional software. The temptation to do this is even greater with the new animations and timeline features added in PowerPoint 2002.

In Wayne's case, the church could not afford to purchase any other package to do what he needed. He opted to develop the music training in PowerPoint, then record it using the Windows Media Encoder, a free download from Microsoft.

If the Windows Media Encoder is hard to use, try Camtasia from TechSmith. It will do screen recordings and output the recordings in many different formats. For more information on Camtasia, check out TechSmith's website at www.techsmith.com/products/studio/default.asp

Faking Time Criticalness

You have decided to stick with PowerPoint to create the presentation. What can you do within PowerPoint to make the best of the situation?

Create Small Segments

The smaller the segment of the presentation linked to a single music file, the less likely it is to drift off the intended timeline. If using a piece of music in its entirety, it will drift. Break the music up into pieces the same length as the animation for each slide so less deviation occurs.

Attaching the sounds to single slides instead of the whole presentation allows more control over the timeline. This will ensure the timing for each slide is as close as possible to the length of the piece of music.

Use Minimal Effects And Animations

The more tasks PowerPoint has to perform to move through the presentation, the less likely it is to remain on the timeline. Coordinating a slide with a complex set of animations to a piece of music may be more than the computer is capable of handling, unless you have a high-powered computer. Now, if you are only going to run on high-powered computers with nothing else running, that won't be much of a problem. Most of us don't have that option.

Use Simple Music

Instead of playing a full score, use the piano version of the music you've chosen. The less complex the piece, the less likely people are to notice things aren't happening exactly on time.

Don't Trigger The Song And The Animation At The Same Time

If you must have complicated animations on a slide that are time-critical, start the animations, wait a second or two and then start the music. An indication of poor settings is stuttering and skipping of the music. Slowing the animations down can help avoid stuttering and skipping, and also make time deviation less noticeable.

Use Lower Quality Sound

The higher the sound quality, the more resources are used to play the piece. Lower the quality to lessen the impact of resource loss.

Test Out Your Presentation With Someone Else

What seems to you as an unacceptable amount of time deviation may not even be noticed by others. Have someone else view the presentation to get an objective point of view.

Ask the tester to watch for any problems with the presentation. Telling her what problems might occur could bring attention to them and the review may become as critical as your own. Be sure to ask her after the presentation whether the music and animation connections were in sync. If she says yes, great. If she says no, find out where you need to do more work.

Last Resort: Connect The Sound To The Action

If it is absolutely necessary a sound and action occur at the same time, attach the sound to the animation or transition. This is the only circumstance in which I recommend connecting the two. You may hear a stutter in the music. If you do, edit the sound to add a short (half-second maximum) empty space at the beginning.

Running A Continuous Loop

Earlier in this book we covered how to create looping presentations and we set up a kiosk to run continuously. When running continuous loops, there are some timing issues to be kept in mind:

- The longer the presentation runs, the more timeline deviation it can experience. There isn't much to do about this, it is the nature of the beast.

- Running presentations for longer than 24 hours without restarting the computer can cause a computer crash. The cause is believed to be a memory leak, but this has not been verified. The solution is to restart the program daily using Windows scheduler. If you want information on scheduling a presentation to restart automatically, check out Tushar Mehta's site at www.tushar-mehta.com. Scroll down the page to Auto Schedule on the menu of site pages and you'll find his tutorial on auto-scheduling PowerPoint.

- PowerPoint 2002 somehow lost the 5-minute reset clock feature for kiosks and self-running presentations, so a presentation running in PowerPoint 2002 may not reset.. Fortunately, Chirag Dalai has developed a free add-in available from OfficerOne at officerone.tripod.com/ kioskassist/kioskassist.html.

It is a good idea to restart the presentation daily. Restarting the presentation resets the time line drift. You may find that continuously looping presentations run more consistently, cause less computer failures and have less problems with sound and animation drifts.

9. Presentation Linking

- ➢ Linking Within the Presentations

- ➢ Absolute vs. Relative Links

- ➢ Traversing the Presentations

- ➢ Hyperlink Example: Create side menus

- ➢ Action Button Example: Exit button

- ➢ Presentation Embedding

- ➢ Linking to the Web

- ➢ Keeping the User Where You Want Them

- ➢ Kiosk Reset

- ➢ Testing

Sam handles employee benefits for her company. When her company went to a cafeteria plan for employee benefits, she was tasked with creating a series of presentations to quickly bring the entire company up to speed on the new plan options before open enrollment. While developing the presentations, Sam realized that she needed to know much more about linking within PowerPoint presentations as well as how to link to material outside of the presentations.

I have to create a series of kiosk-style presentations that pull information from a number of sources and link seamlessly between the sources. I know what has to go in each presentation and I have a good idea of how the employees are going to move around within and between the presentations. I am unclear about how to make sure all of the navigation elements are on each slide and every user understands how to move around. I am also hitting some roadblocks on connecting the information sources and presentations.

When I test my presentations, I am having problems with links not working, documents and forms not linking correctly, and general confusion by the participants about the presentations.

Sam designed her presentations well. Each presentation worked when taken alone. However, when it came time to put the pieces together, she didn't know how to set up her links so everything was viewable.

Linking Within The Presentations

Before Sam starts working on linking the different presentations together, she needs to be sure it is easy for people to understand how to navigate within each presentation. One of the basic premises for navigation within a presentation is the use of a number of icons every self-navigated presentation should have.

Each slide in a self-running presentation, no matter what the presentation's intended use, should have five buttons on it

- **Home**: Returns the presentation to its beginning. If the presentation is a series of menus, this button should return the user to the original menu slide.
- **End**: Ends the presentation gracefully.
- **Next Slide**: Moves forward to the next slide in the presentation. On the last slide, this button should wrap to the beginning of the presentation.
- **Previous Slide**: Returns to the previous slide in the presentation. On the first slide this button should be disabled.

Tip 31: Previous slide vs. Last Slide viewed	Notice we are setting up a link to the previous slide, not the last slide viewed. If you are used to using the back button on a web browser, you need to know previous slide is not like the back button.
	Previous slide takes you to the slide before the current slide. If on slide 7, previous slide will take you to slide 6, whether that is where you came from or not.
	Contrast this with the Last Slide Viewed right click option. This option is only available while running a show or as an action setting hyperlink. It will take you back where you came from, whether that is the previous slide or not.
	If you use both last slide viewed and previous slide, make the difference very clear to those going through the presentation.

- **Help**: Brings up a slide which explains how the kiosk works. Even if you think everything is self-explanatory, add help anyway. Someone will use it. What's more, writing help materials will usually uncover something you forgot to put in the presentation.

In addition, always have a Contact or Email button. This button opens an email window so users can send feedback or questions to you or some other contact point. This allows you to find out where people are having problems within the presentation, find out when things break and maybe even find out how much they like what you did.

The other button some people find useful is the return button. This is the one that looks like a u-turn arrow. This button is pre-programmed to return to the last slide viewed. It doesn't take you to the previous slide in the presentation, but instead it takes you to the last slide you looked at. I don't like to put this button on the master slide, but I do use this on individual FAQ slides, etc., to allow users to quickly return to where they came from.

The buttons should be clear to you and to those using the presentation. Almost everyone knows a picture of a house means home and an envelope means email. For the other buttons, add text to the button to identify it. To add the text, right click the button and select Add Text.

Adding Navigation Buttons

To add the navigation buttons, first go to the slide and title masters (View→ Master). Next, bring up the AutoShapes→ Action Buttons list from the Drawing toolbar (Figure 9-1)

Figure 9-1: Action Buttons Toolbar

Most of these buttons should look fairly familiar. What's more, several of them have been pre-programmed by PowerPoint to perform the action expected based on the picture.

The first one is a blank button, whose face and action are not pre-defined. The house is pre-defined to take you to the first slide of the current presentation. The question mark and circled i are not programmed to any action, but are intended to be linked to the help or information page. The right and left arrows are the previous slide and next slide buttons respectively.

Next, are two buttons you may or may not want to use as they are originally defined. The left arrow pointing to a line returns to the first slide, the right arrow pointing to a line goes to the last slide. I re-program the right-hand one to end my presentation. I don't use the left hand one, unless requested to use it instead of the home button.

To add each button, select the button from the list and click on the slide or click and drag on the slide. The Action Settings window will open.

If you like what is pre-selected, just click OK. To point the button somewhere else or do something else, select the action and then click OK.

For instance, to reprogram the button with the right arrow pointing to a line, I click the drop-down box in the Hyperlink: options and change Last Slide to End Show. If there is a preset action for the button face, clicking cancel leaves the original button action for the button face.

We will go into details on programming custom actions for the buttons later in this chapter.

Put The Buttons Where They Belong

Once all the buttons are created, drag them into position on the slide. Remember, placing navigation buttons on the slide and title masters helps ensure consistency throughout the presentation.

I put buttons across the bottom of my slides, because that is where people usually look for them. Other common placements are across the top or down the left side of the slide. With left-side placement, make sure it doesn't interfere with any menus in the presentation.

"Contact Us" or "Email Us" buttons can be created by dropping in a picture of a mailbox and giving it an email hyperlink. We will step through this process later in the chapter.

After adding her main buttons, Sam's template looks like this:

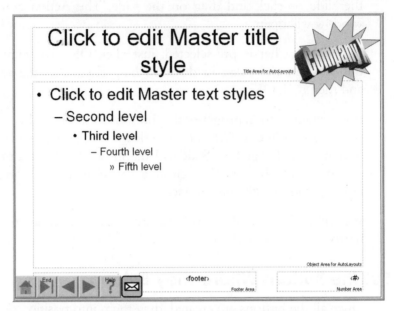

Figure 9-2: Preliminary Template with Navigation

What Do I Hook Help To?

If creating a kiosk presentation, there needs to be at least one help slide. This slide should contain the icons for the common buttons and an explanation of where each button will take the user. In addition, give the user information on how to get around in the presentations. In Sam's case, her help included a linkage map for the presentations.

When I create a single file presentation, I hide the help slide so it doesn't come up unexpectedly. When I create a series of linked presentations, I create the help slide as its own presentation and link to it as well.

The help slide or file finished may not be finished when adding the buttons to the presentation. In this case, there two choices. Don't link the button to anything, but be sure to add a comment to yourself to link it later. Or, create an empty placeholder presentation and link to it.

Absolute Vs. Relative Links

Now that we have the navigation buttons on the master slide, decide what external links need to be created. Before we do that, though, we need to cover one of the biggest pains in PowerPoint: Absolute links and relative links.

Absolute Links

On a computer, each file has a location on a storage device. This location is referenced by using a path. For example, if storing a file called KeySound.wma in the My Documents folder, the full path to the file might be C:\Documents and Settings\MyLogIn\MyDocuments\KeySound.wma. This kind of path is known as the *absolute* path (address).

When inserting this sound file into a presentation, PowerPoint creates a link to it. As long as the presentation is only used on the same machine, there are no problems. PowerPoint knows the path is the same and can always play the sound.

When sending the presentation and the sound file to another computer, because the path is absolute, PowerPoint thinks it will be located on the hard drive at C:\Documents and Settings\MyLogIn\MyDocuments\KeySound.wma. The login on the other machine isn't MyLogIn. Instead, it might be YourLogIn. Poof! The path changed and PowerPoint can't find the file, so the sound doesn't play.

Relative Links

There is another way to reference files. Instead of referencing the absolute path for the file, reference the *relative* path for the file. The relative path is the path you would need to move through to get from one file to another.

Relative links can be quite useful since they let PowerPoint find linked files. But PowerPoint understands only one kind of relative link: When both files are in the same folder before the link is created, PowerPoint creates and understands a relative link between the files. In other words, if the link doesn't contain any folder or drive references, PowerPoint will be able to use the link to find the file, no matter what computer the files move to. If the link contains any folder or drive references, PowerPoint can find the file on the original computer, but not on any other computer.

If the sound file is in a sub-directory of the folder containing the PowerPoint presentation, the relative link would be ...\KeySound.wma. This means go up one level in the folder or directory structure and find the file there. By the same token, if the sound file were in the same folder as the presentation, the relative link would be just the file name.

The Moral Of The Story

When linking files in PowerPoint, whether they are the sound files used up to now, or the PowerPoint and other files we are about to use, make sure all the files are in the same directory as the presentation before linking them to the presentation. Then, when the files are moved to another computer, take the entire folder and there's no need to worry about bad links.

What If My Links Break Anyway?

If links break anyway, wander over to PowerPoint MVP Steve Rindsberg's site and pick up his FixLinks tool. It repairs links and ensures the presentation can still find all its files. The URL for information on FixLinks is www.rdpslides.com /pptools/FAQ00035.htm

Navigating Between The Presentations

Sam developed a message table at the very beginning of her project. Each presentation has defined messages and the messages are applicable to the audiences who are getting the presentations. The next step is to figure out the order the audience members will navigate the slides and create the links based on the information.

When designing complex sets of presentations, step back and look at the information from the audience's perspective. While you may expect the audience to go through the slides in a specific order, they may not. My favorite way to figure out the possibilities is to draw a diagram representing the information and the flow between sections and within sections.

I draw a box for each message, then draw lines and arrows indicating how the messages are linked. For example, Sam's introductory materials include a definitions of the term cafeteria plan, of each employee's individualized plan budget and an overview of each of the benefits the company is offering. For each benefit, there are separate presentations detailing the exact plan information, as well as links to the Internet to get additional information.

Sam lays out an information diagram similar to Figure 9-3:

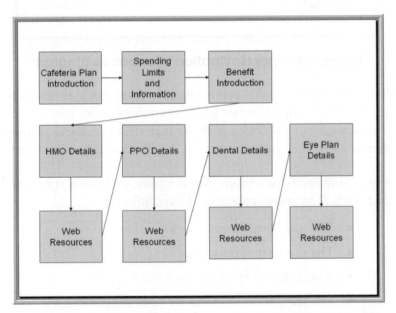

Figure 9-3: Preliminary Navigation Information Diagram

After testing, she discovered employees wanted to jump from benefit to benefit instead of from the pre-defined order she had planned. So the actual path diagram was more Figure 9-4:

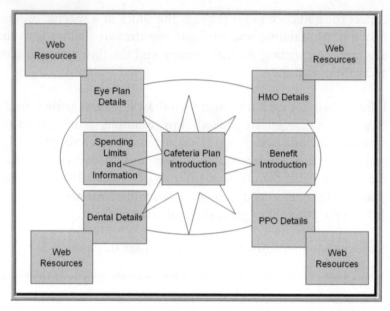

Figure 9-4: Final Navigation Information Diagram

The solution for Sam's presentation is to create a series of menus allowing the employees to jump from section to section on their own. Instead of introducing all the materials in a linear manner, the menus allow audience members to decide what they want to read.

First, Sam needs to change her template to have a menu area on each slide. This menu area should have links to:

- The main introduction slide
- The monetary limits slide
- A slide listing all of the available benefits
- The navigation elements we just talked about

After updating the template, Sam needs an introductory slide containing links to the detail slide for each benefit. This slide allows employees to get from one benefit to another with only two clicks. (One click to get to the list of benefits and a second click to get to the next benefit the employee wants to look at.)

Create a template like Sam's and a number of empty presentations you can use as link destinations. These files will let you work along with Sam as she creates her menu.

Two Ways To Link

There are two ways to link to other content. Create a hyperlink (just like the hyperlinks on the Internet) or create an action setting.

Use the right-click menu to access both the hyperlink dialog box and the action setting dialog box. If you prefer to use the menus, use the Insert menu to add hyperlinks or the Slide Show menu to add action settings.

Hyperlinks

Hyperlinks link to other slides in the presentation, custom shows, other PowerPoint presentations; open other application files (the required application must reside on the computer on which the presentation is run); access web sites on the Internet. Hyperlinks can only be activated by a mouse click or when the cursor runs over an item with a link (called a mouse-over).

Action Settings

Like hyperlinks, Action Settings allow you to move to other locations in a presentation or on the web; they also allow you to jump to other slides, custom shows, programs, or files. In addition, Action Settings allow you to run programs and execute macros. They're kind of like hyperlinks on steroids. An action can be set to occur on either a mouse click or a mouse-over.

Hyperlink Example: Create Side Menus

To add links to other presentations, Sam needs to put all the presentations in the same folder. She then opens the template she used to create the presentations originally and sets up a list of links down the side of the master slide. She knows she will need to reapply the template to each file manually, but also knows that making the change only once lessens the chance she might forget to add the menu to one of the files.

By setting up the menu and its links on the master slide, it becomes available on every slide. The links are not clickable during creation of the presentation, but they become live when run as a show. Since the slide master's elements are inherited by the title master, the title master will have the menu when it is created.

In order to add the menu, Sam needs to make space for the menu on the master pages. She adjusts the size of the 2nd placeholder so it is 1 inch narrower. After adjusting, it looks like Figure 9-5:

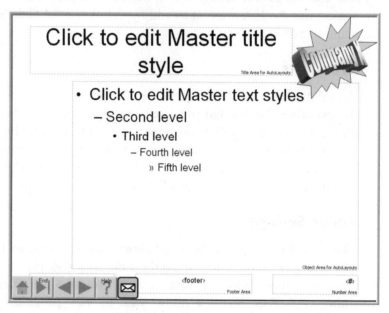

Figure 9-5: Slide Modified for Placement of Menu

Tip 32: Turn on Rulers	Need to know how far an inch is? Turn on the rulers. From the View menu, select Ruler.
	Don't see the word Ruler? Hover over the little double arrow at the bottom to get the whole menu.

Next, Sam adds the menu text. In the space just made, she adds a text box with the following lines of text:

- Changes
- Limits
- Benefits

- Next
- Previous
- Exit

After adding the menu space and text, Sam realizes some of her buttons along the bottom were also on her menu. She decides to use text for the last three menu items and removes the buttons. She feels the text would be clearer than the buttons in these cases. Her master slide now looks like Figure 9-6:

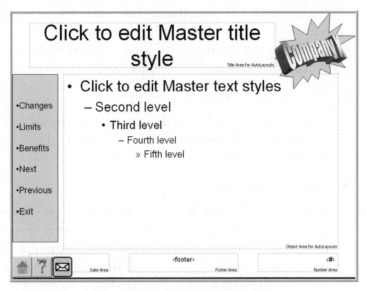

Figure 9-6: Slide with Menu

Sam is now ready to create the first link. She selects the first word (Changes), right clicks and selects Hyperlink. The Insert Hyperlink window appears.

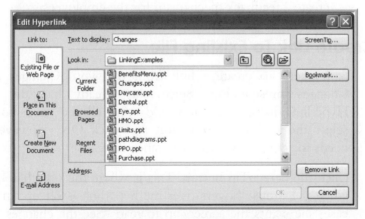

Figure 9-7: Insert Hyperlink Window

Here you can create hyperlinks to locations both inside and outside the document. Let's take a quick look at each type. Then, we will step through the link creation process to create several of the different types.

- Existing File or Web Page

  Creates links to things that already exist. Use this option to create the links from the menu to the presentations containing the information. Use this option to create links to web pages, PDFs and Word documents.

- Place in This Document

  Creates links to other slides or custom shows within the current file. Use this option when we create the links to the individual benefits.

- Create New Document

  This hyperlink is one way to create a brand new PowerPoint document. However, we will not be using this option. Instead, we use Action Settings to create the external PowerPoint file. Why? It is much more flexible and gives us more control over what we need to do.

- Email Address

  Quickly creates a hyperlink opening the user's default email program with an email pre-addressed to the email address defined in the hyperlink settings. Sam uses this option to create a feedback mechanism for the employees.

Create Link To Existing File

Sam needs to create a link from the word Changes to the Changes presentation. Since she already has the Insert Hyperlink dialog open, it would seem all she needs to do is select the correct presentation and click OK. However, she needs to set up some user assistance first.

Click the ScreenTip button. This is where the text that appears when the mouse hovers over the hyperlink is set up. In Sam's case, she wants the screen tip to read "See the changes to our benefits program." Once the screen tip is set up, Sam selects the

Changes presentation in the Insert Hyperlink dialog and clicks OK. The word Changes has changed colors and has an underline. This indicates it is a hyperlink.

Tip 33: Go to a spot in a presentation	Note the Bookmark button in the Hyperlink dialog. If the document you are linking to is a PowerPoint document, it lets you take the user to any specific slide or any custom show within the presentation.

After setting up the menu links to the other presentations, the template looks like Figure 9-8:

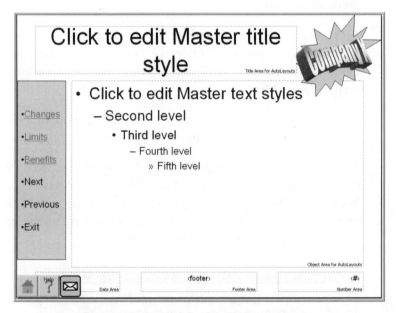

Figure 9-8: Slide with Linked Menu

Create A Link Within This File

Now that we have set up the external links, we will use the same basic process to create links within the file from the words Next and Previous.

Select the word Next, and bring up the hyperlink window. Click the Place in This Document button. Notice the center section of the window now lists places within the document you can link to. Using this list, set up the Next link by setting the hyperlink to Next Slide, remembering to set up a screen tip for it as well. When finished, set up the Previous link by setting the hyperlink to Previous Slide and setting up its screen tip.

Create An Email Link

We will set up the Exit link as an action setting in just a moment. But, before moving off the hyperlinks, one more special case hyperlink needs to be created. The employees need a way to get feedback and questions to Sam from within the presentations. To do this, set up an email link for Sam's envelope button.

Right-click on the picture and select hyperlink. Click on the Email Address button. Notice the center of the window now allows an address to be entered along with a subject for the email (Figure 9-9).

> **Note:** If you have used this option before, you will also see the previous address in the bottom box.

The destination address goes in the Email address box. Notice as soon as you start to type, PowerPoint adds "mailto:" to the front of the destination address. This sets up the hyperlink as a mail item. Next, add "I have a benefits question" to the subject area. Set up the screen tip and click OK.

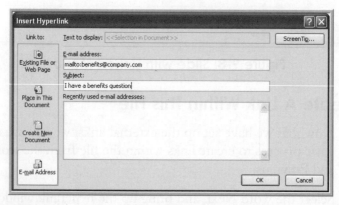

Figure 9-9: Insert Hyperlink Window for Email Addresses

Notice that unlike the text, the shape didn't change to show it is a link. When you run the presentation, the cursor will change to show it is a live link.

Action Button: Exit Button

Now that you understand how the basic hyperlinks work, it is time to take them one step further. We use an action setting to activate the exit menu item, because the Hyperlink dialog doesn't offer this option. Select the word Exit from the list of actions added to the master. Off the right click menu, select Action Settings.

Figure 9-10: Action Settings Window

When the Action Settings window comes up, it defaults to the Mouse Click tab, with no action selected. Click the Hyperlink to radio button and select End Show from the drop down list.

The second tab, Mouse Over, has the same list of actions. However, instead of requiring the audience member to click on the link to activate it, they only have to the cursor across the area. This can be good in some situations, but annoying in others; be careful how you use mouse-over settings

The End Show option tells PowerPoint when the text is clicked, the show will end. Fairly obvious, right? Don't get caught up by the one small caveat in this option. This action setting closes the active presentation only. If there are other presentations open, End Show does not close these, nor does it close PowerPoint. The exception is if viewing the only open presentation. Then the End Show option closes the presentation. If using the Viewer, ending the last open presentation also closes the Viewer. If a file was opened as a show, ending the last open presentation closes PowerPoint and returns to the desktop.

This brings up one of the biggest potential problems with using hyperlinking and action settings to navigate through presentations. It opens each presentation as you jump to them. If you don't close the presentations as you leave them, you could end up with many presentations open, using up valuable resources. .

Tip 34: Play a sound with the action	To play a sound every time the action occurs, click the Play Sound checkbox at the bottom of the Action Settings screen and select the sound. Use this sparingly –too many sounds distract the audience.

Other Action Settings

The process for setting up the other action settings is the same. Click the appropriate radio button, navigate to the action and click OK. Here are a few more tips:

- Run program: - This option assumes the program you want to run is always in the same spot. Now, if creating presentations where you control the machine, this will work. However, if, like Sam, you are creating presentations for others, be very careful using this option. For transportability, it is always better to set action settings to point to an existing document instead of an application. Then, you can place the document in the same folder as the presentation and eliminate broken link problems.

- Run macro: Macros only run automatically if PowerPoint's security level is set to low. If the security level is higher than that, a message appears letting the user know the macro may not run. If using PowerPoint 2003, the warning will appear regardless of the security level setting.

- Mouse Over: Use this sparingly. Unless the users know moving the mouse around is going to cause something to occur, mouse over can have unexpected results. If you use these options as surprise options, know the users will be surprised once or maybe twice. After that, the action becomes an annoyance.

After completing the slide master, Sam created her title master. Since the title master inherits information from the slide master, the menu options and buttons will appear on the title master just as they do on the slide master. If the title master is created already without the navigation elements, copy the elements from the slide master to the title master.

No matter when the title master is created, the size of the placeholders on the title master will need adjusting, just as on the content master. After that, close the master slides, insert a new slide and notice the slide has the new menu.

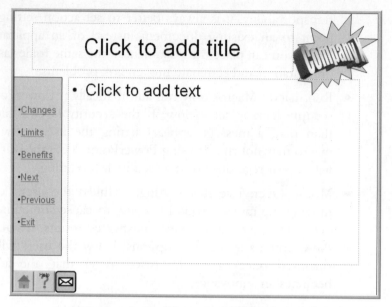

Figure 9-11: New Slide with Menu

When this presentation is run, the links become live. If you move the mouse over any of them, it turns from a pointer to a hand.

Presentation Embedding

There is another way to set up linked presentations. Instead of setting up text or shape hyperlinks, embed the other presentations into the main presentation. By doing this, any potential link breakage is eliminated (since all the files are together). This also ensures the presentations appear more secure than sending individual presentations. After all, in order to edit the presentations, those receiving them have to know they are included in the file.

There are two drawbacks to take into account when using embedded presentations. First, the file may be very large because all of the presentations are in one file. Second, you won't be able to play the presentations using the PowerPoint 2003 Viewer. At the time of this writing, PowerPoint 2003's Viewer doesn't support embedded object execution.

The process for embedding a presentation for chaining is a simple one. Edit the slide where you want to embed the presentation. Insert the presentation by selecting Insert → Object and click on the option to Create from file. Navigate to the presentation you want and click OK. The first slide of the embedded presentation appears on the current slide.

To activate the embedded presentations when the presentation is run, click the slide picture. You can also set up the presentation to start automatically by using Custom Animation. If planning to have users activate the embedded presentations, make sure they understand to click the pictures to start the presentation. When the presentation finishes being run, the show returns to this slide.

Example: Benefit List Slide

As a quick example, let's create Sam's benefits list slide using presentation chaining. Create a copy of the presentation you were just working with. Add a single slide that has a title "Benefits Available."

Using the hyperlink method, the slide would look like Figure 9-12:

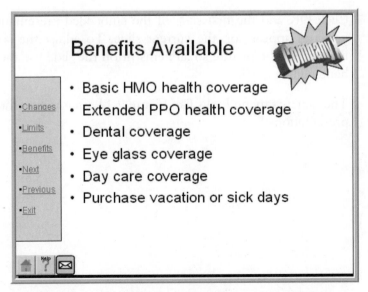

Figure 9-12: Sample Hyperlinked Menu Slide

However, to make this slide really eye catching and user friendly, replace the bullet points with actual presentations by using Insert → Object, Create from file.

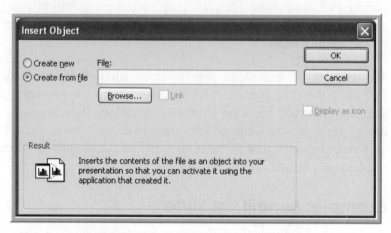

Figure 9-13: Insert Object Window

Navigate to the presentation to embed, and choose whether to display the file as an icon or a thumbnail. Linking is useful only if always sending the external file along. Display as icon is useful if you don't want to give away what the first slide of the presentation looks like.

Click OK and the first slide of the embedded presentation (or its icon) appears on the current slide. To adjust the size and location of the picture so all items fit on the slide use the white handled boxes.

The benefits menu looks like Figure 9-14 after adding the other presentations:

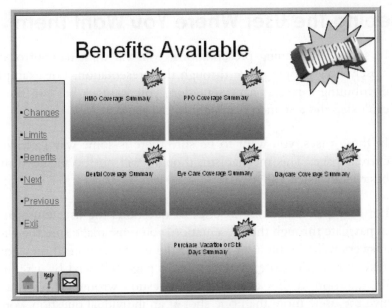

Figure 9-14: Sample Slide with Embedded Presentations

For clarity of printing, I did not include the menu or buttons on the embedded presentations. If you base inserted presentations off the master slides just created, the menus will be on the embedded presentations as well.

Linking To The Web

Linking to the web is done just like any other link. The only difference is the address is not a path to a file on the hard drive, but a URL to a page on the web. Link to web pages using hyperlinks or action settings.

Clicking a link to a web page opens the page with the default browser, as long as the Internet connection and the web page are both available. To insert web pages and have them surfable from within PowerPoint, try out PowerPoint MVP Shyam Pillai's LiveWeb add-in. Information and download links are available on his site at www.mvps.org/skp/liveweb.htm.

Keeping The User Where You Want Them

In some self-running presentations, you will want to control more closely how people move through the presentation. For example, if distributing a test as a presentation, you want to be sure the user can't skip the test and go straight to the answers.

In these cases, you want to be sure there is some way to leave the current page. This mechanism, though, will not be included in the basic icons listed above.

For example, if creating a series of questions the user must answer to navigate through the presentation, you must make sure the clicked answers will take the user to either the next question (if they got the answer right), or to a Wrong Answer page followed by a return to the question (if they answered the question wrong). If you want to give the users more than one shot at an individual question, you will need to develop a macro to handle the looping.

Since the basic navigation buttons are on the master slide, you will need to somehow not show those buttons on the test slides. The process for this differs depending on what version of PowerPoint you are using.

In PowerPoint 2000 or earlier, turn off the master elements and paste in the graphics needed from the master slide to the individual slide. To do this:

1. Right click the slide and select Background

2. Check the Omit background graphics from master box

3. Turn on the header and footer information if it should be showing

4. Go to the master slide (View → Master) and select everything (Ctrl+A)

5. Deselect the two placeholders (Ctrl+click each)

6. Deselect the navigation elements (Ctrl+click each)

7. Copy (Ctrl+C)

8. Return to the slide (View → Normal) and paste (Ctrl+V)

9. With the pasted elements still selected, right-click and Order → Send to Back

Tip 35: Send to Back with a lot of elements selected	If you have a lot of elements selected, it can be hard to right click without unselecting everything or selecting something else.
	There is another way to access the Order menu. If you look at the Drawing toolbar, you will see the word Draw. Click this and a menu shows up. Select Order → Send to back and the elements move to the back without changing the selection.

In PowerPoint 2002 and later, this process is much easier. Since you can have multiple masters, create a master slide that doesn't have the navigation elements and use it instead.

1. View → Master → Slide Master

2. Insert → Duplicate Master

3. Remove the navigation elements from the new title and slide masters

4. When you are ready to create the quiz slides, right click the slide in question and select Slide Design

5. In the Slide Design task pane on the right, click the drop down arrow for the master without the navigation elements and select Apply to selected slides

The Timing Option

Since you are running kiosks, the keyboard is disabled, with the exception of the escape key. What you may not know is the Kiosk mode also disables the ability for the audience to use right-click. So, unless there are navigation elements, users won't be able to move through the slides, right? Wrong.

When setting up the show (Slide Show➔ Set Up Show), it can be set to either manual advance or to use timings, if present. The timings referred to are transition timings and narration timings.

If you really want to control how the presentation is seen, set it up so each slide has a transition time on it. Then, for those slides where users have a choice of where to go next, remove the transition timings and add navigation buttons. This will force the user to choose one of the options in order to continue the show.

You can set up slides to advance on whichever comes first, the passage of the right amount of time or the click of a mouse. If the show is set up this way, be sure to leave enough time for users to read and understand all of the slide content before moving on. With both options set up, they can always advance more quickly than you want them to, but moving slower takes backtracking.

Kiosk Reset

When a presentation is set up as a kiosk, PowerPoint adds a feature you may or may not know about. It automatically re-starts the presentation after five minutes of inactivity. This is good for unattended presentations, not so good for attended ones where there is a lot to read on a single slide.

Having said that, I also need to say in PowerPoint 2002 this feature is broken. The timer doesn't work. So, PowerPoint MVP Chirag Dalal, has created a free add-in to fix the broken timer in 2002: officerone.tripod.com/kioskassist/kioskassist.html (there is no www in this address).

The feature was fixed in both PowerPoint 2003 and the 2003 Viewer, the add-in is only required with PowerPoint 2002.

Testing

Now that Sam has the presentations set up, it is time to find out if the presentation meets the needs of the intended audience.

Just as you must practice a presenter-led presentation in front of a test audience, you need to find some guinea pigs to test the kiosk presentation. Just because it makes sense to you, doesn't mean it will make sense to them.

Who Should Test The Presentation?

In Sam's case, two sets of testers are needed. First, we need a set of typical employees to test the presentation. Next, we need to have representative from Benefits test the presentation.

What Should The Two Audiences Test For?

The employees need to test to make sure they can navigate easily in the presentations, they understand how to use the presentation without someone standing there to help them and the information includes what they want to know. This group will do creative testing. They will be just playing around with the presentation to find out everything they can about the new benefits package and to ensure they can do what they need without getting lost. This group should also be surveyed to make sure the messages the kiosk presentations convey is what the Benefits department wanted to give.

The Benefits representative will do more formalized testing. He should help ensure the content and links for the departments part of the presentation work correctly. He needs to make sure what the employees see is what they should see and the takeaway messages are appropriate.

The testers Sam's second set of eyes. She is ultimately responsible for ensuring everything is right, but may be too close to the project to see problems.

Between the two groups, Sam should also make sure every link is tested. By having someone else test the links, no preconceived notions about what is supposed to happen on a specific slide gets in the way of seeing what really happens.

The final test is a verification of the help file. The test groups should be asked if the help is clear, complete and understandable.

How Should The Testing Be Done?

To do the testing, Sam should copy the entire set of presentations from her development computer to another one. By doing the testing away from Sam's computer, a number of things can be caught that wouldn't be otherwise

- If something doesn't get moved to the testing computer, it will show when testing occurs. If the testing is done on Sam's machine, missing content won't necessarily show.

- If a link is broken, it is better to find it during testing than after the kiosks have been made public. If Sam didn't set up her links properly, running the presentations on the test computer will show it right away. Testing at Sam's machine would never reveal these errors.

- Sam won't be there. If the testing is done on Sam's computer, Sam will be right there, tempted to explain things. By moving the testing to a different system, the testers will get information only from the presentation. The testers should note their problems for Sam to correct.

- Because the presentations were developed on Sam's computer, as the links are followed they will change color just like they do on web pages. On the test computer, the only links will show as having been followed are the ones clicked during testing.

When Should The Testing Be Done?

I believe informal testing should be done early and often. From the first point where pieces of the presentation are available, it is a good idea to have an independent set of eyes looking at things regularly to catch anything Sam misses.

Formal testing should begin when Sam believes the presentation is ready for public use. It will probably take two or three rounds of testing to get everything the way everyone wants it. The general order of the testing should be

- Sam puts the presentation and all associated files on the test computer and does a quick sanity check

- The Benefits representative does his testing and reports results to Sam

- If there were a lot of comments and changes, Sam makes the changes, puts a clean copy of the presentation and all associated files on the test computer. Then the interested parties test again

- When the Benefits representative is satisfied with the presentation, Sam re-loads the presentation on the computer for the employee group to test

- The employee group tests the presentation and reports back to Sam

- Repeat these steps as needed until the presentation is ready for public use

- If anyone other than Sam is going to do the installation or distribution of the presentation files, the installation/distribution process needs to be documented and tested as well

- When everyone is in agreement the presentation is ready for the public, all files should be placed on each computer. Double-check all final files have been included. Then, Sam can throw a party – the project is done!

This page left intentionally blank.

10. PowerPoint And Office

> ➤ Why Use Microsoft Graph?
>
> ➤ Sending to Word and Back
>
> ➤ Emailing Presentations
>
> ➤ Clip Art Gallery
>
> ➤ Word Art
>
> ➤ Equation Editor

Lydia works in Sales Support. Her job is to create and distribute various sales reports to each branch. The data she needs to work with is in Excel, but each branch manager needs to share a PowerPoint presentation with his sales people.

While all of the data is in Excel, I feel much more comfortable in PowerPoint and Word. What I have been doing is copying the data for each slide to a MS Graph table and working on the charts there. This worked well when we only sold a few products through a couple of branches.

The amount of data I process each month has grown as our product line has grown. It is now too difficult to continue manually updating the files. I need a new way to generate the graphs. I have started to learn Excel, but don't entirely understand how to make the links between the products.

Why Use Microsoft Graph?

Lydia started out using Microsoft Graph because it was there. Basically, people use MSGraph because it is integrated into PowerPoint and seems easier to use. The very limits MSGraph places on data manipulation makes it seem easier to use to the novice user.

In reality, MSGraph is more limited than Excel. It has no multi-datasheet capability. It has a limited ability to manipulate and compute data.

Lydia started using MSGraph because it kept some of the data isolated in the PowerPoint presentation. She didn't want the branch managers to be able to edit (and possibly corrupt) the main corporate data sources. What she didn't know was that you can easily insert charts from Excel and then break the links between the data and the graphs.

Using the linking method allows you to do computations and graph creation in Excel but still limit the possibility of data being accidentally changed.

So, How Do I Do It Then?

Let's start in Excel. Lydia needs to build a chart showing the sales trend for the Phoenix Branch for large widgets over the last six months. The data has already been gathered into an Excel spreadsheet for her; she just needs to create her graphs and move them to PowerPoint.

In Excel, she selects the data for her graph and clicks the chart button. She is amazed to find the interface for charts in Excel very similar to MSGraph. After stepping through the wizard, she ends up with a chart which looks like one she is used to seeing in MSGraph. She can either copy and paste the chart directly into the PowerPoint file or she can link to the chart in the Excel file.

To link the chart, Lydia can either paste the data using Edit → Paste Special or insert it using Insert → Object →From File,

Link. In both cases, she can insert the chart so it shows as a chart or as an icon on the slide.

Using Edit → Paste To Add Items

To paste the chart on a slide, select and copy the chart in Excel. Switch to PowerPoint and paste it using Edit → Paste or Edit → Paste Special. With Paste Special, several options become available, such as pasting as an Excel chart object or various types of picture formats.

In PowerPoint 2002 or later, a regular paste of the chart brings up a Smart Tag letting you define how to paste it: as a Picture of Chart (smaller file size) or as the Excel Chart (entire workbook) with all the data included. While this method can save keystrokes, it doesn't give as many options as the Paste Special dialog.

If you do a regular paste of an Excel document in PowerPoint 2000 or earlier, the entire workbook will be embedded in the presentation. This can greatly increase the size of the file.

Using Insert → Object To Add Items

Using Insert → Object to add content creates one of two kinds of OLE elements: OLE links and OLE embedded programs. Both are ways to get information developed elsewhere into the presentation, but they cause drastically different results to the size of the presentation.

There are three ways to insert objects. You can insert a link to a file that already exists outside of PowerPoint, create a new object using another application from within PowerPoint or insert an object that already exists outside of PowerPoint without creating the link.

Object	How to Create	Behavior	Notes
Link	Insert→ Object→ Create From File. Select Link. Browse to File. OR Copy information in other application. In PPT, Edit→Paste Special, choose Paste Link.	Allows file editing in either the other application or PPT. File created outside of PPT and remains outside of PPT.	Links can be updated manually using Edit→Links or automatically at open of file. File can be unlinked easily for distribution of presentation. Smaller PPT file size.
Embed	Insert→ Object→ Create New OR Copy information in other application. In PowerPoint, Edit→Paste Special. Choose, for example, "Microsoft Word Document Object."	Allows editing only from PPT. There is no separate application file (Word document, Excel workbook, etc.)	No need for additional file to be available to presentation. Can greatly increase PPT tile size, as both the file and the server are included.
Embed (existing file)	Insert→ Object→ Create From File. Do not select Link.	File exists outside of PPT, but the two are not connected.	This is a cross between the other two methods. An existing file is used to create the object, but the existing file is not linked to the PPT file. Can greatly increase PPT file size, as both the file and the application are included.

When embedding objects without linking them, PowerPoint creates a new copy of the application used to make the object and puts it in the file. If embedding a Word or Excel file, the change in file size is not very large. However, with other applications, it can be very large. If linking the items instead, the item exists outside of PowerPoint, so the presentation file will not grow as much. The effects of OLE Objects on presentation files will be covered in more detail at the end of Chapter 11.

What If I Want To Change The Chart?

If a chart is pasted as a picture, double clicking it brings up the format picture window. Work with the chart in the same manner as any other picture.

If a chart is pasted as a linked object, it can be edited directly in Excel by opening the file in Excel or by double clicking the chart in PowerPoint, which opens Excel for you. If a chart is pasted as an embedded object, double clicking it will open Excel so you can edit the chart and the data.

To edit a chart created in MSGraph, double-click the chart and edit the data or change the look of the graph with the formatting features in MSGraph.

What About Animating A Chart?

If a chart is pasted as a picture, it can only be animated as a single object – any effects are applied to the entire picture.

On the other hand, if you used a regular MSGraph chart or if the chart is pasted as an Excel object, individual series and data points within the chart can be animated. To apply animation, right-click the chart and select Custom Animation. In the Custom Animation task pane, add an effect. Then, right-click the chart in the Custom Animation task pane and choose Effect Options. Notice there is a new tab called Chart Animation. This tab has two options: Group Chart or Animate Grid and Legend.

The options under Group Chart select how much of the chart this animation is applied to. Depending on the animation effect chosen, the animation is applied to the whole chart, to individual series or categories, or to elements of series or categories.

Available animation effects for charts depend on the kind of chart chosen. Some effects are not available on 3D charts; others are not available on pie charts. Animation of individual elements of a series is also available on only some of the chart types.

PowerPoint won't animate certain elements of a series and not others without using a bit of animation trickery. If several of the animations occur together (with previous or 0 seconds after previous), it will create the effect of several items animating together. You can also ungroup the chart and animate the individual elements.

If you do ungroup the chart, make sure there is an untouched copy of the chart stored somewhere else. When ungrouping the chart, it will disconnect from the Excel spreadsheet or MSGraph datasheet. If changes are made to the Excel data after ungrouping, the data changes won't show in the chart. You will need to:

1. Delete the animated chart

2. Update the data in the chart copy

3. Copy the updated chart

4. Paste the new chart in

5. Ungroup the new chart

6. Re-set your animation

You will find for most charts it takes longer to describe this process than it does to do it.

Tip 36: Preventing Excel data from getting cut off when copied to PowerPoint	There are times when you don't want to bring over charts from Excel, but instead the actual data. This is done with copy and paste just as with the charts. However, there are circumstances where you won't get all of the data.
	When you copy and paste data from Excel, only certain amounts of it are pasted into PowerPoint. It seems to be tied to the size of the data, not the amount of data. If trying to paste an area of Excel data larger than about 13 inches in either direction, the data may be cut off. If you can make the Excel data fit in a smaller area by reducing the font size, it will paste just fine. Once pasted into PowerPoint, readjust the font size back up to large enough to see.
	Quite a bit of research has been done on this problem as it relates to the various versions of Windows and PowerPoint. If you want to read more, feel free to check out the PowerPoint FAQ entry at:
	www.rdpslides.com/pptfaq/FAQ00068.htm

So What Did Lydia Do?

Lydia linked to the Excel object by copying her charts and using Edit → Paste Special → Paste Link (Microsoft Office Excel Chart Object) so she could make any last-minute updates to the corporate data right up to distribution day. When she was ready to send out the presentations, she broke the links leaving her with pictures of the graphs. By doing this, she not only shrunk the size of the PowerPoint file, she also was able to keep the data safe from changes by the branches.

Send To Word And Back

In addition to creating chart presentations for the branch managers, Lydia needs to create a Word document for each product line offering further information on each report. She has been doing this manually and needs to learn more about using the Send To features to coordinate her documents.

The second half of the process is to create Word documents from the presentations that contain additional information for each presentation. What I have been doing is saving my presentation as an outline and using that as the basis of my Word document. I would really like to get more of the graphics into the Word document, but don't know how.

Until now, Lydia has been saving her PowerPoint presentation as an outline and opening that outline in Word, which isn't very efficient. Now, she'll send her presentations to Word using the built-in functionality known as Send to Word. Do a File → Send To → Microsoft Office Word. Options for sending the presentation are:

Figure 10-1: Send to Word Window

The top part of this screen defines what is being set to Word. The content will be used to create a new Word document. Using either of the top two options will create a three-column table in Word. I know, it shows only two columns, but Word adds a column containing the slide number. The next two options create Word files containing just the slide picture and either the notes or blank lines. These files do not contain tables. Use the last option to send your outline and automatically open Word's outline view.

I recommend sticking with one of the top two options or the last option because they seem to give the most flexibility in working with content, while maintaining a reasonable amount of formatting.

When using Send to Word, each slide is inserted into the Word document as a PowerPoint object. This creates a very large file, especially if working with a large presentation. If the presentation is sent using Paste Link break the link in Word by going to Edit → Links and choose Break Link. Once this is done, only the Notes text and the thumbnail images of the slides will be left. Saving this file will create a Word file smaller than the original one. If using just a Paste instead of Paste Link when Sending to Word, there is no way to tell Word to get rid of the PowerPoint hooks in the miniature copies of the slides. You therefore can't make the file smaller.

So, Pictures Of My Slides Are In Word. Now What?

When slides with either lines or notes next to them are sent, the file creates a three-column table. The columns created contain:

- The slide number
- A small copy of the slide
- Either the notes created for the slide or lines for note-taking

A sample row from this table looks like Figure 10-2:

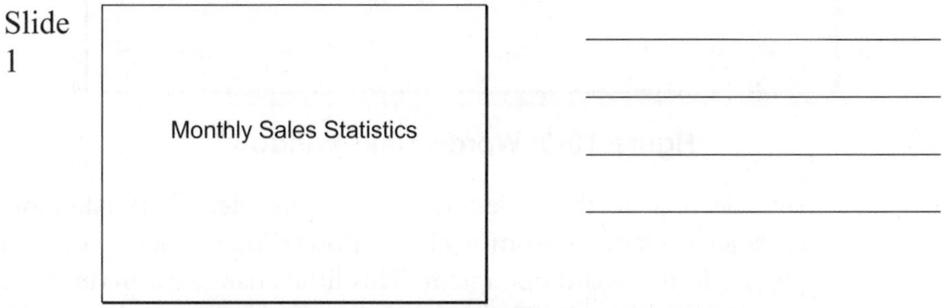

Slide
1

Monthly Sales Statistics

_____

_____

_____

_____

Figure 10-2: Sample Slide Sent to Word

In Lydia's case, she will use that third column to add the additional information the branch managers need to back up each chart. She can work with the document as she would any other Word document, including adding information for the individual branch managers. She can add such items as headers, footers, page numbers, additional text and cover pages. When Lydia has finished making her updates, she will have both a PowerPoint document with the presentation and a Word document containing everything the branch managers need to know to present the reports and charts. Unfortunately, the Word file will be a very large file.

Shrinking And Saving The File

To shrink the Word file, right-click on one of the miniature copies of the slides. From the right-click menu, select Linked Slide Object → Links (or Edit → Links from Word's menus), which brings up the Links window (Figure 10-3).

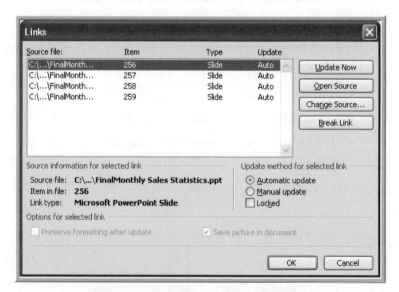

Figure 10-3: Word's Links Window

By selecting all the slides in the list and clicking Break Link, each slide changes from a linked PowerPoint object to just a picture in the Word document. This little change can reduce the file size significantly. The presentation used to create the sample dialog box above reduced from 143KB to 39KB in size by breaking the links.

What About Going The Other Way?

If there is content in Word that needs to turn into a PowerPoint presentation, use Word's File → Send To → PowerPoint menu choice. There aren't any options. Word will automatically open PowerPoint and create a new presentation based off of the Word document.

Keep in mind the content may not transfer the way you expect it to. Anything with a heading style will become a title or a bullet point. For details on the best way to set up the document, review the information about creating outlines in Word found in Chapter 2.

Another way to incorporate content from Word into a PowerPoint presentation is to copy and paste Word tables into the presentation. In PowerPoint 97 and earlier, this creates a Word table. Starting with PowerPoint 2000, this creates a PowerPoint table. There are not many differences in working with the tables, other than the interface used to work with them. If you do want an actual Word table in PowerPoint 2000 or later, you will need to either:

- Use Paste Special and choose to paste the table as a Word object
- Create a new Word object using Insert → Object and work within the Word interface

Emailing Presentations

One thing Lydia needs to do with her monthly reports is distribute them by email to each of the branch managers. However, she has had some major problems when attempting this in the past.

Every once in a while when I send the presentations out by email, the presentation file becomes corrupt by the time the branch manager opens it. What's happening and what can I do?

While sending via email is built into the Send To menu, it is not usually a good idea to send presentations this way. In PowerPoint 2002 or later, sending email directly from PowerPoint may turn on the Compare Document option. Since this will increase the presentation size, I recommend doing the send from outside PowerPoint. Use one of the zip tools to package the presentation, which can greatly reduce the likelihood of file corruption. Because you should already be working with files in the same folder, zipping them is easy.

In Windows XP and later, right-click on the folder containing the presentation and its associated files. Then choose Send to → Compressed (zipped) folder. Windows creates a compressed version of the folder and names the file with the same name as the folder name, followed by an extension of ".zip."

On operating systems earlier than Windows XP, you need to get a copy of one of the compression utilities. I recommend using WinZip. It is the most popular, which makes it likely recipients will be able to uncompress the files. WinZip can be found at www.WinZip.com.

You probably won't notice any significant change in file size after compression. When PowerPoint saves files, it generally does a good job of compressing the data into the smallest space possible. When compressing the folder for emailing, there may not be any compression occurring with the PowerPoint file itself; most size changes are from the compression of the other files in the folder.

Once the files are zipped, create a new email message, attach the zipped file, make any changes desired to the email and send it to the recipients.

Okay, But The Files Are Too Big To Email....

If the files are too big to email, but they need to be distributed to other people, jump ahead to Chapter 15, which covers sharing PowerPoint presentations with others.

Send For Review

What if you need someone else's input on the presentation? In PowerPoint 2000 and earlier, you need to send a copy of the presentation, have the recipient make changes and send it back.

Comparison is done by opening both the old presentation and the changed ones, and manually comparing the slides, one by one, to check for differences.

There is the option of using a routing slip to send the file around. However, the process for reviewing the changes is not very efficient, as there is no easy way to compare the files. In addition, when using the routing slip technology, the slip is routed, but the actual file is not.

PowerPoint 2002 added an easier option called Send for Review. This option sends the presentation to a person or group and receives comments and changes from each person, along with a built-in method to evaluate and incorporate the comments and changes back into the main presentation.

Using Send For Review In PowerPoint 2002 And Later

To send the file, use File → Send to → Mail Recipient (for Review). First, PowerPoint will check that the current file has been saved. If it hasn't, it will prompt to save the file. Next, a new email will be opened with a subject line of "Please review 'Monthly Sales Statistics.'" The subject line is generated from the file name for the PowerPoint file (you can change it if you want). The file will be listed as an attachment. The default text for the email asks the recipients to review the attached document. Add the recipient list to the email. Edit the body of the email to pass along information to the reviewers.

When the reviewers receive the document, they should save it to their hard drive, edit it and save their changes. Then, when they access the Send To menu to send it back, they find a new menu item, Original Sender. Selecting this option creates a return email message with the new version of the document attached. As with when the file was sent out for review, the subject and the message are filled in, but both can be changed. When you receive it, save the attached file with a new name.

If the person receiving the presentation makes changes and sends the file back to you, use Tools → Compare and Merge Presentations to find the changes.

When opening a reviewed file, the following message box appears:

Figure 10-4: Merge Changes Prompt Window

Click Yes to merge the reviewer's comments and changes with your version of the presentation. PowerPoint compares the two presentations and brings up a combined, marked-up copy of the presentation. In addition, you get a new task pane called Revisions on the right side of the screen.

The Revisions task pane is a two-tabbed task pane. Both tabs show the changes made by the reviewers. The List tab shows the changes in a text list. The Gallery tab shows all the changes to a single slide at once. In either the Gallery or List tabs, you can accept or reject the changes individually or all at once.

If no content changes were made to a slide, the task pane reflects that and tells you where the next changes are. Addition and editing of comments show only in the List tab.

Once all changes have been accepted or rejected, save the file again. I recommend saving it under another new name so you have a full trail of the review process.

If, after accepting or rejecting all the changes, the file size is quite a bit larger than it should be, check to make sure revision markings were not missed in the presentation

Tip 37: Using 2003? Check out shared workspaces!	When using PowerPoint 2003, you have another way to share presentations: Share Point Services. If your company uses Share Point Services, you can set up the review email to place the presentation file on the Share Point server. Each recipient sees the same copy of the presentation. When they are ready to make changes to the file, they check out the file from the shared space, make changes and check the file back in. Using a shared workspace for reviewing allows each reviewer to see the changes made by other reviewers. It also makes your job much easier: All the changes made are in one file. When you are ready to review the changes, lock the file by checking it out from the shared workspace. When you open the file, you can see and process the changes and comments by individual reviewer or all at once. Once you have accepted or rejected the changes, save the final version back to the shared workspace.

We fixed the problems Lydia has been having with her presentations. However, we should also show Lydia the other available Office tools. The rest of this chapter will give you a quick overview of the three Office tools you are most likely to use:

- Clip Gallery: Add pre-created pictures and sounds to a presentation
- Word Art: Create graphics based on text formatted and adjusted to your specifications
- Equation Editor: Create embedded equations in line with the other text in a presentation

Clip Gallery

Feel the need to add some punch to a presentation, without creating the items yourself? Consider clip art. Delivered with every version of Office, as well as with individual copies of Office products, Clip Gallery (Office 97 and 2000) and Clip Organizer (Office 2002 and 2003) include sound files, movie clips, drawings and photographs. Each item in the gallery contains not only the item, but also keywords to search and find exactly the item needed.

Clip Art items are added to a presentation via the Insert menu. Use Insert → Pictures → Clip Art for pictures (both drawings and photographs), Insert → Movies and Sounds → Movie from Clip Organizer for movie clips, and Insert → Movies and Sounds → Sounds from Clip Organizer for sound clips.

That's not as complicated as it sounds. Bringing up the Clip Organizer in any of these three ways will give you access to all of the clips.

Once you are viewing the clips, search for specific clips by entering words in the search box. In PowerPoint 2000 and earlier, the Clip Gallery runs in a dialog box. In PowerPoint 2002 and later, it runs as a task pane will appear on the right side of the screen.

If you have clip collections on the computer other than the ones in the Clip Gallery or Organizer, you can import them. The clips are not actually moved from their location on the hard drive. Instead, the location of each clip is stored with the existing clip data.

If the clips delivered with PowerPoint don't meet your needs, add items from the Microsoft website. With the Gallery or Organizer open, look for a link to Clips Online. It will automatically take you the Microsoft clip art web site where you can find more sounds, pictures and movies.

If you upgrade from PowerPoint 2000 or earlier to PowerPoint 2002 or later, old clip items can be added to the new version's Clip Organizer. Unfortunately, the process of importing them will lose the keywords attached to each clip. Since most of the old clip art is found in the new gallery as well, the loss of keywords should not be a problem.

WordArt

On the graphics toolbar, there is an icon that looks like this :

This tool inserts text as a graphic element instead of as just plain text. The elements created with WordArt are used to add punch to a slide. For example, look at these two pieces of text:

Figure 10-5: Comparison Plain Text to WordArt

The first one is typical plain old formatted text. The second is a WordArt element. The text has been re-formatted to be 3D, shadowed, curved and tilted, in less than a minute!

When viewed in color, there's simply no comparison between the two as to which grabs attention most. When viewed on a PowerPoint slide, the WordArt element will grab attention much more than the flat text.

To create the WordArt element above, I clicked the WordArt button and this dialog appeared:

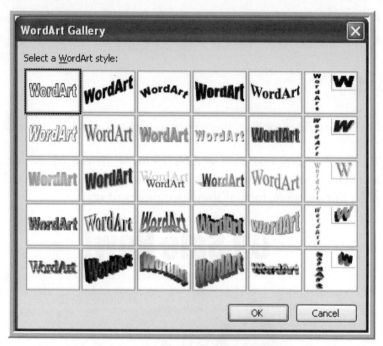

Figure 10-6: WordArt Gallery Window

I chose the third selection in the bottom row. This brought up a text entry box and I entered the text. I used the default font and size, but you also have the option to bold or italicize the text. Once the text is formatted, click OK and the element will be created and inserted onto the current slide.

Play around with the options on individual WordArt elements and you will find there is much more customization available than just font changes. You can change the shape, direction or angle of the element. In short, you can change everything about the element with just a few clicks. WordArt elements can also be animated using PowerPoint's Custom Animation options.

Equation Editor

The other Office tool you may find useful is Microsoft Equation, .commonly referred to as the Equation Editor. This tool quickly inserts scientific and mathematic symbols into presentations.

The Equation Editor is accessed via Insert → Object → Create New Object Select Microsoft Equation. This brings up the Equation Editor interface:

Figure 10-7: Equation Editor Window

By clicking the symbols at the top of the screen and selecting from the menu options, you can insert a wide variety of characters from various fonts.

> **Note:** Because Equation Editor is a separate application, you cannot insert equations into text placeholders or boxes on slides. The equations are inserted as individual elements. They do not show up on the outline and so they will also not show up if the outline is exported using Send To Word.

This page left intentionally blank.

11. Keeping Your File The Right Size

> ➢ Turn Off Fast Saves

> ➢ Accept Changes

> ➢ Pictures: How Big Should They Be?

> ➢ Sounds: Quality vs. Size

> ➢ Linking vs. Imbedding

> ➢ Fonts

> ➢ OLE-Related File Bloating

The company Bryan works for has just expanded its product line and doubled the number of products it sells. Bryan has been tasked to create and distribute a product catalog which the employees at the branch offices can use to quickly become familiar with the new products. He has created a series of presentations, each of which describes one of the products. However, he has a problem…

I have finished creating the product description presentations. They look great. The photos are wonderful, the narration and sounds with the pages are clear and understandable, and the text and animations are perfect. Unfortunately, when I add up the file sizes, the project is too big to put on the business card CDs the company planned to distribute.

When I took a look at Bryan's presentations, I found he had an even bigger problem than he thought. The presentations looked great, but three of them were over 100MB in size. Not only were they too big to distribute in a batch, the individual presentations were too big to run smoothly on some machines.

Turn Off Fast Saves

I know you did what I said at the beginning of the book and turned off Fast Saves. Bryan did, too. Unfortunately, the company president didn't. So, when Bryan got back the review copies, each one the president had opened and changed had increased in size.

One problem with Fast Saves is other people reviewing the presentations are probably going to have it turned on. What can you do? You can train them to turn it off, but this isn't always going to help. So, if the file size has suddenly grown during review time, re-save it with a new name just to be sure.

When Bryan re-saved the presentations using File → Save As on his machine, the size on each decreased. Unfortunately, they didn't become quite as small as they were when they left his computer for review. This was because the changes made by the president had not been processed.

Accept Changes

In addition to having Fast Saves on, the company president had made sure the reviewing features were on. This helped him track what changes he had made to the file and to communicate those changes to Bryan. When Bryan opened the files, he got an "Accept changes?" message for each one.

When Bryan realized the reviewing features were on, he accepted the appropriate changes and saved the document. The file size decreased to about where it was before the review. Now, Bryan is ready to work on optimizing the presentation file size even further.

Tip 38: Problems with a file you sent out for review? Help is here!	Ever send a file out for review, accept the changes, save the file, and still see popups asking whether you want to review the changes when you open the file? One clue all changes have not been accepted is a file just won't shrink in size even after you've accepted changes. It happens sometimes. Here's what's going on.

Sometimes, when you accept changes, not all the change flags within the document get cleared. In these cases, you might think the file has been disconnected from the reviewed files, but it hasn't.

To fix this, open the file and make a slight change such as adding a space in a sentence or adding an extra empty paragraph. Save the file with a new name. Close the newly renamed file. Reopen the original file. Do a Tools → Compare and Merge Documents. Select the new file to compare against. You have not changed files, you are still looking at the original file. You have added the changes from the second file to the original file.

Using the reviewing features, delete all changes on the current slide. Close the file. When prompted to save changes, say yes. This will save the original file and clear out the reviewing information from it.

When you re-open the file, you should receive no indication there are changes waiting for you to accept or reject.

What happened was when you rejected the slight change, you cleared out all the reviewing information in the file. This shrinks the file back down to its original size and cleans up all the reviewing marks.

I have seen cases where resolving the reviewing situation shrinks the file by more than 75% of the original size.

Pictures: How Big Should They Be?

It is now time to cover one of the hardest topics for some PowerPoint users to understand: picture resolution. You are probably used to thinking about the resolution of files in terms of dpi (dots per inch). That isn't how PowerPoint works. Because PowerPoint is primarily a screen application, it works in pixels – dots on the screen.

Think about a picture that was 4 inches by 4 inches, scanned at 100 pixels per inch. If you insert that picture into PowerPoint at 4 inches by 4 inches, the picture displays at 100 pixels per inch. If you use the handles to change the size of the picture down to 2 inches by 2 inches, you still have same number of pixels covering less area. On the other hand, if you use the handles to stretch the pictures to 8 inches by 8 inches, the pixels need to cover twice as much area as the original so the picture becomes blurry.

PowerPoint cannot display a picture at a higher resolution than the monitor. For most monitors, the resolution is less than 100 pixels per inch.

How Does That Help With File Sizes?

If the pictures are saved with many more pixels than can be displayed, the file is unnecessarily enlarged. PowerPoint is designed to create on-screen shows. These shows are displayed on monitors that have a much lower resolution than a printer, usually around 72 or 96 PPI (pixels-per-inch). Unless creating print files, reduce the picture quality for on-screen use instead of leaving it at super-high print quality.

If creating presentations which need to look absolutely perfect when printed, you need to make a choice. In any given file, you can either have super-high resolution photographs or you can have a small file size. If both are needed, keep two versions of the presentation, one for print and one for distribution. This is not a perfect solution, but that's what happens when you stretch the boundaries of the program.

How Do I Do Compress The Pictures?

PowerPoint 2000 And Earlier...

PowerPoint 2000 and earlier versions don't have a built-in way to compress photographs. Use a separate program to compress the pictures for the best balance between quality and size. Some of the options I recommend are:

- Use your favorite graphics program and save duplicate versions of the graphics, which are optimized for screen. Lower the resolution to 96 or 100 PPI (the math's easier on 100), experiment with different compression levels on JPGs, try index color on TIF if the option is available, see how a PNG looks, etc. Once you have created a smaller-sized image which meets the requirements, save it as a new image file and insert that image into PPT. Don't overwrite the original files, as you may want them later.

- Steve Rindsberg, a PowerPoint MVP, sells the *RnR Presentation Optimizer*. The Optimizer can remove most of the common causes of bloat in files in addition to right-sizing the pictures. Details on the tool, including current prices, are available on the RnR website at www.rdpslides.com/pptools/FAQ00013.htm

- Two other commercial solutions are *NXPowerLite* from Neuxpower Solutions Ltd. www.nxpowerlite.com/ and *PointLess* from Impact Labs, Inc. portal.impactlabs.com/ImpactLabs/DesktopDefault.aspx?t abid=54. Both are reputed to be good tools, but I don't have personal experience with either.

PowerPoint 2002 And Later...

In PowerPoint 2002, a great option was created that compresses photos one at a time or all at once. It also removes any parts of the pictures that have been cropped. To show how it can change the presentation file sizes, we are going to create a sample presentation and work with the tool.

Open a new presentation. Give the first slide a layout of title only. In the title type "Picture Compression." Elsewhere in the slide, create an eight-pointed star using the autoshape tool. Grab the yellow diamond and pull the points in so the points are obvious, but not too skinny. Now, right click the autoshape and selecting Format→ Autoshape.

From the Colors and Lines tab, use the drop down list for the fill to change the background to a picture. (I am going to use the picture of the water lilies from the sample pictures.) Your shape should look something like Figure 11-1:

Figure 11-1: Insert a Graphic in an AutoShape

Save the presentation and note its file size in Windows Explorer. Mine is about 118KB in size, your size may be different. Now we are going to optimize the presentation for on-screen use.

Right click on the star and select Format Autoshape. Go to the Picture tab. In the lower left corner of the window you will see the Compress button. Click it and the Compress Pictures window will appear (Figure 11-2). Another way to access this window is to click the Compress Pictures button on the Picture toolbar.

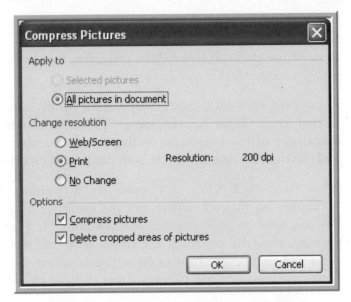

Figure 11-2: Compress Pictures Window

Because we only have one picture in this file, PowerPoint doesn't give us a choice between this selected picture or all pictures. Usually, you will have to select one or the other. Next, decide what resolution you want, based on the final destination of the presentation. When selecting a new resolution, PowerPoint will tell you the approximate dpi it will use. For this exercise, select Web/Screen.

Wait A Minute: Microsoft Talks In dpi?

Yes, here the compression levels are specified in dpi, not ppi. Since the print world works in dpi, Microsoft figures when asking for compression for printing it is best to describe the target in dpi. For completeness, they decided to give you the target dpi for screen use as well.

Back To The Compression Process...

Once you know how far to compress the pictures in the presentation, decide if you also want to:

- Compress the pictures
- Delete cropped areas of the pictures

While the first option seems obvious, it really isn't. Since Compress Pictures can also be used just to delete the cropped areas of the pictures, PowerPoint gives you the option to turn off the compression if you don't want it.

In this case, we want to both compress the picture and crop the unused areas. What unused areas? Those areas outside the boundaries of the autoshape, or those removed with the crop tool (on the Picture toolbar) are both considered cropped areas.

When you click OK, you may get a warning reading, "Compressing Pictures may reduce the quality of your images. Do you want to apply picture optimization?" If you get this warning, click the checkbox for Don't show me this warning again and then click Apply. (To continue seeing the warning every time you compress pictures, don't click the checkbox.)

You will return to the Picture tab of the Format AutoShape window. Click OK to return to the slide. Nothing will appear to have changed. The picture should look the same. The difference will only show in the file size. Test the presentation in full screen mode to prove it to yourself, then do a Save As and save the file with a new name. Your file size should be smaller. Mine's down to 58KB, yours may not go down as far.

Quite a savings, isn't it? In general, compressing from high resolution photographs to web/screen use will cut the file size to about half of what it was. The higher the resolution of the photographs, the bigger a difference you'll see.

Tip 39: Elements in the presentation but not on any slides	Sometimes, when designing a presentation, you will find you don't need a certain element on a slide, but you still want to have it available for use. The quickest way to do this is to drag the object off the slide and onto the gray area surrounding the slide. If you drag your image off the slide, be sure you check each slide for extraneous objects when finished creating the presentation. Zoom out so the slide is smaller and the area around the slide shows. Delete anything in this area you aren't using. Leaving these items in the file can cause bloat.

Sounds: Quality Vs. Size

Changing the compression on his photographs shrunk Bryan's presentations to a size he could distribute more easily. But before he sent them out, he decided to see what else we could optimize. The next thing we looked at was his sound files.

Just as with photographs, optimizing sound files involves finding a balance between quality and file size. If you have super-high quality sounds in the presentation, the size of the files will reflect that. How high the quality of the sound files needs to be depends to some extent on will be used for sounds. Voice-overs and narration can be lower quality, while music should be of a higher quality. In addition, look at whether you really need to use 16-bit stereo sounds for a presentation that will only be played through a computer's speakers.

In general, sound quality and effects such as volume and fades will have to be adjusted outside of PowerPoint. PowerPoint MVP Geetesh Bajaj's Indezine has a great page (www.indezine.com/products/sound) with up-to-date information on a wide variety of sound editors in a wide variety of price ranges, from free on up.

If using PowerPoint 2002 or later, you have a volume setting on the Sound Setting tab of the Custom Animation Effect Options for the sound. You can't use the volume setting for all sound types, only those which don't get volume control from your computer's system volume control.

Can't use it for these types	Can use it for these types
CD Audio	AIF
WAV	AIFF
MID	AIFC
MIDI	AU
MP2	M3U
MP3	SND
MPA	WMA
RMI	

No matter what version of PowerPoint you use, you can adjust the quality of the sounds from within PowerPoint when recording narration. To record narration, go to Slide Show → Record Narration. The resulting window allows you to start narrating.

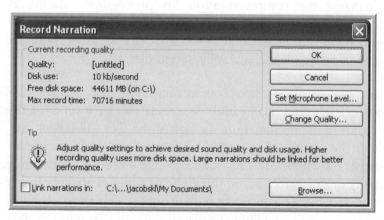

Figure 11-3: Record Narration Window

Before starting narrations, adjust the quality of the sound files by clicking the Change Quality button.

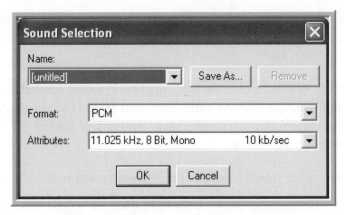

Figure 11-4: Sound Selection Window

Click the drop down for Name; there are three default sound setups: CD Quality, Radio Quality and Telephone Quality. Select each in turn and notice the changes in the Attributes box.

The default choice for recording is CD quality, 44KHz at 16-bit stereo. This will take the most space at 172KB per second of sound. You will need only 46 KB per second if you change to 48KHz at 8-bit mono. The change from stereo to mono won't be noticeable in most situations and the higher sampling rate should help cover the quality differences.

Radio quality reduces the sound quality and records in mono, taking only 21KB per second of sound. Telephone quality is very low quality sound, but takes virtually no space at 10KB per second. However, telephone quality is often the most appropriate choice for voice narration. It will sound good enough, without taking too much space.

Once sound quality is selected, click OK and return to the Record Narration window. Click OK to start the presentation and record the narration. In addition, PowerPoint will note where in the narration the slide transitions and other clicks occur.

If you don't want the narrations embedded in the PowerPoint presentation, click the checkbox for Link narrations in, set the path for the files to the same folder as the presentation and off you go. Why wouldn't you want them embedded? Because if the files aren't embedded, you can edit them in a sound editor to correct mistakes. Since the sound files will be recorded as WAV files, you can re-embed them later.

The best way to determine what quality of sound needed for a given presentation is to record some narration at each of the three default settings. Play the narration back through a couple of different speaker sets and listen.

By testing his sound levels, Bryan learned two things:

- First, none of the branch employees would be listening to the presentation on high quality speakers, so using radio quality was more than good enough for the product catalog. This cut the size of his sounds to less than 20% of the size he had originally used. While he could have re-recorded the sounds to get the savings, instead he used a sound editor to reduce the quality (and size) of the sound files.

- Second, he discovered the desktop computers used by some of the managers didn't have speakers at all. So, when he distributed the CD, he had to include a note that the product catalog included sounds and needed to be played on a system with external speakers.

Linking Vs. Embedding

If embedding all the graphics, sounds and other objects, the file size may be quite large. This is not unusual. You can shrink the size of the PowerPoint file by linking these files instead of embedding them. This won't necessarily shrink the overall space required for the presentation, since the extra files must be included when distributing the presentation.

If sound or graphic files are linked, be sure to put the linked files in the same folder as the presentation before linking to them and keep them with the presentation when distributing it.

Fonts

Another space eater in files is the fonts. If embedding fonts when saving the file, the presentation file size will increase by the size of the font file. Need a refresher course on embedding fonts? Review Chapter 4.

This is not always a large contributor to file bloat, since font files are usually less than 100K in size. There are two situations where fonts can contribute to large amounts of file bloat. The first is if Arial Unicode is embedded. The other is there are a lot of embedded fonts in a single file. Both of these situations will cause the file to bloat in a perceptible fashion.

Master Slide Elements

One more place to look for causes of file bloat is on the slide masters. If you have cleaned up everything you can think of, but the file is still much larger than you think it should be, look at each of the masters. There may be something included which shouldn't be.

Sometimes, a graphic will be placed on the slide or title master. Since this picture shows on each slide, you would expect the file size to grow with each slide added. Luckily, this doesn't happen. The file will grow with the first slide added, but after that, PowerPoint keeps using the same copy of the image and adds a link to the image location within the file. However, if that graphic is severely oversized, it will still increase the size of the file unnecessarily.

As Bryan learned, the same is not true of backgrounds on the masters such as the handout and notes master. Objects placed on the other masters are just like objects placed on individual slides. They are independent objects.

One of Bryan's files had a case of file bloat with no cause he could find. He went to the slide, title and notes masters: nothing there. Finally, he looked at the handout master. Bingo! Someone had placed a large copy of the company logo on the handout master as a background. Deleting the graphic from the handout master shrunk the file size to where he expected it to be.

OLE-Related File Bloating

After cleaning up everything in his presentations, Bryan still had one presentation that was extraordinarily large. He could find no reason for the file size. I suggested he check the file for the two different kinds of OLE objects: OLE links and OLE embedded programs.

OLE links and OLE embedded programs are a common cause of confusion for PowerPoint users. Both are ways to get information developed elsewhere into a presentation, but they cause drastically different results to the size of the presentation.

OLE Links

Use OLE links to link to the output of another program. If you wanted to include an existing Word file in the presentation, but still wanted to be able to edit that file in Word, use an OLE link to get the file. To do this, Insert → Object and select Create from file. Then, browse to the file on the hard drive and link to it by clicking the Link button in that dialog.

There is a potential problem with linking to a file. Since PowerPoint uses absolute addresses when linking files, distribution of the presentation can be a little tricky. If sharing the presentation, place the file to be linked in the same folder as the presentation and then link to it.

OLE Embedded Objects

When creating a file from another application while running the presentation, use an embedded object to do it. These objects are also called OLE Servers. There are two ways to create these files:

- Insert → Object → Create new
- Insert → Object → Create from file

The only difference between these two options is whether the data exists before bringing it into PowerPoint. If it exists, you are creating a new copy of the data inside PowerPoint.

When embedding objects (using Insert → Object → Create from file) without linking them, PowerPoint creates a new copy of the application used to make that object and puts it in the file. If embedding a Word or Excel file, the change in file size is not very large. However, if you use other applications, it can be very large.

So, Are You Saying Don't Use Servers?

I am not suggesting never to use OLE servers. There are very logical places for them, especially if the presentation is designed to train users on a specific application. I am suggesting you decide ahead of time whether you need either the application available within PowerPoint or just the file itself and work from there. Another way to look at this is whether you will need the data outside of the presentation. If you need it outside the presentation, use links and don't embed the server. If you only want the object to exist inside the presentation, then use embedding.

You will also find the servers are the way to go for the insertion of certain Office application items. If adding an equation, for example, do it via Insert → Object → Create new. If you don't want the overhead of the server, do the following:

1. Insert the equation using Insert → Object → Create new

2. Copy and delete the equation (or cut the equation)

3. Use Edit → Paste Special to paste the equation back in as a picture

This creates a non-editable equation, so don't do this until the equation is right. But doing this will break the connection with the application, which will save space in the presentation file.

The following table summarizes when to use each of the different types and how to work with them.

OLE Object	How to Create	Behavior	Notes
Link	Insert/Object/Create From File. Select Link. Browse to File. OR Copy information in other application. In PPT, Edit→Paste Special, choose Paste Link.	Allows editing of file in the other application or from within PPT itself. File created outside of PowerPoint and remains outside of PowerPoint.	Links can be updated manually using Edit→Links or automatically at open of file. File can be unlinked easily for distribution of presentation. Smaller PowerPoint file size.
Embed (Server)	Insert→ Object→ Create New OR Copy information in other application. In PowerPoint, Edit→Paste Special. Choose, for example, "Microsoft Word Document Object."	Allows editing only from within PowerPoint itself. There is no separate application file (Word document, Excel workbook, etc.)	No need for additional file to be available to presentation. Can greatly increase PowerPoint tile size, as both the file and the server are included.
Embed (existing)	Insert→ Object→ Create From File. Do not select Link.	File exists outside of PowerPoint, but the two are not connected.	This is a cross between the other two (need a word here, just not sure what!). An existing file is used to create the object, but the presentation and existing file are not linked. Can greatly increase PowerPoint file size, as both the file and the server are included.

How Do I Find Out Which Way Things Were Added?

If there is an object you suspect was embedded instead of linked, double click the object. If the application opens, it's embedded. If not, it's linked.

However, most times you won't know which object or objects to check. In these cases, you can tell which type of objects were added by checking the properties of the presentation. Once you know which types of objects are embedded, you can find the actual objects much easier.

To check the properties, go to File → Properties and look at the Contents tab.

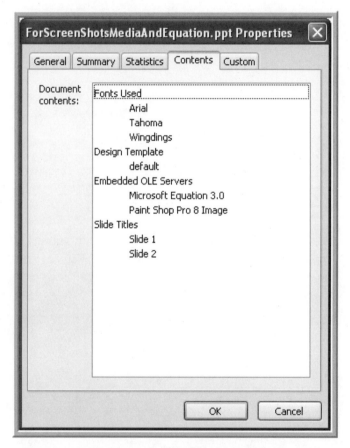

Figure 11-5: Presentation Contents Properties

Bryan found out that unnecessary embedded servers were causing the bloat in his last presentation. When Bryan looked at the properties of the presentation, he noticed there were entries for several embedded objects. In this case, one of the managers had used Insert → Object → Create new to insert a picture. As you can see from Figure 11-5, this added the entire

PaintShopPro server to the presentation. Instead of adding the picture this way, Bryan copied the picture and created a new picture file from PaintShopPro. He then did an Insert → Picture → Create from file, found his file and inserted it. This shrunk the file size down to normal and made the presentation more usable.

12. Printing

➢ Black And White, Grayscale, and Color

➢ Printing Posters

➢ Common Gotchas

Rachel has worked with PowerPoint for many years, but has done little with printed presentations. Now, she has been asked to use some of her slides as printed promotional materials. She has been using color schemes for online work, but now she needs some help making sure what she has created will look right when printed.

All of the presentation development I have done has been for on-screen presentations. I very seldom print slides. When I do print materials, I send the slides to Word and print them on a black and white laser printer.

Now, several of the slides I created to introduce the corporate color scheme have been chosen for use as part of the corporate identity project. The slides need to be printed quickly and cheaply for proofing, as grayscale sheets for review, as full-size color posters for posting at the offices and as flyers for distribution to company employees.

I know I am not going to get exact color reproduction when I print, but can you help me get something close?

Rachel has two different problems with her project: the printers and the paper size.

- She needs the same materials to be printed in three different formats: a black-and-white laser printer for the review copies, a color inkjet for the posters and gray scale options on either printer for the flyers. She needs to ensure the printers have the same fonts available and the slides are set up for printing in all three color modes.

- She needs to ensure what she has designed can be scaled for use as posters. The slides were created for on-screen use, but the printed posters will be on large paper. The posters will need to be larger, but they will also have a different proportion between the length and width than the on-screen presentation. To solve this problem, Rachel must ensure the pages have been set to scale without problems.

Color, Black And White, Grayscale

PowerPoint prints in three basic modes: Black and White, Grayscale, and Color.

Black and white printing takes the screen colors and turns them into black and white. This is what Rachel originally planned to use for creating her review copies. However, as we shall see in a moment, this did not create the slide printouts she wanted.

Grayscale printing takes each pixel on the screen and interprets it as black, white or a factored gray. Rachel needs to determine if the default grayscale printing shows enough detail to allow proofing or if a custom color scheme just for printing will yield better results.

Color printing takes the screen colors and re-interprets them for color printing. Since printed colors are created differently than onscreen colors, you are almost guaranteed to get different colors than desired. To solve this problem, we are going to create a specific color scheme for printing and test the colors until they are as close as possible to the ones we want.

Before We Start...

Before starting on the details of each of the three printing modes, we need to understand some basics of how printers work. For the purposes of this book, I am going to review the basics of laser printers and inkjet printers. If using another kind of printer, refer to the manufacturer's web site for information on how the printer works.

No matter what kind of printer is used, the quality of the printout is defined by the resolution of the item being printed. The resolution is measured in dots per inch (dpi). The more dpi, the finer the printout will be. If the resolution of a computer screen were converted to dpi, the results would be between 76 and 100 dpi. However, most laser printers create output of 600 to 1000 dpi (super-high quality laser printers can have even higher dpi ratios). Most inkjet printers create output with a minimum of 200 dpi. If converting PowerPoint files optimized for the screen for use on high-quality printers, go back to the original graphics to get reasonable quality printouts.

Laser printers print by hitting a photosensitive drum with a laser. The drum picks up toner on the places the laser hits. This toner is transferred to the paper as it goes by. The paper and the toner are heated to fuse the toner into the paper. Laser printers print quickly and cleanly. Most laser printers use a single reservoir of black toner to create their output. Some laser printers create color output by using multiple reservoirs in the basic CMYK colors. (Remember CMYK? We covered it in Chapter 5.)

Inkjets print by spraying colored ink from a reservoir onto the paper. The percentage of each color applied to a specific spot on the paper is defined by the printer driver. Inkjets print slower than laser printers. Some lower quality inkjet printers will also leave extra ink on the paper. In addition, older inkjet printers may create smudged or blurred printouts. If using the printer's photo resolution mode, you can get better quality printouts – but they print much slower.

Black And White Printing

As I said, pure black and white printing takes the color slide and outputs it as just black and white. This usually does not create the effect you want. Compare this screen shot of a test slide in pure black and white (Figure 12-1):

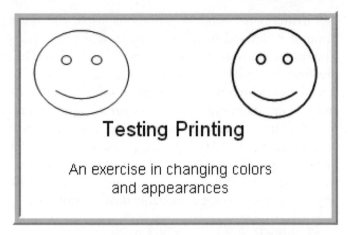

Figure 12-1: Black and White Slide

With this screen shot of the same slide in grayscale (Figure 12-2):

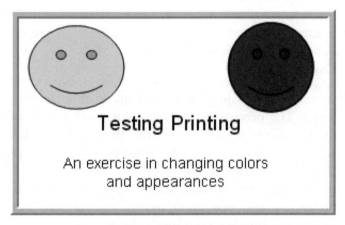

Figure 12-2: Grayscale Slide

As you can see, the black and white version has no fill on either of the smiley faces, while the grayscale one has fill, but it isn't the right fill. In the actual slide, the right hand face is filled with a light blue color and the left hand one with a dark blue.

To see this effect, create a slide with two autoshapes on it. Fill one with a light color, the other with a darker color. Change the line color on the darker shape to a contrasting color.

Now, print preview the slide by going to File → Print Preview. What you see will depend on what printer is defined as the default printer. If a black and white printer as the default, the preview will show in grayscale. If a color printer for the default, the preview will show in color.

Tip 40: No Print Preview?	If running PowerPoint 2000 or earlier, you don't have a Print Preview option under the File menu. In this case, turn on the Black and White view in order to see how the slide will look in black and white or grayscale. You can also print a test page to see how it will look on the printer.

On the right side of the Print Preview toolbar, there is an Options dropdown arrow. Click on this arrow and slide down to Color/Grayscale. Slide over to the right. Change the value to Black And White. Notice what happens to the slide.

When printing in black and white mode, PowerPoint takes each element on the slide and reduces it to two-bit color. Each pixel is either on (black) or off (white).

Tip 41: Other print preview options	Most of the print preview options are things covered in other parts of this book. However, there three options to explore
	• Scale to fit paper: This adjusts the slide size to best fit on the paper in the printer.
	• Frame slides: Creates a box around each slide before printing. This box is not an element on the slide; it's just a printing element. You can't edit the box. The frames are useful if using printed transparencies with paper frames and need to know how much of the slide will show inside the paper frame.
	• Printing order: This option defines whether slide thumbnails print across the page or down the page when printing handouts. It is only available if printing 4, 6 or 9 slides per page.

Grayscale Printing

Grayscale printing interprets the contents of the slide to determine how much black ink to put on the paper. The result is an image of the slide with the colors replaced by various shades of gray. The darker the color of a given pixel, the darker the gray; the lighter the color of a given pixel, the lighter the gray.

As shown in Figure 12-2, this method comes closer to the actual look of the slide than the pure black and white method does. But, it may not be as close as wanted.

Rachel didn't like the way her colors looked in grayscale, so she created a test slide with swatches of each of the colors used in the presentation. She printed this slide in both color and grayscale. She distributed these two test prints with the full review copies. This eliminated the need for printing all of the applicable slides to the color printer (saving time), while still allowing the reviewers to see what the colors would look like when used together.

Color Printing

Color printing produces a full color printout of a slide. Unfortunately, since printers create color differently than the display does, the printouts probably won't match the colors on the screen.

To adjust for the color differences, set up a color scheme just for printing. First, create a slide with blocks of colors on it. Set each block to one of the colors in the color scheme. If there are additional colors in the presentation, be sure to create a block for each of those colors as well. Print this test slide to the color printer.

Now, compare the printed swatches to the colors on the screen. Create a new color scheme based on the current scheme and adjust the colors one by one. When the colors are the way you want them, apply the scheme to the test slide and print it again. Repeat this process until each of the color scheme swatches prints the way you want.

Before going any further, open the template. Add the new color scheme to the template and re-save it. Now, each presentation using this template will have the color-print color scheme ready when needed.

Since you have been working in the color scheme up to now, the color changes have been automatically applied to the slides in the presentation. Next, you need to determine the adjustments needed for the other colors in the presentation. Repeat the print-and-check process until all the colors are right. Then, find where each of those colors is used and change the objects to the new colors.

Once finished adjusting the colors, print a few test slides. If all looks as you want, print the whole document.

What About The Flyers?

For her flyers, Rachel had planned to print the slides using the black and white printing option on her color printer. However, when she tried this, she found the elements within the slide were not clear enough. The light colors came out as white and the darker colors came out black. The colors she had the worst problems with were the ones in the background of the slides. To adjust this, she went to the black and white view of her slides and used the Settings button on the Grayscale toolbar to find the perfect color combination for the flyers.

Printing Posters

Rachel's next task was to print full-sized posters of some of her slides. Unfortunately, PowerPoint will only let you set a maximum page size of 56 inches by 56 inches. Rachel needed a poster much bigger than that.

PowerPoint is not designed for printing large posters. There are better tools to do the job, such as MS Publisher, etc. However, since Rachel's content is already in the form of PowerPoint slides, she needs to figure out a way to print the posters.

The way to do it is to set up the page size as a smaller, but equally proportioned page. Then, when printing to the poster printer, put the poster paper in the printer and use Scale to fit paper to enlarge the slide.

The option to scale slides to fit the paper in a printer can be found in two places. First, you can set this option via the Options dropdown box on the Print Preview toolbar. You can also set this option directly in the File → Print window via a checkbox near the bottom of the page.

When creating posters by scaling slide sizes up, be sure to run a test print before creating the final poster. You may find some of the graphical elements need to be adjusted for quality reasons.

Poster Dimensions vs. Screen Dimensions

Another problem Rachel ran into was the difference between the ratio of the height vs. the width of the screen and the ratio of the length vs. the width of the paper for the flyers.

Rachel's screen shows were set up for the default screen size of 10 inches by 7.5 inches. Her posters were supposed to be 23 inches by 35 inches. The ratios between these two are vastly different. When Rachel changed the dimensions, she found the elements on the slides had moved around and the background graphic had been stretched.

Before sending the posters to print, she went back and adjusted the poster content so it looked the way she needed it.

Common Print Gotchas

While we have covered the worst of the printing problems you are likely to run into, there are a few other things to keep in mind when creating PowerPoint files to be printed.

Print Files Are Bigger Than PowerPoint Files

When sending a presentation to the printer, it will grow in size. Since PowerPoint compresses its files when it saves, the file expand back to full size as it is spooled.

Further, any graphics linked to the presentation will be sent to the printer with the file. This also will affect the size of the spooled file.

Another cause of huge print files is the use of gradients as fills and backgrounds. Because gradients are complex to print, they swell the spool file.

Finally, if using fonts in a presentation not native to the printer (or if using a printer that doesn't store fonts), PowerPoint will put the font information in the spool file. This too will affect the final spool size.

My File Prints Slowly Or Causes Print Errors

PowerPoint files can be huge, especially when compared to Word or Excel documents. This means the printer has to work harder to print PowerPoint documents. Some printers don't have enough memory to print PowerPoint files. If this is happening, there are a few things to try.

- Print the presentation a few slides at a time. This will slow you down, but should let the file print.

- Print the slides without the background graphic. This will lessen the load on the printer.

- If neither of those suggestions work, try another printer. Some printers just aren't able to handle the load involved when printing graphic-intensive files.

- Check to see if there is a newer driver available for the printer. Install it.

- Finally, try upgrading the printer or the memory in the printer. The printer may not have the power to print what you want it to.

If the file consistently causes print errors on a specific slide, try deleting and re-creating that slide. The slide may have a corrupted element on it. If this is the case, be sure to create an extra backup of the presentation. Sometimes this is an indication the presentation is on its way to being corrupted.

How Do I Print Animations?

In PowerPoint 2000 and earlier, there is a nifty feature which prints each animation step of each slide. This feature was removed in PowerPoint 2002.

To access the feature in PowerPoint 2000 and earlier, bring up the print dialog box. Under Print what, select slides with animations.

To get this functionality in PowerPoint 2002 and later, use a free add-in, *Capture Show,* from PowerPoint MVP Shyam Pillai. www.mvps.org/skp/cshow.htm

Why Don't My Pages Center Correctly?

Few printers print edge to edge. So, when printing PowerPoint files, the slides, notes, handouts, etc., print only within the area the printer can use. To make matters worse, most printers that don't print edge-to-edge also have a larger non-printable area on one side of the page than on the other.

A printer has to grab the paper from the tray, so it leaves a wider margin on that side. You don't notice this effect with most other documents, because most other documents have margins. When printing a PowerPoint file, you haven't set up margins since you want the slides to fill the whole screen.

Printing notes pages will generally work better than printing slides. The best way to avoid this problem is to send the document to Word. There, set up the margins to be equal so the problems won't be quite as noticeable.

To print a full slide per page, with the slide printed on the page, you will also be better off sending the slides to Word. Just as with the notes pages, you can set up the margins in Word to compensate for the unequal margins the printer may cause when printing slides.

One Of My Slides Won't Print. Why?

A problem with a single slide generally means there is something on that slide the printer doesn't like. The most common cause is having something run off the edge of the slide. If you can, crop the item to remove the parts located outside the boundaries of the slide. (By the way, some printers are fussier about this than others are. Try printing to another printer.)

Another cause of pages not printing is a file on its way to corruption. Before doing anything else with the file, save it under a new name, just in case.

This page left intentionally blank.

13. Saving Your Presentation

➢ PowerPoint Files: PPT vs. PPS extensions

➢ PowerPoint and HTML

➢ Templates: Where Are They?

➢ Password Protection & Information Control

Curt runs a communications consulting company. He has a series of presentations that discuss communicating across cultures. Curt's newest client wants to make his presentations available to employees around the world...

I may be a communications expert, but I am not a PowerPoint expert. My latest client wants to send my presentation to a number of their remote offices. I don't want to send the presentations to the home office for distribution without some kind of protection on my intellectual property.

I need to send both a PowerPoint presentation and a set of HTML files. I really am not sure how to send the files so they open without going through the editing interface. I also don't understand what to do with the HTML request.

Curt has a number of problems we need to address. He is used to sending files for speaker-led presentations, so he has never worried about making his presentations open at the first slide. This is the easy one to fix. He also needs to figure out how to save his presentation for use over the Web. This is a little more complicated, but still quite addressable. His last problem, controlling the information in his presentation, is a little harder to address.

PowerPoint Files: ppt Vs. pps Extensions

PowerPoint files can have a number of different extensions: ppt, pps, pot, etc. We need to look at each of these individually to determine what the differences are and which one Curt should use to distribute his presentation.

ppt

PPT files are regular PowerPoint files. When double-clicked on a computer which has PowerPoint installed, PPT files open in the editing interface for PowerPoint. (The normal interface we have been using to edit and change presentations throughout this book.) If PowerPoint is not on the system, but the viewer is, PPT files are opened in the viewer.

pps

PPS files are PowerPoint Show files. They are no different from PPT files, other than the last letter of the extension and what that extension is associated with. PPS files are supposed to open directly in show mode. This means when a PPS file is double-clicked in Windows Explorer, the show should start.

To open a PPS file for editing, open PowerPoint and then use File → Open (or the folder button) to open the presentation.

pot

POT files are template files. They are the design templates used to set up a standard look for slides within a presentation. We will discuss where they are hidden on a machine at the end of this chapter. We will discuss how to create them in Chapter 16.

POT files do not generally contain any content. Instead they contain master slides, color schemes, font attributes and the other master pages.

ppz

You may come across one other presentation file extension in PowerPoint 2002 or earlier, PPZ. In Chapter 15, we will discuss Pack and Go, which was the distribution mechanism for PowerPoint 2002 and earlier. When you Pack and Go a presentation, the process creates two files: one is the same as the presentation, but with an extension of PPZ and the other named Setup.exe The PPZ file contains the packaged presentation but, unfortunately, it can't be opened on its own. It can only be opened by opening the Setup.exe file created with the same Pack and Go.

PowerPoint And HTML

The other way Curt needs to distribute his presentations is via the Web. His client wants the employees to be able to view the presentations via the web interface.

The first thing Curt needs to do is convert his presentation from PowerPoint to HTML. Once he has done that, he will publish the files to the web so his client can view the pages.

There are two ways to create web content from PowerPoint presentations: Single file web page (MHT) or multiple file web page (HTML).

Tip 42: What is an MHT file?	MHT stands for Multipurpose HTML. It was originally developed by Microsoft as a way to package HTML pages for email. Think of MHT files as HTML folders – the single MHT file contains all the HTML and related files necessary to display the presentation.
	In PowerPoint 2003, this process is called Save as Single File Web Page. In PowerPoint 2002, it is called Save as Web Archive. There was no MHT option for PowerPoint 2000 and earlier.

To save a presentation as web content, use File → Save as, Select either Web Page or Single File Web Page from the Save as Type dropdown list. (You can also use the File → Save as Web Page. This will bring up the Save As window, but defaults to one of the web options instead of Presentation.)

When one of the save as web options is selected, two new buttons will be added to the save screen: Publish and Change Title. The Publish button customizes more of the HTML content. The Change Title button changes the tile of the HTML pages. Because the Change Title button brings up the same screen as one of the buttons on the Publish as Web Page screen, we will look at the whole process from the Publish screen.

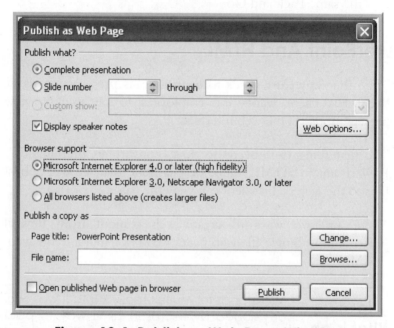

Figure 13-1: Publish as Web Page Window

By the way, just because your browser isn't listed doesn't mean it won't support PowerPoint's HTML. It just means the pages may or may not work. And if they do work, they may look different than intended.

As you can see from Figure 13-1, the Publish as Web Page screen defines:

- How much of the presentation to publish (all of it, a slide range, or a custom show)

- Whether the notes information is available on the web

- What browser(s) to support

- What to title the presentation (using the Change button near the bottom of the screen)

- Where to save the presentation (using the Browse button near the bottom of the screen)

- Whether you want to see the presentation in your Web browser when it is done being converted

It is usually a good idea to create a directory to hold the HTML results. It makes it easier to find them after the conversion has completed.

In addition, from this screen you can customize a wide range of options specific to web content. To access these options, click the Web Options button. A six tabbed window will appear.

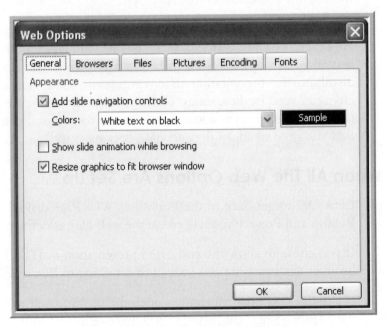

Figure 13-2: Web Options Window

Do I Really Need To Worry About These Options?

Generally speaking, no, you don't. Once the options have been set to create the web pages the way you want them, PowerPoint will keep the settings on the computer until they are changed. However, there are a couple of these settings you do want to investigate.

Adjust the General tab options to your preferences. To make the site easy for people to use, turn on the navigation elements. It is also a good idea to set the colors to one of the presentation-based color schemes. Why? If you don't, you lose the ability to make the web version match the appearance of the presentation. Whether you select Show slide animation while browsing or not will depend on the presentation and audience. This setting determines whether the animation is on when running the presentation from the web.

The options on the other tabs usually don't need to be changed. However, as Curt learned, there is one circumstance where several of the options need to be changed: when you need to distribute the presentation to environments using non-native character sets. In these cases, click the fonts tab and ensure the correct character set is selected. In some of these cases, you may find you need to adjust the encoding options as well.

When All The Web Options Are Set Up...

Click OK to get back to the Publish as Web Page dialog. Click Publish and PowerPoint will create the web files as defined.

If you chose to show the converted presentation as HTML, the browser window will open instead of returning to PowerPoint.

If you didn't choose this option open the files yourself to check the results. Since the process will have returned you to the PowerPoint interface, switch to Windows Explorer and navigate to where the files were saved.

If you chose to create an MHT file, you will see one additional file in the directory. If you chose to save as HTML, you will see a new directory. The name on this new folder is the file name you defined, with "_files" added at the end. In this folder, you will see PowerPoint has taken the single presentation file and created

- One gif file and one HTML file for each slide (called slide0001, etc.): This the slide picture and the HTML to run that slide.

- An outline.html file: This file allows for easy viewing of the outline from the special opening page PowerPoint has created for the HTMLed presentation.

- A buttons.gif file: This is the picture of the navigation buttons, if you chose to include them.

- A series of XML, JS, and CSS files: These are used to actually run the web version of the presentation.

In addition, if the presentation had sounds or movies, those files will also be in this folder.

Tip 43: Get your sounds out of your presentation	Ever been in the situation where you have a presentation with embedded WAV files, but you need to edit the sounds? Save the presentation as HTML.
	In the resulting folder you will find one sound file for each sound in the presentation. Edit these files and re-insert them.

Running An Htmled Presentation

To see what the presentation will look like to the Internet audience, open it in your own browser. To do this, open the browser and do a File → Open. Navigate to the folder where you stored the HTML version of the presentation.

If you saved the presentation as a single file web page, select and open the MHT file. If you saved the presentation as a set of web pages, select and open the file frame.htm from the folder named after the presentation.

When you open either of these files, you will see the first slide on the right side of the screen, the outline down the left side of the screen and some buttons at the bottom of the screen.

To see the static slides, either click on the slide title in the outline pane or click on one of the arrows at the bottom of the screen.

In addition, you will find buttons on the web page for expanding and contracting the outline. If you set the web publish settings to show notes and there are notes for the current slide, those notes will show underneath the picture of the slide. To hide the notes, click the word Notes or the checkmark next to it. (If there isn't a checkmark, it means there are no notes for that slide.)

Tip 44: My slide show doesn't animate on some computers	In order for the presentation to animate when running through a browser, the animation plug-in for the browser must be installed. To find this plug-in for Microsoft Internet Explorer, search the Microsoft site for "PowerPoint 2003 Add-in: Office Animation Runtime." **You won't need this add-in if the computer has PowerPoint 2002 or later installed.**

Click on the slide show icon to see the presentation full-screen. Navigation while the presentation is running is pretty limited. If the designer has put navigation buttons on the slides, use them to move around in the presentation. Unlike the fully functional right-click menu when running the presentation directly, when running the HTML version there are, at most, three options on the right click menu: Next, Previous and End Show.

Tip 45: Navigation in slide show	Even though you don't have as many options on the right-click menu when running a show been to HTML, you can still use a couple of the presentation shortcuts. Exit the presentation prematurely by pressing the escape key. Skip around in the presentation by entering the slide number using the keyboard and then pressing enter.

Using Html To Fix Presentation Problems

Saving a presentation as HTML and then opening the HTML files using PowerPoint allows certain problems within the file to be cleaned up. One use for this is to correct the inconsistencies that can cause corruption. Another use is to remove double byte fonts. Use this process to remove embedded sounds and graphics so they can be edited elsewhere. If you use this method to work with the presentation, be sure to save the HTML version under a different name when you re-open it with PowerPoint.

Can't find the MHT or HTML files? Make sure the Files of type dropdown box shows All PowerPoint Presentations instead of Presentations and Shows when you File → Open in PowerPoint. You can also set this to All Web Pages to see only the HTML pages.

If you open a regular HTML page as a presentation, PowerPoint will try to interpret the page content as a slide. Try it out and see if you like what you get. You may find the results are what you need, you may not.

Use this process to replace sounds within the presentation and clean up situations where you believe corruption may be in process.

The other thing Curt needs to think about with the PowerPoint-to-HTML process is whether the audience will see and hear what he has spent so much time and energy creating.

In the web environment, you have much less control over what the audience sees. Because of the nature of a web page, the audience can change how they see almost everything within a single page.

In addition, there are a few PowerPoint features that may not work as you would wish within the HTML environment.

Things That Don't Work The Way You Would Think

When converting a presentation to HTML, test the presentation to ensure it converted the way you want. Before beginning that testing, there are a few things to keep in mind about converting presentations to PowerPoint.

Sounds

Because HTML is page-based, sounds which play on an HTML page do not usually continue to play when you move to the next page. The same is true of presentations converted to HTML. Sounds play on the slide where they are set to start, but do not continue to play when slides change.

This can be a big problem for those presentations which depend on music or narration. Once you move off the slide with the sound, the sound stops. Fear not, there is a solution: Hand-edit the HTML files created by PowerPoint.

This process is different if running 2000 and earlier or 2002 and later, as so many things are.

PowerPoint 2000 and earlier

1. To make the sound play across slides, you need to update one of the files PowerPoint created during the HTML process and build a text file to control the sounds.

2. To make the coding easier, when you create the new text file name it playsound.htm. This file should read:

```
<html>

<head>
<meta http-equiv=Content-Type
content="text/html; charset=windows-1252">
<meta name=ProgId content=PowerPoint.Slide>
<meta name=Generator content="Microsoft
PowerPoint 10">
<link id=Main-File rel=Main-File
href="../PRISMTest.htm">
<link rel=Preview href=preview.wmf>
```

```
</head>
<P><EMBED
SRC="http://www.URLForSoundFile.com"
type="application/mpeg" NAME="Music"
ALT="Classical Music Piece Plays in the
Background Here" ALIGN=LEFT WIDTH=20%
HEIGHT=31%><BR CLEAR=LEFT><BR><BR> </P>

</html>
```

Note: Replace "http://www.URLForSoundFile.com" with the actual URL for the sound file.

3. Save playsound.htm in the folder PowerPoint created when it converted the presentation.

4. Change the frame.htm file to add a small column or outside frame for the sounds. To do that, change the line

   ```
   <frameset cols="*,495">
   ```

   to

   ```
   <frameset cols="*,25,495">
   ```

   This will change the main frame from two columns to three columns and define the width of the new column.

5. Add the actual frame which will contain the sound file. To do that, find the last two frame commands in the frame.htm file. These lines start with "<frame src". Add a blank line between the two commands. On that line, add the following command:

   ```
   <frame src=playsound.htm title="Sound"
   name="SoundSpot">
   ```

PowerPoint 2002 and later

You only need to add one line to the frame.htm file and to the fullscreen.htm file, if it exists. Inserted between the <html> and <head> tags, the following line will set the HTML up to play the sound file.

```
<bgsound src="yourmusic.wma" loop=infinite>
```

Note: Replace "yourmusic.wma" with the name of the sound file.

These changes will play a single sound or piece of music across all slides, no matter where the audience enters the presentation or which direction they go from the entry slide.

Things Don't Always Show

One problem with web content developed from PowerPoint presentations is certain content doesn't show when the presentation is run. This can have two different causes – either the files are not available to be viewed or the files available are too big to download.

When the files are not available, you will see empty boxes (some may have red x's) instead of graphics. To prevent this, be sure to put all of the files from the web folder up on the web server. If any of the content is not moved up to the server, the pages will not display correctly. The most common issue is the HTML files get moved to the server, but the graphic. This means the slides themselves never get onto the server and unable to be activated from the HTML files.

One way around this problem is to use MHT files. Since everything is in one file, you don't have to worry about forgetting to upload something. Upload the MHT and all content is included, because it's all contained in the MHT file.

When the files uploaded to the server take up too much disk space, they load very slowly and the audience may think the presentation is not working at all. The internet connection used by the audience may be too slow to process the pictures in a timely manner. Be sure to test the access to the presentation on both broadband and dial-up connections. If presentations are too big for access by audiences, see Chapter 11 for information on how to decrease the size of graphics. This should decrease the size of the files enough to get around speed problems.

I Need To Create Web Content That Is Section 508 Compliant

Section 508 compliance measures how accessible content is to viewers with disabilities. Accessibility issues covered by 508 include visual limitations, hearing impairments, movement limitations, color vision problems and other disabilities.

Web content created by PowerPoint's HTML conversion process is not fully Section 508 compliant. If Section 508 compliance is required, check out PowerPoint MVP Steve Rindsberg's PPT2HTML tool. This tool creates more standardized HTML pages from PowerPoint presentations. The other advantage to using PPT2HTML is the code generated to display the slides is much easier to understand and work with.

The down side of PPT2HTML is it doesn't re-create PowerPoint animation. It does maintain slide transitions. If animations are needed for the presentation to be understood, you probably won't be satisfied with the results.

Full Screen

PowerPoint presentations run as web content do not automatically play in full-screen mode. PowerPoint MVP Michael Koerner has developed an on-line presentation that will step you through the process to make presentations run in full-screen mode. Find Michael's presentation at www.oldfco.ca/tutorial/

Templates: Where Are They?

PowerPoint templates are special files which are intended to add formatting to a presentation. We will address creating templates in Chapter 16. Right now, I want to work with you to find where template files are on the PC.

Template files have the extension "pot." When Office is installed, the basic templates are added to the computer's hard drive. The location for these templates depends on the version of Windows.

- Windows 98 or earlier: Template folder will be located in the same path as the rest of Office.

- Windows 2000 or later (or an NT machine of any kind): Templates will be in two different places. The bulk of the templates will be in the Documents and Settings directory, in the All Users folder structure. You will probably have to navigate down a few more levels in the directory structure to find them. In the directories under your user ID, there are more templates. These are the ones you created or acquired for your own use.

To find the default template location on the machine, attempt to save a file as a template. This should automatically change the path to the templates directory. It would be a good idea to take note of the path to this file for later use.

Another way to find the templates is to use the search ability built into Windows Explorer and search for "*.pot". This should bring up a list of all of the PowerPoint templates on the computer.

Templates And PowerPoint 2003

Microsoft changed how PowerPoint 2003 references templates. Templates delivered with PowerPoint 2003 are listed as From design template on the new presentation task pane. These presentations are stored in a location similar to C:\Documents and Settings\Your name\Application Data\Microsoft\Templates

Any templates you add to the machine will probably show up when you use From design template. If they don't, they can also be reached by clicking On my computer under the templates section of the new presentation task pane. You may find this interface easier to use to find templates. These files are stored in the same location, but listed differently on the screen.

PowerPoint MVP Sonia Coleman has an excellent tutorial on the template location at her site www.soniacoleman.com /Tutorials/PowerPoint/PowerPoint_2003__templates.htm

Where Can I Find More Templates?

There are many places on the web with templates available for sale or free download. Several of these are listed in Appendix A. If you need something not referenced in the Appendix, do a Google search (www.google.com) on "free PowerPoint templates." You will get more results than you could ever use!

Password Protection & Information Control

Before we talk about using passwords to protect presentations from theft, misuse or modification, I need to go into what several of my friends call...

The Protection Rant

Any information put in front of someone on a computer can be used for purposes other than what you intended. Any information provided on screen can be taken via screen shots, screen recorders or scanning of a printed copy. Our challenge is to make this at least a little more difficult for those viewing our content.

This is not to say content *should* be taken, this is just to say it *can* be. You have to decide how much you trust the people to whom you are showing the presentation. In Curt's case, he needs to decide whether he trusts his client to protect the design and content of his presentations or whether he is going to make them go through extra work to edit or change the slides.

Most people are not going to steal your work. My experience has been that those who want to use work created by someone else will generally ask permission to use the work and give credit to the original source.

Does this mean I don't believe in protecting intellectual property? No. I believe intellectual property is some of the most valuable property in the world today. However, the value of information can be dependent on how easy it is to access and use the intellectual property.

Password Protection In PowerPoint

Having had my rant, you (and Curt) are still in the position of needing to password protect the presentation to make it harder for people to steal. In PowerPoint 2000 and earlier, you can't do it natively. In PowerPoint 2002 or later, you can.

PowerPoint 2000 And Earlier....

There are several good file protection options available to users of PowerPoint 2000 and earlier:

- Zip the presentation and put a password on the zip file. This will require the receiver to have some way to unzip the file, but it requires the least effort on your part. Once the receiver has opened the zip file there is no other protection on the PowerPoint file. (This option is especially useful if you need to zip the file for protection during emailing anyway.)

- Get SecurePack. This PowerPoint add-in from Shyam Pillai lets you control access to the presentation and all the related files through a single interface: www.mvps.org/skp/securepack/index.htm

- PrezGuardPro, from AlaDat, works along the same lines as SecurePack in that it creates a secure package for the presentation and its files: www.aladat.com

Another option for securing the presentation is to distribute it in some medium other than PowerPoint. Some examples include:

- Turn the presentation into a PDF, then use Adobe Acrobat's password protection mechanisms

- Use PowerPoint to save the file as jpegs and use a movie creation tool to bring the jpegs to life.

- Create Flash or other movies with a screen recording tool. If you are going to do this, check out Camtasia from TechSmith. (www.techsmith.com) It is the one I like best. If you prefer, you can also use the free Microsoft Movie Maker.

- Distribute a show within a show. Create an empty presentation and use Insert → Object to add the main presentation. One word of warning: If the recipients are going to use the PowerPoint 2003 viewer to view the presentation, they will not be able to click the included presentation to activate it. To make sure this isn't a problem, set up animation that starts the inner presentation as soon as the first slide of the outer presentation comes up. There is a way around this method. If the inner presentation is double clicked from the editing interface of PowerPoint, it opens. This way the entire set of slides can be copied and pasted into a new or existing presentation file.

- If sending a presentation to a group of computer novices, change the presentation format to PPS and they may not know the presentation can still be edited. If you wish to go one more step, right-click on the file in Windows Explorer and use the properties to set the file to Read-only. Be careful with this though: Many people know how to remove Read-only from a file's properties. Read-only and PPS do not offer much file protection at all.

PowerPoint 2002 And Later....

As with so many of the features we have investigated in this book, PowerPoint 2002 and later allow you to easily add passwords to the presentation, giving you some control over the use of the file by others.

Passwords can be added via a number of different screens. You can go to Tools → Options and use the Security tab. You can go to File → Save As, and select the Security options from the Tools drop down on the right side of the window. In either case, the screen that comes up looks like Figure 13-3:

Figure 13-3: Presentation Security Options

There are two levels of password protection for files. You can require a password to open the presentation and you can require a password to modify the presentation. This allows you to determine both who can open and view the file, and who has rights to actually change the file.

Once you have set the password, the person receiving the presentation must have a password to open and/or change the document. This only works if recipients are using PowerPoint 2002 or later. If recipients try to open the presentation with one of the earlier versions of PowerPoint, or with the PowerPoint 97 viewer, they will receive an error message. This is because the earlier versions don't know how to handle the passwords and can't interpret the file.

Information Rights Management

Office 2003 added an option called Information Rights Management (IRM) to the protection arsenal. IRM allows you to define not only who can access your documents, but for how long the document can be accessed.

IRM is available with Office Professional and higher. It can be added to individual Office programs by downloading an application from the web. If using PowerPoint in an environment where Windows Server 2003 is in use, you may find the IRM services are already available on the computer or from your friendly system administrator. If you don't have the IRM client installed on the computer, you will be prompted to download it the first time you try to use one of the IRM options.

Access to the settings is through the File → Permission dialog.

To learn more about how to use IRM in the Office System 2003 environment, check out this URL from Microsoft: office.microsoft.com/assistance/preview.aspx?AssetID=HA01 0397891033

This page left intentionally blank.

14. For Presenters: Getting Ready To Present

➢ You Are The Expert

➢ Notes Pages

➢ Handouts

➢ Practice

➢ Slick Presenting Tricks

If you are reading this chapter, you are likely creating PowerPoint content will be presented by a live presenter. Whether the presenter is you or someone else, there are a number of things you can do to make sure the presentation is the best possible.

As you already know, I came into the PowerPoint world as a stand-up trainer. Developing content and delivering it live was my life. In the process of learning to use PowerPoint to support my training sessions, I learned quite a bit about the things that can bite presenters and the things that can make things easier on presenters.

For that reason, rather than using someone else as the example in this chapter, I am the example. You are going to get to know me from a different angle than you have seen so far. You are going to see Kathy the presenter, instead of Kathy the writer.

You Are The Expert!

The most difficult thing about getting a presentation ready to go live is being sure you are confident in what you are doing. For that reason, I am going to share with you the best advice I ever got:

The audience is on your side. Really, they are. They want you to succeed. They want to learn from you. They wouldn't be there if this weren't the case.

So, when finalizing the presentation, do it from the viewpoint of "I can do this." If you keep that phrase in your mind, you will be much more comfortable than you could imagine.

Does This Mean You Won't Be Nervous?

I hope not. I still get nervous before I train, talk or present. I think it helps you be better prepared. If the event isn't important enough for you to be nervous, you will come off as un-attached and disinterested. You want the audience to know what you are about to say is important. You want them to know it matters to you they "get" what you are saying.

That doesn't give you permission to be un-prepared. It does give you permission to have butterflies in your stomach, to worry a little about your opening sentences, to worry a little about the audience and the environment, and to prepare.

If nerves are getting in the way of the preparation, there are a few simple tricks to try which will limit the effect of the nerves.

- Breathe deep. Yawn, even. Yawning relaxes the face and the neck. It is impossible for your jaw to be tight if you are yawning. In addition, a yawn removes excess carbon dioxide from your system. This means you have to breathe in more oxygen to compensate.

- Leave the room for a minute. By leaving the room, you can make an entrance when you return, which will do a lot to focus the attention of the audience. Leaving the room also gives you a little exercise, so you loosen up. (If you can take a bathroom break, even better. You will be away from the audience and able to focus.)

- If you can't physically leave the room, do it mentally. Turn your back to the audience, close your eyes and think of the ten things this presentation is going to do for you. You aren't going to lose track of the audience, but you will refocus yourself.

- Take a slow drink of water. Yes, water. Not pop, not coffee, not anything else. Water is clear. If you spill it, it will dry and not show. The act of drinking will relax you almost as much as a yawn. In addition, it will prepare your throat for the torture it is about to endure.

- Warm up your voice. I do a couple of quick sentences from a play or a basic theatrical warm up. Others do true vocal warm-ups. Both achieve the same things: They prepare your throat and larynx for the stress of talking to a group.

- Shake out your arms and legs. Stretch your back. Remember, presenting is work. If you haven't warmed up, you may find you regret it later. Think this only applies to long presentations? Think again. Your poor feet and legs are about to hold your entire body weight for an hour or more. Don't they deserve as much preparation and warm-up as your voice?

Still nervous? Don't worry. Focus on what you need to say and what you need the audience to hear, and your nerves will calm down. Remember: Public speaking is the number one fear for Americans. World wide, it is in the top ten fears. Few people in the audience want to do what you are up there doing. They will respect you just for trying, especially if you have done your homework and followed the tips in this book.

Slow Down!

When presenting, you will tend to talk faster than normal. The spaces between your words will disappear, and the vowels and the consonants will slur together. This will make it very difficult for the audience to understand you.

If you practice breathing while you speak, you will slow down. If you aren't sure how to slow down the presentation, tape yourself talking through it. Now, listen to the tape. Can you understand the words? If not, try it again. Just the act of being conscious of your speed will slow you down.

The other need for slowing down is to ensure you aren't saying too much. Give people a chance to ask questions. Get them involved. The more they are involved, the more they will remember.

Give breaks. If you are going to speak for more than an hour, take a formal break, if possible. If the schedule doesn't allow for real breaks, make sure you get people up out of their seats for a minute or so. A great friend of mine says the mind can only absorb what the seat can endure. Keep this in mind when you speak.

Even Though You Are The Expert...

Remember you are also human. You don't have to know everything. If a question comes up you can't answer, tell the person asking you will get back to her. (Then do!) If you make a mistake, admit it. Allow the audience to know you are human, just as they are.

Ever been in one of those slick sales presentations where the sales person had an answer for everything? How did you feel at the end of the presentation? Did you connect with the speaker, or did you feel they thought they were better than you? Remember that feeling when you speak. If you are too glossy and detached, the audience will know it.

One of the best ways to improve how you speak is to listen to others. Pick up tips and techniques from the good speakers. Learn and improve by seeing what doesn't work.

Now that you are ready, let's do the final few stages of getting your materials ready. First up: the notes pages.

Notes Pages

Notes pages in PowerPoint allow you to add supplemental materials to the presentation. You type information into the notes area and it travels with the presentation to remind you what to say.

There are two different approaches you can take to slide notes. You can use them as full scripts, with every word and action recorded in the notes area. You can also use them as a place to hold additional information, resources and things you may forget about.

I don't use the script approach. I come close to the script when I develop presentations others are going to present, but I don't like being told what words to say, so I don't like to tell others what to say. However, if the slide is fairly complex, I will give extended hints of what to say and when to click.

When content has to be presented word for word, such as when I am presenting facts and figures, I will put the exact wording in my notes. I may not follow it, but it is there.

Another example is when I am presenting safety-related information. As a volunteer Girl Scout trainer, there are times when what I am training comes straight from one of the Girl Scout publications. This is especially true when training new leaders. I want to be sure what I am telling the leaders matches exactly what they are going to read in the books. This information will be written out so I don't say it wrong.

So, what do my notes pages look like? They generally are short chunks of text giving extra information. I use formatting and codes to tell myself and the other presenters what each little blurb or chunk is for.

If a paragraph is about something I know I tend to forget, I preface the note with the letters REM (for reminder). If it is a reference to more information, I preface it with REF (for reference). If I need to be sure the audience gets a particular point, I bold the note. If I want to verify they understood something, I will put in a question to ask them and italicize it.

One other use for notes pages: If you need to remember to customize the presentation for each audience, the notes area for the title slide is a great spot to record what needs to change. Sometimes, the reminder can be as simple as "Customize customer name, date, location." Other times, the title slide notes page includes questions I need answered before I start the presentation.

So, What Do You Do With The Notes?

Once finished with the presentation and the notes, I print them out to use during practice runs. I don't use these notes during the actual presentation unless I have not gotten enough practice time.

For others, the best way to use the notes is the multiple monitors set up, which is built into PowerPoint. This allows you to have the notes and slides show on the laptop screen while only the slides show up on the projector or main monitor. (If you need a refresher on setting up the multiple monitors, check out Chapter 3's sections on setting up the show.)

Another use for the notes section is to share information with the audience. If putting together a class, use the notes area to hold questions, quizzes, etc., as well as the extra resource information.

A Word Of Warning

If using PowerPoint 2000 and earlier, it is not a good idea to save the presentation while working in the notes view. This has been known to cause people to lose the notes from their file. The problem doesn't occur in more recent versions of PowerPoint, or if it does, it hasn't been reported.

Instead, when you are done with the notes for a slide, switch to the main view or the slide sorter view and save the presentation from there.

Changing The Look Of Your Notes

Control the look of the notes pages by making changes to the Notes Master. The default master is laid out as a portrait 8.5" by

11" page. It has an image of the slide at the top and space for notes at the bottom.

The Notes Master has several lines of dummy text to show the current text format and indentation levels for the notes. You can change the look of notes by clicking on the text in the Notes Master and changing the formatting.

In addition to changing the way the text on the notes pages looks, you can also turn on and off the header and footer. To do this, view the Notes Master and do View → Header and Footer. Click the Notes and Handouts tab and set the elements up as you want them.

Only One Page Per Slide

You can only have one page of notes per slide if using PowerPoint notes. You cannot have notes pages not attached to slides. If you need extra space within the notes pages, change the size of the picture of the slide, or remove it from the notes page by selecting it and then hitting Delete on the keyboard.

I don't recommend removing the picture of the slide from the notes master. It is a useful tool for telling at a glance which notes go with which slides.

Handouts

There are two kinds of PowerPoint handouts: Those which have just slides on them and those which have either notes or space for notes next to each slide. Both kinds of handouts can be created in PowerPoint, but there are better ways to do them.

Handouts In PowerPoint

Handouts in PowerPoint are generated by bringing up the print dialog and selecting Handouts from the Print What list. Once Handouts is selected, choose how many slides per page to print. The options are:

- 1 slide per page – centers the slide on the page, taking into account the margins needed by the printer

- 2 slides per page – half-sized slides stacked one on top of the other

- 3 slides per page – three slides, each at quarter-size, running down the left side of the page, with lines for notes next to each slide

- 4, 6, or 9 slides per page – small versions of each slide, printed in rows of two or three, order of the slides determined by the order radio buttons (horizontal or vertical)

In addition, you can define what you want to see on the page besides the miniature slides. You can turn on and off the header and footer elements just as you did on the Notes Master. In fact, if these elements are set to show on the Notes Master, they will show on the Handout Master as well. You can also add graphical elements to show behind the miniature slides by doing Insert → Picture, creating an autoshape or changing the background.

When viewing the handout master, a new toolbar will appear on the screen:

Figure 14-1: Handout Master View Toolbar

While it would appear from this toolbar that you can change each of the layouts individually, you can't. You can view each, but any change you make to one of the views is made to all of the views. You also can't adjust the size of the miniature slides.

Better Options

I don't use the handouts as PowerPoint creates them. Instead, I use another tool to create my handouts. There are two tools I use regularly: Word and Shyam Pillai's Handout Wizard.

Word

To use Word to create handouts, do a File → Send to and send the presentation to Word. Remember to select paste link to decrease the file size later.

If you want notes to be visible in the Word handouts, send the slides three to a page with notes next to them. If you don't want the notes visible, send the slides three to a page with lines.

Now, you have a Word document you can edit and adjust as you see fit. You can add title and section separation pages, additional resource pages, quizzes and exercises, etc. Once you have it set up the way you want and the PowerPoint file is finalized, break the links between the two files and you are all set.

PowerPoint MVP Shyam Pillai's Handout Wizard

Another option for creating handouts is a great tool developed by Shyam Pillai. This tool creates customized handouts directly from PowerPoint. It will allow you to create layout templates, add graphics and determine what exactly you want printed.

Yup, you read that right. You can even use the HandoutWizard to create gorgeous handouts for custom shows, individual slides or slide ranges. What's more, this great tool allows different sections of the presentation set up to create handouts using different handout templates.

Want to learn more? Check out the Handout Wizard webpage: www.mvps.org/skp/how/

Practice

Okay, the presentation has been created, the notes written up, the handouts printed, and they look quite good. Are you ready to present?

Not quite. Actually, you have the most important piece of preparation yet to do. You need to practice the presentation.

Practicing the presentation means running through the actual slides while saying the words you want the audience to hear. You should practice several times by yourself or in front of a mirror or camera. Then, when you think you are ready to present, it is time to add a test audience.

Test Audience

The test audience should be made up of people who will be honest, yet kind. If at all possible, the test audience should be a cross-section of the actual audience. If that isn't possible, instruct them on what the real audience will be like so they can evaluate you realistically.

The job of the test audience is to help you polish your presentation and anticipate problems and questions. Their job is not to pick on your particular presentation style. (Though if you make a huge gaffe, they should be willing to comment on it.)

Don't be afraid to ask the test audience the hard questions. Don't be afraid either of their answers. Take it as a learning experience and grow your presentation skills.

You can't over-practice. What most people consider an over-practiced presentation is really one where the presenter has lost touch with the content, the message and the audience. As long as you keep connected, practice will only make you better.

Final Practice

Once you have fully practiced the presentation, it is time for the real test. You want to do a timed practice of the presentation in the actual location where you will be speaking.

I know this isn't always practical. If you can't get full practice time, you should at least get time to verify the machine set up, the room layout and where you can move. The more time you can get in the actual room, the higher the payoff will be.

The extra time running through the material in an unfamiliar location will allow you to verify everything is working. In addition, it will let you brainstorm techniques for working in the space you have been assigned.

This is especially important if you have been practicing in a small space and are actually presenting in a much larger space. You will need to test out how the microphone and sound system work with your voice. You will also need to check out how you and the presentation work in the available lighting.

Slick Presenting Tricks

You have practiced, prepared and tested. You are ready to give the presentation. This section will give you some tips for moving through the presentation with ease.

Keystrokes You Need To Know

The first thing to do is to memorize some very important shortcuts to use when presenting. While a presentation is running, either right-click and select Help or press F1. A window will appear which lists the key combinations to use during the presentation to wow the audience.

I recommend you bring up the Help window and learn what options are available. These are the ones you will use most frequently:

- B and W – Blank the screen. Typing a "B" turns the screen into a black screen. Along the same lines, typing a "W" turns the screen into a white screen. Depending on the presentation environment, you will use these keys to hide slides while you talk about things not on the slides. To bring the slide back again, either press the same key again or press the spacebar.

- Number followed by Enter – Typing a number followed by the Enter key takes you directly to that slide. If you have a list of the slide titles and numbers, you can go to any slide in the presentation without the audience knowing you went out of order.

- Escape key – End the show. This is a great way to leave the show in a hurry. It will return you to the PowerPoint interface or desktop, depending on where you started.

I am not going to go over the rest of these great navigation tools. Instead, I recommend you play with them and get comfortable with the ones you are most likely to use.

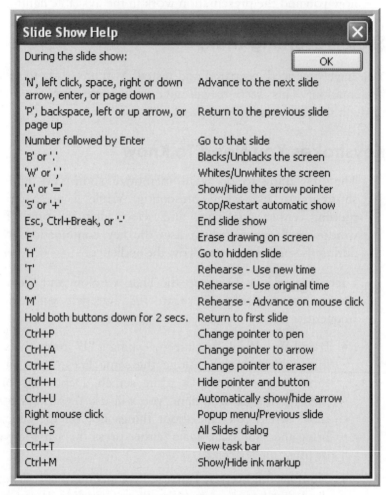

Figure 14-2: Slide Show Help Window

Tip 46: Out of time before you are out of slides?	If you run out of time before you run out of slides, you can easily cover the fact by typing B or W to blank the slide, do a quick wrap up and ask for final questions. The audience won't know you had more slides if you don't tell them.
	Why not just hit escape? Because you don't really want to go to the desktop or the PowerPoint interface while summarizing. You want the audience looking at you, not the desktop.
	Practice this move a few times and it will become more natural. You never know when you will need it.

Use The Pen

Need to make a note on a slide during the show? Right-click on the slide and change the pointer to a pen. In most cases, you will also find a button at the bottom left of the slide that looks like a pen. It will change from pointer to pen as well. Once the pointer changes to the pen, draw all you want. Note unless you are using PowerPoint 2003, the drawings won't be saved.

Need to save the annotations in an earlier version? You could use print screen to capture the final drawings or notations on any particular slide. Or, you can use a facility called the Meeting Minder which I will cover later.

Need to change the pen color? That's on the buttons and the right-click menu, too. Just select Pen Color and slide over to the color needed.

Using 2003?

With 2003, you are not limited to changing the color of the pen – can select the type of pen as well. The choices are a ballpoint pen, a felt tip pen or a highlighter.

If you have a computer that uses an electronic pen for control instead of a mouse, you may have an option called inking enabled. This allows you to write on the screen and have

PowerPoint understand what you write. You can even turn it on and off from the right-click menu.

Need to run another program during the presentation? Right-click, Screen → Switch Programs. You can also use ALT+Tab to switch between programs.

Meeting Minder

Meeting Minder lets you take minutes and assign action items during the presentation. When activated, a new two-tabbed window will appear.

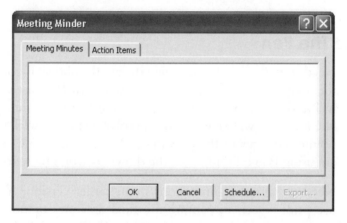

Figure 14-3: Meeting Minder Meeting Minutes Window

The Meeting Minutes tab allows you to enter anything you need to remember about the meeting. At the end of the presentation, you will be prompted to save the meeting minutes. If you say yes, the minutes will be saved with the presentation.

As soon as you make a change to a set of meeting minutes, the export button will become active. Use this button to send meeting minutes to either Word or Outlook when done. If you save the notes but don't export them, you can export them later by bringing up the Meeting Minder and clicking Export.

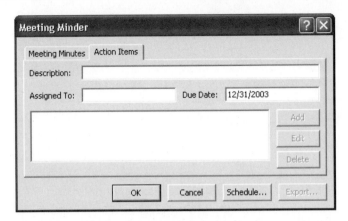

Figure 14-4: Meeting Minder Action Items Window

The Action Items tab allows you to create and assign action items during the presentation. This is quite useful for noting changes to the presentation or the content. Each action item is tracked within the presentation. Just as with the minutes, you can export the action items to Word or Outlook.

The schedule button creates a meeting, but only if Outlook is installed and an account has been set up on the computer.

Meeting Minder was removed in PowerPoint 2003. Microsoft felt the inking capabilities added with Office System 2003, combined with One Note, was a better solution for taking notes during presentations. You will have to judge for yourself.

Other Cool Tricks

- Need to see the speaker notes? Right-click, Screen → Speaker Notes, or click the folder icon at the bottom left and select Speaker Notes. Be aware if you do this on the primary monitor, the audience will see the notes as well. If pulling up a reference, this can be a good thing. If you have a full script in the notes, it probably isn't.

- Bring up a list of slides by using the folder button at the bottom left of the screen or by right-clicking. From either option, select the slide number off the Go to slide list. Or, slide over from the custom show item and select a show to run.

This page left intentionally blank.

15. Sharing

- ➤ How Do I Know Which Viewer to Use?

- ➤ Preparing to Share

- ➤ 2003: Package for CD

- ➤ Pack and Go for PowerPoint 97 or 2000

- ➤ Pack and Go for PowerPoint 2002

- ➤ Do it Yourself AutoRun CDs

One thing almost all PowerPoint users have in common is the need to make presentations available to other users or other computers. If you look through the case studies in this book, almost all of them include moving presentations from one computer to another.

Sharing presentations can be easy if you take the time to learn about what you are doing and prepare for the presentation move. If you don't prepare for the move, sharing presentations can be a real pain!

In October of 2003, Microsoft did something that made every PowerPoint users life much easier: They released a new Viewer for the first time since 1997.

The PowerPoint Viewer for 2003 supports almost every PowerPoint feature, action, animation and effect used in PowerPoint 2002 or 2003. If using an older version of PowerPoint to create the presentation, use the older viewer instead of the 2003 viewer.

How Do I Know Which Viewer To Use

Tip 47: A quick way to find the Viewers	If you don't feel like searching the Microsoft site for the Viewers, check out PowerPoint MVP Steve Rindsberg's PowerPoint FAQ site. Links to the Viewers can be found there on this page: www.rdpslides.com/pptfaq/FAQ00153.htm

Before sharing presentations, download and install the correct Viewer from Microsoft's site. Go to www.microsoft.com and do a search for "PowerPoint Viewer." One of the links will bring up the download page for the PowerPoint Viewer 97 and another for the 2003 Viewer. Download the one needed and install it in a folder on the hard drive. Write down the name of this folder for later use.

PPT Version	Which Viewer?	How to Pack	Notes
2003	2003 Viewer	Package for CD	Can copy directly to CD (Windows XP required) or to folder on hard drive. Will not run embedded presentations
2002	2003 Viewer	Pack and Go. Don't include Viewer	Creates setup.exe and PPZ file. Recipient must unpack. Audience will need to download and install 2003 Viewer from the web. Viewer shows all 2002 animations and transitions. Will not run embedded presentations
2002	2003 Viewer	Manually add files and 7 Viewer files to Staging folder.	Recipient doesn't have to unpack. Use best practices with regard to linked files or use third-party utility such as PowerLink Plus or FixLinksPro to resolve links. Will not run embedded presentations
2000	97 Viewer	Pack and Go. Include Viewer	Creates setup.exe and PPZ file. Recipient must unpack. Viewer won't run animated GIFs; won't show picture bullets
97	97 Viewer	Pack and Go. Include Viewer	Creates setup.exe and PPZ file. Recipient must unpack.

No matter which viewer you are using, there are a few things to know before using it:

- The 2003 Viewer does not let you activate embedded presentations. It will allow you to activate linked presentations. If you need to use embedded presentations in a distributed presentation, use the 97 Viewer.

- Neither Viewer supports VBA or PowerPoint macros. If the presentation needs macros to run, the people receiving it will need the full PowerPoint application in order to run any code included in the presentation. Microsoft determined adding support for VBA to the Viewers was a security risk.

- The 2003 Viewer supports password protection at multiple levels. This is a good thing for developers who want to protect their proprietary slide shows. If you do share a password-protected presentation, send the password to allow the presentation to be opened, even if you don't want to share the modify password. You can have different passwords on each of the presentation files.

  The 97 Viewer does not support passwords, so if the presentation needs password protection, use the 2003 Viewer.

- Both Viewers need to be installed once they are downloaded from the web. Once installed, they can be used on the computer or you can copy the files to a CD, USB drive or other device and run them.

  If distributing a presentation on CD, you can include the files created when the Viewer is installed. This way, those receiving the CD do not need to install the CD on their computers.

- The 2003 Viewer will run on Windows XP (any version), Windows 2000 (Service Pack 3), Windows 98.SE, Windows ME or any Windows Server product from 2003 on. If the recipients of the presentation are running an older version of Windows, they will not be able to see the presentation.

Preparing To Share

If there is *any* chance you are going to share a presentation, create that presentation so that links to other files won't be lost when the file is shared.

The first step in preparing to share the presentation is to create a folder for all the presentation files, sound files, movies files and other linked files.

As you build the presentation, put a copy of each linked file into this directory and link to that copy. This will save you much heartache later on. (If you need a refresher on setting up links correctly, go back to Chapter 9 and review especially the information on Absolute vs. Relative links.)

2003: Package For CD

In addition to adding a new Viewer in 2003, Microsoft also cleaned up the interface for creating CDs and folders with presentations to be distributed. The feature is now called Package for CD. We will walk through the packaging process using a presentation I created for Daniel's class from Chapter 7, Adding Movies. This presentation is the lifecycle of a rose.

Before beginning the packaging process, it is a good idea to have the 2003 Viewer installed on the computer. When you have downloaded it from the Microsoft site, double-click the ppviewer.exe file. This will install the Viewer on the computer. At the end of the installation, you will be told the Viewer can now be run from the computer's Start menu. The first time the 2003 Viewer is run on any given computer, the license agreement will have to be accepted.

When you select File→ Package for CD in PowerPoint, the window in Figure 15-1 will appear:

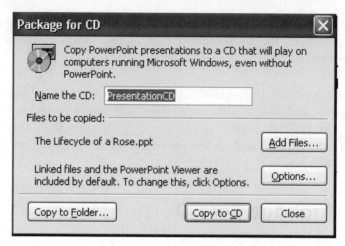

Figure 15-1: Package for CD Window

If running on any version of Windows earlier than Windows XP, the Copy to CD button will not be clickable. You will need to do a Copy to Folder and then write the presentation to CD using your own CD writing software.

Notice the program tells you up front linked files and the Viewer will be included by default.

Package For CD Options

Clicking the Options button on the Package for CD window brings up window in Figure 15-2:

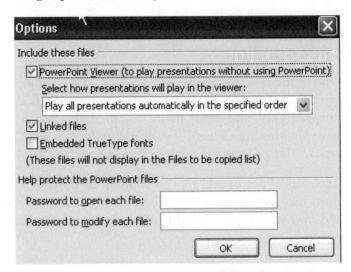

Figure 15-2: Package for CD Options Window

Using these options you can:

- Turn on and off inclusion of the Viewer

- Select how your presentations will play:

- Turn on or off inclusion of linked files

- Turn on or off embedding of fonts

- Set Open and Modify passwords for the top level PowerPoint files

If you already have a password assigned, you will see this when PowerPoint saves the presentation:

Figure 15-3: Presentation Password Reassign Message

Most of the time, the defaults for these options are what you want. The things you are likely to change are the font embedding and the password protection. Remember, if you set a password, make sure those who receive the files and need the passwords have them.

Link Recognition

One of the new features of Package to CD is its link recognition system. Package to CD will go through the file, find all linked presentations and add them to the file list. If multiple presentations are chained together, the Package for CD feature repeats this process for every presentation in the link list.

Click Add Files to add files in addition to those linked directly from one of the PowerPoint files. A browse window will open, and you will be able to add other files from the computer or network.

Basic Copy To CD

For our first example, we are going to do a "vanilla" copy to CD from a Windows XP system. Change the name of the CD to anything you want. I try to keep it short, with no spaces, and make it clear what is on the CD. In this case, I change it to RoseLifeCycle. Click Copy to CD.

As long as you have a blank CD in the drive and are using Windows XP, Copy to CD will run, gathering files and writing them to the CD. It will tell you (via a message box) as it copies the files to the CD. If you don't have a blank CD in the drive, you will be prompted that the files cannot be written because the CD is not writable. Put a blank CD in the drive and try again.

When the process is finished, it will close the CD and bring up this window:

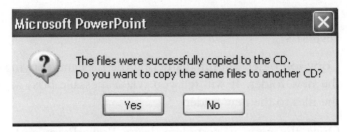

Figure 15-4: CD Copying Finished Message

Click Yes to make another copy. The program will prompt for another CD and copy the files to that new CD.

Click No if finished with this presentation. You will be returned to the Package for CD window.

Basic Copy To Folder

Now, let's package to a folder. This is useful for creating folders to be emailed or for creating presentation sets for storage on a USB drive. It is the only option for packaging when running a version of Windows earlier than Windows XP. It is also the only option if you do there isn't a CD or DVD burner on the computer.

Clicking Copy to Folder brings up the Copy to Folder window (Figure 15-5):

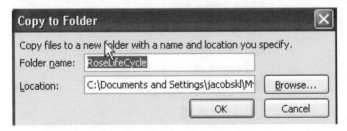

Figure 15-5: Copy to Folder Window

The folder name will default to the value for Name the CD entered in the previous screen (Figure 15-1). Change it if you wish. The default location for the folder is the PowerPoint file default, the one specified on the Tools→ Options→ Save tab. To change the location, click Browse and navigate to where you want to save this folder. When you have selected the location, click OK.

Copy to Folder will run, gathering the files and copying them to the new folder. It will tell you (via a message box) as it copies the files to the new folder.

Once the copy is complete, leave PowerPoint and copy the contents of the new folder to the CD, USB storage device or other location. Be sure to only copy the contents of the folder, not the folder itself. When finished, if you don't need to copy the packaged information anywhere else, delete it from the computer.

What Files Are Packaged?

Package for CD saves the PowerPoint files individually so they can all be accessed and edited. The list of files saved in the folder in my example is:

Figure 15-6: Sample Package for CD File List

Because we used Copy to Folder instead of Copy to CD, there is no autorun.bat. Instead there is a play.bat file. If you look at the files copied to a CD, you will see autorun.bat is there and play.bat is not.

What Next?

The next step is to test the presentation. If you did a Package To Folder, navigate to the folder and double-click the play.bat file. The presentation should start. If it runs the way you want it to, you are ready to either zip the folder together for emailing or copy its contents to the media you will be using to move it.

If you packaged directly to CD, remove the CD and re-insert it. The presentation should start. If it runs the way you want it to, you are finished. Distribute the CD at will.

No matter how you distribute the packaged presentation, make sure you provide instructions for running the presentation.

Pack And Go For PowerPoint 97 Or 2000

Pack and Go is the feature in older versions of PowerPoint which packages presentations, along with other files specified, into a pair of compressed files for distribution. For simplicity, we will refer to this process as PnG. We will work through the PnG process using the same presentation we used for the Package for CD process.

The first step to doing a PnG is to download and install the old Viewer. Once done, open the presentation in PowerPoint. Select File → Pack and Go. This will bring up the first screen of the PnG wizard.

Figure 15-7: Pack and Go Wizard

This screen provides an overview of the PnG process on the left side of the window. The green box is the current step, the red box is the end of the process. After you are familiar with the process, you can click the Finish button at any time to accept the default options. (Note that from here on, I will only show the right-hand pane of the window. To see what happens in the left pane, follow along on your machine.)

Click Next. Tell PowerPoint which presentation to pack.

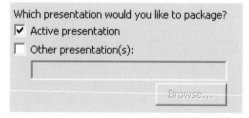

Figure 15-8: Pack and Go Presentation Selection Window

The options are the currently active presentation, another presentation or both. If you select Other presentation(s), browse to the file's location on the computer. We will pack the currently active presentation, so make sure that box is checked and click Next.

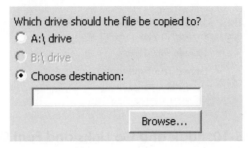

Figure 15-9: Pack and Go Destination Selection Window

Decide where the results of the PnG process will be saved. Notice that the only options are the floppy drive or Choose destination. You will generally want to choose a destination on the hard drive to save the resulting files. I always create a folder just for the packed items. It makes it easier to find and test later on.

Tip 48: Don't PnG directly to removable media	There is a temptation to save files directly to removable media, such as a CD drive or a USB drive. Don't give in to this temptation.
	The first reason to save to the hard drive is because you will want to test the PnG output before you make the CD. It is always a good idea to save directly to the hard drive and move the files to the removable media after you know everything works right.
	Another reason is PowerPoint versions before 2003 don't know how to write to a CD. Unless your version of Windows has built-in CD writing and re-writing, don't save directly to the CD.
	(Tempted to PnG to a floppy? Don't. A single floppy isn't big enough to hold the two files PnG makes. Spanning floppies during a PnG is a good way to corrupt the packed presentation files.)

Once the destination folder is selected, the next step is to decide what is going to be included with the PowerPoint presentation file(s).

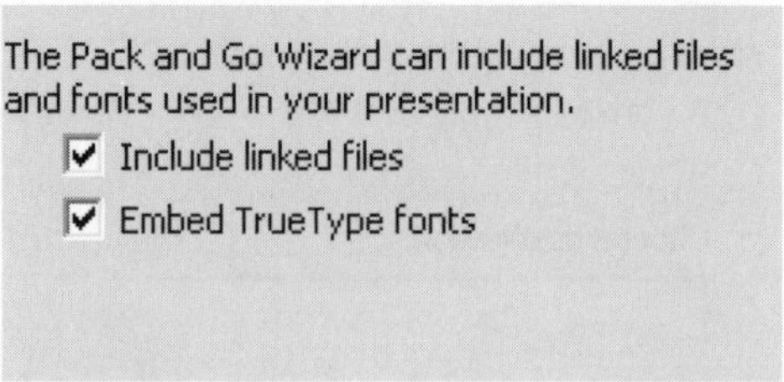

The Pack and Go Wizard can include linked files
and fonts used in your presentation.

☑ Include linked files

☑ Embed TrueType fonts

Figure 15-10: Pack and Go Links and Font Options

Select what else to pack with the presentation: linked files and/or TrueType fonts.

If there are files linked to the presentation, the Wizard will try to find them for packing if Include linked files is checked. If non-standard fonts are used in the presentation, you will probably want to embed them in the presentation. Otherwise, what the recipient sees may not be what you created. If you don't remember which fonts are the standard fonts, review Chapter 4.

Once you have set up what will be included with the presentation file(s), the next step is to decide whether to include the viewer in the PnG files.

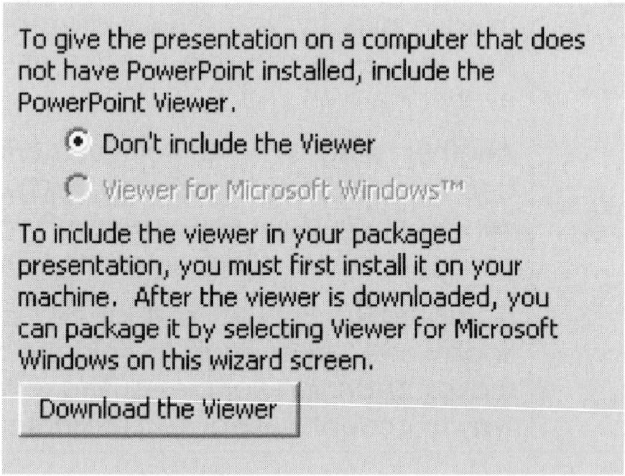

To give the presentation on a computer that does
not have PowerPoint installed, include the
PowerPoint Viewer.

⦿ Don't include the Viewer

◯ Viewer for Microsoft Windows™

To include the viewer in your packaged
presentation, you must first install it on your
machine. After the viewer is downloaded, you
can package it by selecting Viewer for Microsoft
Windows on this wizard screen.

Download the Viewer

Figure 15-11: Pack and Go Viewer Selection Window

For PowerPoint 2000 or earlier, download and include the 97 Viewer. Click the Download the Viewer button. When the 97 Viewer is downloaded, install it on the computer. Then switch back to PowerPoint (which will still be running), select Viewer for Microsoft Windows and continue.

Figure 15-12: Pack and Go Final Window

You are done telling the Wizard what you want packed. When you click Finish, the wizard will put the presentation files together and create two files in the directory you specified:

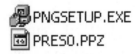

PNGSETUP.EXE
PRES0.PPZ

Figure 15-13: Pack and Go Presentation Files

PNGSETUP.EXE is the file the recipients will double-click to unpack the presentation. It will unpack the other file (PRES0.PPZ) and create copies of the presentations, linked files and embedded fonts for use by the recipient. If the 97 Viewer is included in the PnG process, it will unpack those files as well.

Testing And Distributing PnG Files

To test the packed presentation, unpack it. Double-click on the PNGSETUP.EXE file. Pack and Go Setup will start.

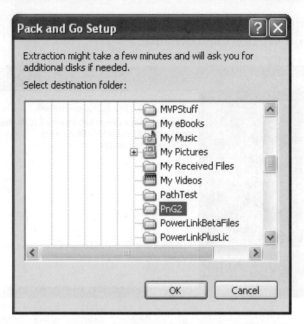

Figure 15-14: Pack and Go Setup Window

First, it will ask where to unpack the unpacked files to. The unpack location must be an existing directory. If you packed to a separate directory, select that directory to unpack. If not, click Cancel and create one now; then double-click PNGSETUP.EXE again. Select the folder and click OK.

If a folder that is not empty is selected, you will receive a warning. As long as none of the files in the directory have the same names as the presentation or linked files, click Yes and continue. If you click No, you will be prompted for a new directory.

The unpack process will now run. When it is complete, it will ask if you want to run the slide show now. Select No. If you select Yes, the presentation will run with PowerPoint. Since we are distributing the presentation with the Viewer, we want to test it with the Viewer.

Now, we need to test the presentation using the Viewer. To run the 97 Viewer, go to the folder where the installed Viewer files are saved and double-click the file pptview.exe. If the 97 Viewer was included in the PnG, it will have unpacked with the presentation so it will be in the same folder as the presentation. From the Viewer, navigate to the folder where the files were unpacked. In addition to the files for the 97 Viewer, you should see the presentation and any linked files. Select the presentation. Click Open. The presentation will start. Run through it and make sure it looks and works as it should. If it does, you are ready to distribute the presentation. If it doesn't, make changes to the original file and repeat the entire Pack and Go process.

After you have fully tested the presentation, you are ready to distribute it.

Copy the files to a CD or other removable media. If you are going to send the files via email, zip the PPZ and the PNGSETUP.EXE files that PnG created together and send the zipped file.

No matter how you are distributing the presentation, be sure to include directions on how to unpack and run the presentation. If the recipient needs to download and install a viewer, tell them where to find it and how to install and run it.

Pack And Go For PowerPoint 2002

If you decide to use PnG for a PowerPoint 2002 presentation, you will want to follow the directions in the previous section. However, do not include the 97 Viewer; use the 2003 Viewer. When using PnG with PowerPoint 2002, you will always take the default of Don't include the Viewer. When sending the presentation on, either tell the recipients to download and install the 2003 Viewer directly from the web or include the files for the 2003 Viewer on your CD.

To test the presentation with the 2003 Viewer, access it from the Start menu. (When using the 2003 Viewer, the license agreement must be accepted the first time it is used.)

Do It Yourself AutoRun Cds

If you don't want to worry about PnG, you can create an autorun CD. Neither Viewer needs to be installed on the recipient's computer if it is included with the presentation on removable media; it will run directly from any media. This makes it much easier to share presentations.

Create a new folder on the hard drive. Call this folder Staging. This folder will be the holding area for the files to distribute.

Copy the Viewer and its associated files from C:\Program Files\Microsoft Office\PowerPoint Viewer to the Staging folder.

Figure 15-15: Staging Folder File Listing

One of the files in this folder is pptview.exe. This is the executable for the Viewer.

Go to the folder with the presentation. Copy the presentation and all associated files to the Staging folder.

Since you're bypassing the automatic Pack and Go process, you'll need to embed the fonts by opening each presentation in the Staging folder and saving it with fonts embedded. Otherwise, what the recipient sees may not be what you created. If you don't remember which fonts are the standard fonts, review Chapter 4. To embed the fonts, open each presentation file in the Staging folder and save it with the fonts embedded.

Test the presentation with the Viewer. Double click pptview.exe. Tell it which presentation to run and click OK. Run through the presentation and test it completely. If there are changes to be made, make them and re-test. If you find a broken link, find the file, copy/paste it to the staging folder, open the presentation file where the link problem occurred and recreate the link.

To create an auto-run CD (one that will run the presentation as soon as a CD is put in the drive), the Viewer must be told what to run.

Using a text editor like NotePad, create a text file called autorun.bat. In this file, type the following line:

```
@pptview.exe /L "playlist.txt"
```

Save the autorun.bat file to the Staging folder. Next use the text editor to create a file called playlist.txt. In this file, type the complete name of the presentation (name and extension). Save this file to the Staging folder.

These two files will combine to run the presentation using the 2003 Viewer when the CD is placed in the drive – if the drive is set up to autorun.

If you want to be sure the presentation can be easily run even if the CD isn't set to autorun, create a third text file called play.bat which is a copy of autorun.bat. When this file is double-clicked, it will call the Viewer to run the presentation automatically.

Once all testing is complete, the presentation is ready for distribution. Copy all the files in the Staging folder, including the text files you just created, to a CD or zip the directory and email it with unzip directions. If sending the files on CD, make sure to include instructions for running the presentation from the CD using play.bat – in case the recipient's computer is not set up to autorun CDs.

This page left intentionally blank.

16. Creating Your Own Template

➢ Master Slides

➢ Template Color Schemes

➢ The Other Masters

➢ Saving and Distributing Templates

Remember Rachel? Her boss was so thrilled with how the printed materials came out she was asked to formalize her PowerPoint designs into corporate templates.

All of my presentations are based on the standard PowerPoint templates delivered with Office. However, for each look I have done some tweaking and nudging. I now need to pull all of what I have done together in to a set of formal corporate PowerPoint templates.

I don't know what to do. I know all about applying the various masters, but I don't know what goes into making a fully functional template.

Template creation is much like the work done when determining the look of the presentation. The difference here is scope. Instead of deciding what a single presentation will look like, consider what a number of presentations will look like. In addition, you have to consider the non-slide elements of the presentation file.

Templates in PowerPoint are made up of a number of elements

- Master slides, which come in pairs: the Slide Master and the Title Master. These slides contain the common elements and formatting for the slides in the presentation. All of the slides in the presentation are based on one of these two masters. The Slide Master is inserted automatically. The Title Master you have to create yourself.

- Notes master: This page generally contains a small picture of the slide at the top, with a placeholder for speaker's notes on the bottom. It also can contain headers and footers, dates and page numbers. Changeable items on this master include the size of the slide and the format and placement of the various text items. (This master is only applied to new files. If applying the template to an existing presentation, copy and paste the notes master from the template to the notes master for the file.)

- Handout master: There are a number of views for the handout master, one for each printable handout style. You cannot change the size or position of the slides or the lines on handouts. All you are able to change on these masters is the content and style of the headers and footers (including dates and page numbers) and the addition of printed background elements. Furthermore, although there are six handout masters, changes made on any given handout master are reflected on each of the other handout masters. (This master is only applied to new files. If applying the template to an existing presentation, copy and paste the handout master from the template to the handout master for the file.)

To ensure the template is complete, format each of these masters. You can start the template from either a blank slide, from another presentation or from another template. We are going to start from a blank slide, as it is the most complex process. If starting with masters from another presentation or template, you are already that far ahead.

Master Slides

To create a template, you must work on the slide master (View →
Master → Slide Master):

Figure 16-1: Default Master Slide Template

Create A Background For Your Slides

Decide what you want on the presentation background. There
are several choices, all of which are found by right-clicking on
the master slide and selecting Background. This will open the
Background options dialog. At the bottom of this dialog is a
white-filled box with a drop-down arrow to its right. The
options you see – More Colors and Fill Effects – should look
familiar, as these are the same options you see whenever you
use any of the Fill commands.

- Create a plain colored background - Select More Colors
  from the drop-down in the Background dialog. You will
  see a default set of eight colors to choose from, as well as
  other options. If you do not like any of the default colors,
  select More Colors and pick a color from these expanded
  options.

- Create a gradient background - Select Fill Effects from the drop-down list in the Background dialog. The first tab on the resulting window lets you pick either a pre-created gradient or create your own. Play around with the options and see which one you like.

- Use an existing texture square for the background - Select Fill Effects from the drop-down list. The second tab shows a list of available textures. Since textures are graphics, the picture will be tiled on the slide to create a full background. If you have a graphic to use as a tile, click Other Texture and select the graphic.

- Create a patterned background - Select Fill Effects from the drop-down list. The third tab shows a set of 48 possible patterns. The two boxes at the bottom of the tab allow the background and foreground colors for the pattern to be chosen.

- Use an existing graphic for the background - Select Fill Effects from the drop-down list. The fourth tab is used navigate to and select the graphic. It previews the selected graphic once. Whereas texture makes the graphic into a tile for the background, picture stretches it to cover the entire slide. Select Lock picture aspect ratio to prevent the image from being distorted.

Once a background is selected click OK to return to the Background dialog. Here, either preview the background or apply it to just the current slide or all slides. In this case, the slide master is the only slide, so after previewing, click Apply.

One More Step

Before you go much further, set up the color schemes based on the colors chosen for the background. For information on choosing and setting up the color scheme, see Chapter 5.

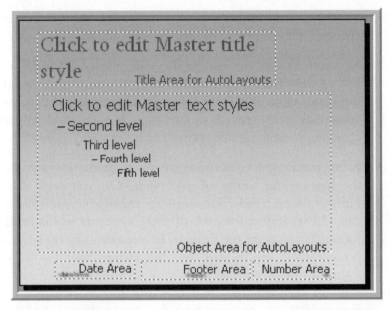

Figure 16-2: Setting a Background on the Master Slide

Determine Which Elements Will Show On Each Slide

The next step is to decide what additional elements need to be on each slide. Examples are company logos, signature shapes and graphics, and design-related items. In addition, you may want a picture or a graphic on each slide.

Add graphical items by creating them with autoshapes or WordArt, importing pictures and graphics from other programs, or by adding clipart. Insertion of these items is done using the Insert menu.

Be careful with what you add. The items added here will show up on every slide. You want to be sure you are not adding so many items you leave no room for the elements of the individual slides.

If you decide to add items to the master purely for design purposes, such as shapes and swooshes, keep them clean and consistent with the colors used in the background. Even better, use colors from the color scheme (the first eight color blocks on the color choices). This way, if the color schemes are changed, the elements will change accordingly.

No matter what you add to the slide master, what colors you use, or what fonts and typefaces you use, subtle is almost always the better choice. It is always easier to add impact by changing something that started simply than it is to add impact by changing something that started out glaring and outlandish.

Next, you need to determine what – if anything – will show in the header and footer of each slide. Do you want the slide number on each slide? Do you want the date on each slide? You can add static text for each of these elements to the header or footer. If you want the fields to be automatically updated as the presentations are created, use the Header and Footer dialog found on the View menu. Be sure to notice the bottom check box on this window. It allows the footer elements on the content slides to be turned on, but leaves them off of the title slides.

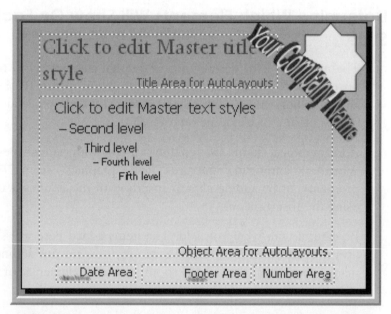

Figure 16-3: Master Slide with WordArt and Graphics

Format The Text On Your Slides

Now that the graphic background of the slides done, it is time to be creative with the text. Format the text on the master slides just as you would on a regular slide (select the text, Format→ Font, make changes). You can change the font, the color, the size, etc. Make sure the font color is complementary to the background, but will still show from the necessary distance.

Having said that, keep in mind other people will be using this template. If you pick fonts not on the common fonts list from Chapter 4, be sure you have permission to share the fonts when you distribute the template.

In PowerPoint 2000 or earlier, fonts cannot be embedded in the template. If using non-standard fonts, be sure those using the template have them as well.

Next, change the indent on the sub-bullets by clicking on the text and using the margin markers to adjust the indent. The margin marker is on the ruler. It looks like two triangles pointing at each other, with a rectangle below the bottom one.

You can also change the look of the bullets (Format → Bullets and Numbering). If you really want to get fancy, select a picture for the bullet (if using a picture bullet, only people using PowerPoint 2000 and later will be able to see them).

It is a good idea to give the users an extra visual clue about the outline level by making sure the bullets for each level are distinctly different. You can change the shape and the color on regular bullets. On picture bullets, make the changes outside of PowerPoint. No matter what you use for bullets, the size of the bullet will be determined by the font size for the text.

Tip 49: Showing text on a busy background	Right-click the placeholder and select Format Placeholder. This will bring up a dialog which changes the look of the text placeholder and apply a font to all the text in the placeholder. If you change the color of the placeholder's background, I recommend turning on the Resize AutoShape to Fit Text option in Tools → Options. This allows the colored area to grow and shrink automatically with the text on the slide.

Define The Default Animations For Your Slides

The next item to define for the template is the elements will become visible when the presentation is running. While I prefer not to use animation on my master slides, I do know it is sometimes needed. If you need it, set up animations on the masters in the template. Just be sure the animations and transitions are only used where they add to the message of the content and the presentation.

If master animation, the first thing to define is how the text on content slides will look when it comes in and when the focus moves on to the next piece of text. To set the animations for the placeholders, select the placeholder and apply whatever animation and effects you have chosen. See Chapter 6 for information on applying animations and effects.

You may also want to animate the logo in some manner so it stands out. If the logo is animated, be sure the animation isn't going to become repetitive for those viewing the presentation. Animation of a logo on the content master is a sure way to overwhelm the audience. If you must have an animated logo, consider placing it on the title master only.

To adjust the animation for items in the header or footer of the slides or for other graphics on the master, apply the animation to those placeholders on the master as well. You can't access these elements from anywhere other than the master.

If you plan to set up a preferred transition for all of the slides in presentations using this master, set the transition on the slide master and the title master using Slide Show → Slide transition. While I don't recommend putting animations and effects on the masters, I do recommend putting transitions on the masters. They can be changed later, but by putting transitions on the masters, you give other presentations based on this template a head start on consistency.

Finally, if this template might be used to create kiosk presentations, put the basic five navigation buttons on the master. If the files created from the template aren't kiosks, the presentation designer can always remove these elements from the masters. However, by placing them here, you make the navigation interface to the presentation more consistent.

Create The Title Master

Now the slide master the way you want it, it is time to leverage that work and create the title master. You could have created the title master at any point previous to this. However, by creating it after creating the slide master, you will have less work to do.

To insert a title master, select New Title Master from the Insert menu. Note you must be in Master View (View → Master) to access this command. You will see a slide that looks much the same as the slide master, but with different placeholders. Chances are good you will find there is little more you need to customize at this point. However, you should check the following items

- Check that the graphics still look proportional to the slide. Because there is considerably less text on a title slide, you may enlarge or change the graphics to catch the readers' notice.

- Check that the fonts on the slide look the way you want them. They should be large, easy to read and yet still stand out from the rest of the presentation.

- Decide whether the background needs a tweak to stand out from the main slides. You may want to change the color or the graphic.

- Decide whether you really want those footer text areas to show on the title slides. Decide if they are distracting from the impact of the title slide.

- Add animation to any logos or other graphic elements you use. Since the title slide will be used less frequently, animated items here are more acceptable.

Multiple Masters

In PowerPoint 2002 and later, you can have more than one master in a given file. This also means templates built into PowerPoint 2002 and later can have multiple pairs of master slides. This is a great thing for template designers.

For example, the template I designed for this chapter has two pairs of masters. When you look at the Slides tab of the taskpane on the left side of the screen in the Master Slide view, you see:

Figure 16-4: Multiple Master Templates

One great use for the multiple master pairs is the navigation buttons. Create two masters, one with buttons and one without. The masters can even be otherwise identical! Then, no matter which type of presentation – speaker-led or kiosk – is being built, the correct navigation options will be available.

When templates with multiple masters are applied to a presentation, PowerPoint will bring up this message:

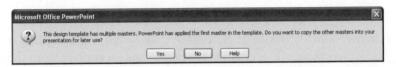

Figure 16-5: Multiple Master Templates Warning Message

The users of the template can decide if they want all of the masters or just the first one. So, be sure if you include multiple master pairs, the first one is the one most likely to be used. If you didn't create it first, select that pair of masters and drag them to the top of the list.

Template Color Schemes

For each template, define one or more color schemes. These schemes define the default colors for the following elements

- Background
- Text and lines
- Shadows
- Title text
- Fills
- Accent
- Accent and hyperlink
- Accent and followed hyperlink

To access the defined color schemes in PowerPoint 2000 and earlier, right-click and select Slide Color Scheme . This will bring up a two-tabbed dialog. The first tab shows the color schemes already defined for the template. The second tab is used to create and use custom color schemes. You can either use one there or define your own. If you change color schemes, be sure you select Apply to All so the the title and slide masters stay consistent.

To access the defined color schemes in PowerPoint 2002 and later, bring up the Slide Design taskpane. Click Color Schemes to bring up the existing color schemes. To change a scheme or add a new one, click Edit Color Schemes at the very bottom of the task pane.

But wait – this is a brand new template! How can it have color schemes already defined? Remember we based this template on the Blank template. The Blank template has several color schemes already defined.

One more note – if using a picture or a texture for the background, changing the background color in the scheme will not change the color of the slides. They will continue to have the graphic as a background. Even so, especially in PowerPoint 97 and 2000, it's important to change the background color to something similar to the background graphic so you'll be able to see the text as you type on the slides. If you leave the background color to one which matches the text color, you won't be able to see what you're typing.

I recommend you create at least four color schemes for each template: a light background-based scheme, a dark background-based scheme, a black-and-white scheme and a gray-scaled scheme.

By having these color schemes, the users of the template have pre-created diversity for those times when they need to add punch to a slide or presentation. You also allow them to select the colors they want to use based on the environment where the slides will be used.

Rachel created seven color schemes. Since her company logo has three base colors in it, she made a color scheme with each of the colors as the background; then she varied the use of the other colors in the other elements on the masters. She also created a black-on-white color scheme and a grayscale scheme. Finally, Rachel made a very dark version of one of the corporate colors and a very light version of one of the other colors. She based her last two color schemes on these to ensure presentations built with the template would be visible in almost any environment.

The Other Masters

Now that you have the slide masters set up, it is time to customize the Notes and Handout Masters. For each of these, there are only a few things to customize, but they can be important.

Handout Masters

The handout masters are set up to show the handouts as they will be printed. Notice the background for the page behind the slides is white, instead of the background you picked for the slides. Change the page background by right-clicking on the white area and selecting Handout Background, but notice it is not changed automatically. Notice also the header and footer choices are separated from the choices for the slides, but the choices are basically the same.

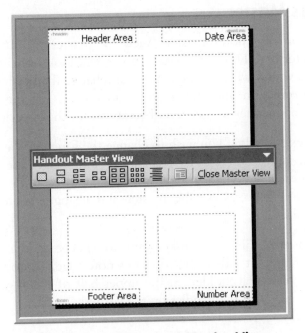

Figure 16-6: Handout Master View

Let's start with the background. You can change the background easily. Think about the impact before you do so. If you are going to print handouts, do you want an overly active background? So, while it is tempting to change the background of the handouts, be careful when you do so.

The other change available here is the choice of content for the headers and footers. This information can be customized by going to Header and Footer under the View menu. When you're in Notes or Handouts Master View, this menu option brings up the second tab of the Header and Footer dialog, which allows you to make similar choices to the ones you made for the slides. Here, it is generally a good idea to put the header and footer information on each page for the convenience of the audience members.

To test how the handouts will look when printed, insert a range of test slides and do a test print. It is the only way to see exactly how the changes made to the Handout Master will print.

Notes Master

From the notes master (View → Master → Notes Master), determine how the speaker notes will look both in the Notes View and when printed. You can change the header and footer information and the background colors. Do this in just the same manner as was described above for the handout master.

Next, decide if you wish to change the font and the text size for the notes entered. To change the font, select the sample text where it says Click to edit Master text styles in the lower of the two big boxes on the master and change the formatting as desired.

Another thing you may want to change is the size of the PowerPoint slide attached to this note page. To do this, click on the slide placeholder on the upper half of the page and adjust the size with the handles on the corners.

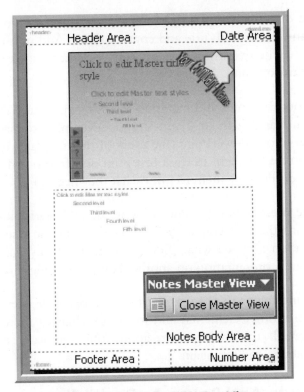

Figure 16-7: Notes Master View

Saving And Distributing Templates

You will want to save your hard work for sharing and reusing. Select the Save As option (File → Save As) and change the type to Design Template (*.pot). When you switch from presentation to template, the list of files showing in the Save in area should change to the location where the rest of the templates reside.

If you used fonts other than the standard ones, be sure to save the fonts with the template. To do this, select Save Options from the Tools drop-down when doing the Save As (this option is not available for templates in PowerPoint 2000 and earlier).

Before sharing this template, use it to create a test presentation with each of the defined color schemes. Starting from scratch, open a new presentation using the template. Type in some dummy text. Verify the text slides look the way you want them to look. Insert a graphic or other style of slide and make sure it also looks the way you want. Insert both title and content slides. Add non-text slides to make sure the graphs, movies and other elements look good on the chosen background.

Check out the notes and handouts pages to make sure they look the way you want them to. Even if you never plan to print notes or handouts from PowerPoint, the users of the templates may want to. You don't want them to do a test print and find out the template's masters don't allow them to print what they need to.

Run the presentation in slide show mode and see it automates and transitions the way you want it to. Have someone else look at the presentation and see what they think of it. Finally, have someone else create a presentation on another computer using the template.

If you find things to change, open the template file, view the master slides (and other elements) and make the changes there. Once you have saved the changes, re-apply the template to the test presentations and test again.

Distribute And Reuse As Desired!

Now that you have created a masterpiece of a template, you can share the template by sending the file to others who need it. However, be warned a template file is not always small. The smallest ones I have created are about 40 KB in size (you can create smaller ones if you use no graphics or effects). Embedding fonts can also increase the size.

40KB doesn't sound very big does it? Well, let's look at that from the other side. If my template has a large graphic in it, plus some music and a couple of fonts, it can become quite large quite quickly. In fact, I changed one template from 50KB to over 900KB, just by adding a sound, two fonts and a picture.) The more you add to a template, the larger the file will be.

What About Credit?

If you want to make sure presentations created with your template are identified as yours, go to File → Properties and change the information on the Summary tab. Few people will look there for information, so the template should stay marked as yours.

This page left intentionally blank.

17. Macros In PowerPoint

> ➢ What's a macro?

> ➢ Plan Macro

> ➢ Record, Edit and Test Macros

> ➢ Create Toolbar

> ➢ Create Combined Macro and Add to Toolbar

> ➢ Change to Add-in

> ➢ Distribute Add-in

Larry has a standard set of promotional presentations he uses to introduce potential clients to his services. He has been hand-editing a dummy presentation to target the presentations to each potential client.

I have created a presentation with "dummy" client information. Right now, I search for and change each client name and contact, and target the goals to the work they are interested in hearing about.

I would like to learn how to do this more quickly so it doesn't take as long to prepare the presentations.

What Larry needs to do is to develop macros allowing him to make his changes quickly and easily, so he has more time to spend on other jobs.

What Are Macros?

Macros are added code that can repeat or automate tasks within another program. Think of them as a translation of what you want PowerPoint to do into a language the computer can understand. The code used to create macros for PowerPoint is written in Visual Basic for Applications, or VBA. The VBA commands available for PowerPoint are referred to as the PowerPoint object model.

Macros are very useful little toys. They can run while designing and editing a presentation or they can run while the presentation is being displayed.

Macros that run while in edit mode reduce the tedium in creating the presentation by making it easier to do certain tasks such as the changes Larry needs to make to modify his presentations for the potential clients. Rather than editing each slide by hand, he is going to build a series of macros allowing PowerPoint to ask him what to change and then make the changes for him.

Macros that run during a presentation allow slide elements to turn on and off, change slide elements, get text or other input from the participants, or record data about the presentations.

More extensive macros perform complex tasks easily. Some of the most requested macros can be found in the PPT FAQ, as well as on the sites run by PowerPoint MVPs Shyam Pillai and Chirag Dalal. URLs for these sites can be found in Appendix A, Where to Find More Help.

While there is not a single book on VBA for PowerPoint, you can find some information in the PowerPoint help sections on macro creation and the VBA language. There are also several good VBA resources on-line which are also listed in Appendix A. You can learn a lot about VBA and macros by recording and customizing your own macros.

My best suggestion for learning to use macros is to read and join the PowerPoint newsgroup (see Appendix A for information on accessing it). Questions are posted daily on how to make various macros work. If you are having a coding problem, feel free to post it to the group. Tell us what PowerPoint version you are using, what you are trying to do, what is happening, and what the code is you have already written. The more details you give, the more likely you are to get quick help.

PowerPoint macros can be created by either recording functionality or by using the Visual Basic Editor. In most cases, you will start by recording the basic process you wish to automate and then adjust the resulting code to do exactly what you want, when you want.

Why adjust the code? Because when you record a macro, you record an exact set of steps. PowerPoint doesn't know you really meant to record a process. You generally will need to edit your macros to tailor them to your specific situations.

As your VB skills expand, you will be able to create macros from scratch in the VB editor. This skill set is beyond the scope of this book. We will touch on it at the end of this chapter so you have resources to use for more advanced macro work.

Tip 50: Save your work!	Every time you get ready to run or record a macro which is in development, save the presentation file. It is also a good idea to use new file names for these temporary copies.

Macro Process

The basic process Larry went through to create his macro has seven steps:

1. Plan what the macro needs to do

2. Record, edit and test each basic macro

3. Create a toolbar with buttons to run each macro individually

4. To make it easier to run the series of macros, create a routine that will call each macro in turn

5. Add a toolbar button to run the full process macro

6. Change the macro to an add-in

7. Distribute the add-in

Plan The Macro

Just as you shouldn't jump into a presentation without knowing what you want to say, you shouldn't just start recording macros for the sake of recording. Ideally, you should figure out what the basic steps your macros need to perform. Then build each step. Once you have all the steps built and tested, you should combine them into one process.

Larry knows what he wants the macros to do to his presentation. Before he starts to record his macro, he needs to plan the steps that actually need to happen in order to make the changes. Larry comes up with the following steps for his macro:

1. Select the old client name

2. Replace the old client name with the new client name

3. Select the dummy client contact information

4. Replace it with the new client contact information

5. Select the dummy client goals

6. Replace them with the new client goals

When Larry looked at the steps, he realized each pair of steps could be done at the same time. This chapter will work through the creation process for Larry's macros.

I recommend you create a blank presentation and save it as DummyClient.ppt and work along. This way, you don't have to worry about messing up any of your existing material, but you will still be able to learn how to create simple macros. You can always add your macro to other presentations later. Or, as you will learn at the end of the chapter, you can create an add-in containing the macros.

What Should "Dummyclient.Ppt" Look Like?

When the entire process is done, DummyClient.ppt needs to have slides with summary client information and goal information in the presentation. The final presentation should have the slides in Figure 17-1 and Figure 17-2:

- A title slide with has a client name of "New Client, Inc." and contact information such as a person's name, address and phone number

New Client, Inc.

Main Contact:
Jane Doe
400 E. West Street, Suite 1921
Sometown II 12345
555-234-5678

Figure 17-1: Client Title Slide

- A content slide with a placeholder for the goals

Project Goals

• Goal 1:

Figure 17-2: Goal Content Slide

If you want to create these slides so you can see what the macros will do, go ahead. Just be sure the presentation where you create the macros contains only a blank slide to become the title slide and a slide with the title "Project Goals." The goals themselves will be added to the blank text placeholder by the macro you'll create.

Record The Macro

The first step in creating the basic macro is to turn on the macro recorder by going to Tools → Macro → Record New Macro. This window will appear:

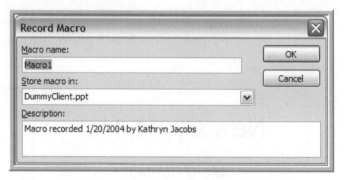

Figure 17-3: Record Macro window

Name the macro CreateClientName. It is also a good idea to give it a description, such as "Finds dummy client name and changes it to real name." The default location for storing the macro is the presentation named DummyClient.ppt, because that is the file open and being used. Clicking OK will start the recording and the Stop Recording toolbar will appear on the slide workspace.

Tip 51: Macro Names	I was taught to run the words together in my macro names and use capitalization to identify the words. That doesn't mean you have to do it that way. You can't use spaces, but you can use underscores instead of spaces. The most important thing about your macro names is that they be descriptive and understandable.

Now perform the steps you want in the macro:

1. Move to the first slide

2. Place the cursor in the title placeholder

3. Type the new company name

Click the square button on the Stop Recording toolbar to end recording of the macro. Do not click the "x" to close the toolbar, as this will not stop the recording, only close the toolbar. If you do close the toolbar, stop the recording by going Tools→ Macro→ Stop Recording.

Once the macro is recorded, you will want to customize it. Remember, the computer doesn't read your mind; it reads your keystrokes and mouse movements. You need to make sure what the macro recorder recorded is what you meant to do. Frequently you will find, because the computer recorded *exactly* what you told it to do, you will need to edit the macro.

Edit The Macro

The macro is edited in the Visual Basic Editor. Go to Tools → Macro → Macros to bring up the Macro window.

Figure 17-4: Macro Window

Click the Edit button to bring up the VB Editor, with the new code showing. The code should look something like this:

```
Sub CreateClientName()
'
' Adds client name to slides
' Macro recorded 1/20/2004 by Kathryn Jacobs
'

ActiveWindow.Selection.SlideRange.Shapes("Rectangle
2").Select
ActiveWindow.Selection.ShapeRange.TextFrame.TextRange
.Select
ActiveWindow.Selection.ShapeRange.TextFrame.TextRange
.Characters(Start:=1, Length:=0).Select
    With ActiveWindow.Selection.TextRange
        .Text = "Dummy Partners"
        With .Font
            .Name = "Arial"
            .Size = 44
            .Bold = msoFalse
            .Italic = msoFalse
            .Underline = msoFalse
            .Shadow = msoFalse
            .Emboss = msoFalse
            .BaselineOffset = 0
            .AutoRotateNumbers = msoFalse
            .Color.SchemeColor = ppTitle
        End With
    End With
End Sub
```

The first line, Sub CreateClientName, is the name of the macro. The last line, End Sub, tells VB the macro is finished.

The lines starting with a single quotation mark are comments. Comments explain what this macro is supposed to be doing. They are also a great place to note changes things in the code. Comments are good things. The better the comments, the less you need to remember about the code. Any time you do something tricky or unusual, add a comment about what you did and why.

Each of these areas will be in all macros created. They are the shell of the macro.

The section we are most interested in are the three lines starting with "ActiveWindow." (If you look at the code in the VB Editor, you will see all of the information is on one line. It word wraps here in the book due to its length.)

What's This "With" Stuff?

The VBA command "With" tells VBA the next few lines should be assumed to start with what comes after the With. These commands are commonly called "With clauses." It is a way to prevent having to repeat some of the content. Let's look at the first With clause in the macro:

```
With ActiveWindow.Selection.TextRange
        .Text = "Dummy Partners"
```

These two lines are saying "For the next line, assume the variable to the right of the equal sign really starts with ActiveWindow.Selection.TextRange." The ".Text" attribute is understood to be "ActiveWindow.Selection.TextRange.Text."

The other With statement in the code makes it clearer why you would want to use the With clauses. Instead of typing:

```
ActiveWindow.Selection.TextRange.Text.Font
```

in front of each of the next 10 lines, the With .Font gives the attributes for the font. With clauses not only make it easier to type and edit the code, once you get used to reading them, they make it easier to understand the code, too.

In VBA-speak, those periods are called separators because they separate one VBA term from another. You can use With clauses to repeat any set of terms, as long as you set your With clauses up to end where a separator would appear if you were typing the whole command or clause.

Back To The Code

This code is good, except it has a major gotcha in it. Because the recorder records exactly the steps you perform, it will always add the text you typed. Of course, we don't always want to add "Dummy Partners." We want to be able to set the new name to whatever we want.

To make this change, we need to use a variable for the new name. Variables are places VB can store data so you can reference it by a name instead of by the exact value.

To change the macro, insert a line in front of the first ActiveWindow line. In this line, type

```
NewClientName = "Dummy Partners"
```

The next step is to tell the macro to use the variable, NewClientName, instead of a fixed value in the existing code. To do this, replace Dummy Partners in the .Text line with the variable name, NewClientName. The first With clause should now look like this:

```
With ActiveWindow.Selection.TextRange
        .Text = NewClientName
```

Now, we need to close and save the macro. You can do this via File → Close and Return to PowerPoint, or by using Alt+Q. This will return you to the presentation. Save the presentation.

Next, do a test run of the presentation. On the slide, remove any text you added. To run the macro, do a Tools → Macro → Macros. Make sure the macro name is selected, then click Run. The screen will flash and the text Dummy Partners will appear in the title placeholder on the title slide.

What happens if the macro runs a second time? The name is added after the existing text. For this reason, always run this macro on a slide with no existing title text.

We are now going to record the steps to add the contact name and address. Repeat the recording process, adding the following text to the sub-title placeholder:

- Linda Lyle
- 2300 Southern Dr.
- MyTown MM 67123
- 555-666-8888

When recorded, the new macro, "CreateClientContact," should look like this:

```
Sub CreateClientContact()
'
' Create the contact name, address, and phone number
slide
' Macro recorded 1/20/2004 by Kathryn Jacobs
'

ActiveWindow.Selection.SlideRange.Shapes("Rectangle
3").Select

ActiveWindow.Selection.ShapeRange.TextFrame.TextRange
.Select

ActiveWindow.Selection.ShapeRange.TextFrame.TextRange
.Characters(Start:=1, Length:=0).Select
     With ActiveWindow.Selection.TextRange
          .Text = "Linda Lyle" + Chr$(CharCode:=13) +
"2300 Southern Dr." + Chr$(CharCode:=13) + "MyTown MN
67123" + Chr$(CharCode:=13) + "555-666-8888"
          With .Font
               .Name = "Arial"
               .Size = 32
               .Bold = msoFalse
               .Italic = msoFalse
               .Underline = msoFalse
               .Shadow = msoFalse
               .Emboss = msoFalse
               .BaselineOffset = 0
               .AutoRotateNumbers = msoFalse
               .Color.SchemeColor = ppForeground
          End With
     End With
End Sub
```

Wondering what "Chr$(CharCode:=13)" means? That is adding the hard return between the lines of text on the slide. As the text is changed to variables, we will create a variable for that too. Modify the new code to look like this:

```
Sub CreateClientContact()
'
' Create the contact name, address, and phone number
slide
' Macro recorded 1/20/2004 by Kathryn Jacobs
'
'Set up new line variable and contact information
variables
```

```
      NewLine = Chr$(CharCode:=13)
      NewContactName = "Linda Lyle"
      NewContactStreetAddress = "2300 Southern Dr."
      NewContactCityStateZip = "MyTown MM 67123"
      NewContactPhone = "555-666-8888"
'Find the place the stuff goes

ActiveWindow.Selection.SlideRange.Shapes("Rectangle
3").Select

ActiveWindow.Selection.ShapeRange.TextFrame.TextRange
.Select
'Do the replace
ActiveWindow.Selection.ShapeRange.TextFrame.TextRange
.Characters(Start:=1, Length:=0).Select
      With ActiveWindow.Selection.TextRange
          .Text = NewContactName & NewLine &
NewContactStreetAddress & NewLine &
NewContactCityStateZip & NewLine & NewContactPhone
          With .Font
              .Name = "Arial"
              .Size = 32
              .Bold = msoFalse
              .Italic = msoFalse
              .Underline = msoFalse
              .Shadow = msoFalse
              .Emboss = msoFalse
              .BaselineOffset = 0
              .AutoRotateNumbers = msoFalse
              .Color.SchemeColor = ppForeground
          End With
      End With
End Sub
```

For the remainder of this chapter, I leave the addition of comments to you.

What About Formatting My Text Pieces?

The code we are creating in this chapter is designed to use the text formatting as defined in the template and on the existing slides. That's what each With .Font clause does. Since Larry is working with an existing, formatted presentation, this isn't a problem; each of his With clauses will pick up the font information from the template. However, to change the formatting on the slides, change the text attribute values in the code.

To make the font different, change Arial to another font name. Same goes for the size and the other attributes. If you really want to be slick, create variables for the font attributes and make the changes to the variables instead of after each equal sign.

Creating A Macro From Scratch

Repeat the recording process for the goals to create the remaining macros. These macros will be much like the ones we just did. However, when you get ready to run these macros, you will want PowerPoint to move from one slide to the next.

The macro to change from one slide to the next is not one that will easily record. Instead, we are going to create the macro from scratch. You can create this macro from any slide in the presentation. Go to Tools → Macro → Macros and type in the name for the new macro, ChangePage. As soon as you start to type, a Create button will appear. Clicking the button will bring up the VB Editor and place the cursor between the comments and the End Sub command. You are ready to create the macro.

First, add a comment describing what the macro is going to do. Next, move the cursor to the first line after the comments. Type in the code you

```
Sub ChangePage()
' Change from one slide to the next
' Macro created 1/20/2004 by Kathryn Jacobs
'
    ActiveWindow.View.GotoSlide
Index:=ActiveWindow.Selection.SlideRange.SlideIndex +
1
End Sub
```

As you type, a box comes up containing various VBA objects. These objects work together to make the instructions that are the macros. Objects are separated by periods, commas, parentheses and operators. As you type, the VBA environment will try to guess what object you are looking for. When it shows the object you want, you can type the separator to select the object you want.

Since the editor knows which objects can go with which other objects, the guesses are generally pretty close to what you want. Taking advantage of the guesses can save you keystrokes while typing the code and help make the code more likely to run correctly.

When you have finished typing in the lines of code above, close the VB editor and return to PowerPoint. Do a test run of the macro to make sure you move from the current slide to the next slide. If you run the macro from the last slide in the presentation, it will give you an error. Why? Because there is no slide number plus one in the presentation. If you get any other errors when you run the macro, go back to the editor and check for and correct any typographical errors.

When the code runs cleanly (that's computer speak for when it works), you are ready to create the rest of the macros.

Creating A Macro From Another Macro

To easily create the goals macro, we are going to copy the code from the contact information macro and adapt it to our use.

Give the new macro a name and click Create. (I used CreateGoals in this example.) Scroll up through the code window to find the contact information macro. Select the comment and code lines (not including the End Sub), copy them, move back down to the CreateGoals macro and paste them.

Edit the copied lines so the macro looks like this:

```
Sub CreateGoals()
'
' Macro created 1/20/2004 by Kathryn Jacobs
'
'Set up new line variable and contact information
variables
    NewGoalLine = Chr$(CharCode:=13)
    NewGoal1 = "Goal 1: My First Goal"
    NewGoal2 = "Goal 2: My Second Goal"
```

```
        NewGoal3 = "Goal 3: My Third Goal"
        NewGoal4 = "Goal 4: My Fourth Goal"

'Find the place the stuff goes

ActiveWindow.Selection.SlideRange.Shapes("Rectangle
3").Select

ActiveWindow.Selection.ShapeRange.TextFrame.TextRange
.Select

'Do the replace
ActiveWindow.Selection.ShapeRange.TextFrame.TextRange
.Characters(Start:=1, Length:=0).Select
    With ActiveWindow.Selection.TextRange
        .Text = NewGoal1 & NewGoalLine & NewGoal2 &
NewGoalLine & NewGoal3 & NewGoalLine & NewGoal4
        With .Font
            .Name = "Arial"
            .Size = 32
            .Bold = msoFalse
            .Italic = msoFalse
            .Underline = msoFalse
            .Shadow = msoFalse
            .Emboss = msoFalse
            .BaselineOffset = 0
            .AutoRotateNumbers = msoFalse
            .Color.SchemeColor = ppForeground
        End With
    End With

End Sub
```

Test and correct the macro until it runs the way you want it to.

Making The Macros Easier To Run

As these macros are written, Larry has to edit each macro to make his changes. That really isn't any easier than what he was doing. Larry would like the macros to ask him what information should be on the slides and automatically place his answers in the right places.

The way to do this is to use input boxes. Input boxes are dialogs that pop up when you run the macro and ask you to provide information you want the macro to use.

To create an input box in a PowerPoint macro, use the InputBox function. InputBox is used to get input from users by opening a message box where they can type in text. This information is then passed to a variable.

We are going to change the variables in the macros we just created to use Input boxes instead of having the text *hard-coded* into the macro. ("Hard-coding" is the term for when the value for a variable is set in the code and the only way to change it is to edit the code.)

To set up the input boxes, edit the CreateClientName macro. Replace

```
NewClientName = "Dummy Partners"
```

with the following code:

```
NewClientName = InputBox("What is the name
of the client company?")
```

Test the change and make any needed corrections. Once it is right, you can make the same kind of changes within each of the other macros by replacing the quoted text with the InputBox function.

You don't need to edit each macro separately. The VBA editor will move between macros in a single edit session. If you do edit more than one macro at a time, be sure to test each one thoroughly to make sure they all work at the end.

When creating the input boxes for the goals, make sure the goals still say which goal they are. You can either place a reminder in the prompt for the input box and have "Goal 1:" typed before the goal, or you can add "Goal 1:" and so on to each goal line. The two ways these variables can look are:

```
NewGoal1 = InputBox("What is the first goal
of this project? (Format is: Goal 1: Goal)")
```

or

```
NewGoal1 = "Goal 1: " & InputBox("What is
the first goal of this project?")
```

Create Toolbar

Now that Larry has all of his macros defined, he would like to be able to run them without going through the macro interface every time. To do this, he needs to connect his macros to a toolbar.

To connect macros to a toolbar, first have a toolbar defined. Go to Tools → Customize and click on the Toolbars tab. Click the New button, give the toolbar a name and a new toolbar will appear on the PowerPoint desktop.

Next, click the Commands tab. Scroll down the list in the left hand box until you find Macros. Select it and a list of the macros should appear in the right hand box. Click and drag each of the macros to the toolbar. My toolbar looked like this:

Figure 17-5: Custom Toolbar with Macros

Once the macro names are on the toolbar as buttons, change them to other text or icons. We are going to change the face of the ChangePage button to a graphic instead of text.

If you closed the Customize window, bring it back. Right-click on the ChangePage button, select Change Button Image, slide over and select an image for the button. Next, right-click the button again and click Default Style. This will change the button from text plus an image to just the image.

Tip 52: Want more button faces?	PowerPoint MVP Shyam Pillai has created an add-in that gives you all the possible button faces provided by Microsoft. Since most of these are hidden from you as a general user, this is one of the most useful add-ins available for macro developers. Find the add-in at www.mvps.org/skp/faceid.htm

If you want to change the rest of the buttons, feel free to do so. When I finished mine, the toolbar looked like this:

Figure 17-6: Custom Macro Toolbar with Icons

Close the customize window. You have created a macro toolbar!

Tip 53: Customize all of PowerPoint	Use the Customize window to change what shows on what menu and in what order, as well as changing all of the toolbars and creating new ones.
	Play around with creating your own toolbars. You will find it is a great way to make PowerPoint even more usable.

Create A Combined Macro And Add To The Toolbar

Being able to create a toolbar for the macros gave Larry an idea. He decided the next logical step in his project was to make one macro that would call each of the others in turn. Since it was going to use existing code, he knew it would prompt him for most of the inputs he needed.

To call one macro from inside another, you place the called macro name in the code area of the calling macro. Larry figured out the order in which he needed to call the macros and created a macro called UpdateToNewClient with this code:

```
Sub UpdateToNewClient()
' This macro calls the other macros to update the
presentation to the new client information
' Macro created 1/20/2004 by Kathryn Jacobs
'

    CreateClientName
    CreateClientContact
```

```
ChangePage
CreateGoals

End Sub
```

Once Larry had his new macro tested and ready to go, he added it to the existing toolbar and gave it an icon. When done, his new toolbar looked like this:

Figure 17-7: Macro Toolbar with Combined Macro

What If Larry's Pages Weren't Next To Each Other?

If Larry's presentation had slides between the contact information slide and the goals slide, he could make one of two changes to his macros. The first way would be to change the ChangePage macro so instead of adding one to the page location, he used a variable which asked for input using an InputBox. The other way to make the change is to change UpdateToNewClient so it called ChangePage the correct number of times.

To use a variable and an InputBox to make changes, create a new variable in ChangePage filled by an InputBox asking how many pages to skip. Then, instead of adding the number 1 to the current slide index, add the new variable to the current slide index. When complete, the code for ChangePage would look like this

```
PagesToSkip = InputBox("How many more slides
until the goals slide?")
ActiveWindow.View.GotoSlide
Index:=ActiveWindow.Selection.SlideRange.Sli
deIndex + PagesToSkip
```

To do it the other way, Larry needs to add a loop to his macro that will repeatedly call ChangePage until the right number of pages gets skipped.

First, he needs ask how many pages to skip. To do this, he creates the new variable in UpdateToNewClient and fills that variable using InputBox. He then uses a For loop to call the macro that number of times. A For loop says do this for every number between my start point and my end point.

After making the code adjustments, the UpdateToNewClient code looks like this:

```
Sub UpdateToNewClient()
' This macro calls the other macros to update the
pitch presentation to the new client information
' Macro created 1/20/2004 by Kathryn Jacobs
'

    CreateClientName
    CreateClientContact
    PagesToSkip = InputBox("How many more slides
until the goals slide?")
    For I = 1 To PagesToSkip
        ChangePage
    Next I
    CreateGoals

End Sub
```

Add-Ins: PowerPoint's AutoOpen And AutoClose

Now that Larry has his full set of macros, he would like to have the toolbar always available. To do this, he needs to turn the macros and the toolbar into a PowerPoint *add-in*.

An add-in is a special type of PowerPoint file. It contains no slides, only compiled macro code and the toolbars to run that code. Whenever you create an add-in, save two versions of the add-in file. The first version is a regular PowerPoint file with the macro code and any slides you need. The second version is the add-in itself. When you create the add-in file, you will be unable to edit anything within the file. In order to make changes or additions in the future, you need have a regular PowerPoint file with the code and slides where you can make the changes.

In Larry's case, part of the reason for splitting the code off into an add-in is to separate the code from his static presentation. Once the code has been split, he can use it on any presentation file that has a title slide with company contact information and a content slide with goals information. By using the add-in, he doesn't have to worry about always starting with the same presentation file, he just has to be sure the file he is using is set up to enable the macros to run.

So, how do we turn our macros into an add-in? Once the macros are finished, it is a two-step process:

1. Create Auto Open and Auto Close routines that will load and unload the toolbars

2. Create and test the add-in file

Create AutoOpen And AutoClose Routines

Many Office applications have the ability to create macros that run whenever the application is opened or closed. These macros can be stored in the default template. In PowerPoint, you can create these same macros, but they must be placed in an add-in before PowerPoint will run them.

When the add-in is loaded, it won't automatically run or load toolbars unless an AutoOpen macro is created. In the same manner, if you don't close the add-in when you close PowerPoint, you won't be able to use it next time PowerPoint opens. To get around this problem, you need to create an AutoClose macro that closes the add-in and removes any toolbars it has created.

These macros can't be recorded, as they aren't action-based macros. They have to be hand-coded. Sounds like a real pain, huh? Lucky for you, PowerPoint MVP Steve Rindsberg agrees. He has created a page on the FAQ containing the exact code needed to create these two macros. In addition, the page contains links to two other great resources on creating add-ins. Read the pages and you will fill in all the blanks on turning the macro into an add-in. The FAQ entry can be found at

www.rdpslides.com/pptfaq/FAQ00031.htm

Larry's AutoOpen And AutoClose

After Larry read through the process given in the FAQ, he added these two macros to his PowerPoint file:

```
Sub Auto_Open()
    Dim oToolbar As CommandBar
    Dim oButton As CommandBarButton
    Dim pButton As CommandBarButton
    Dim qButton As CommandBarButton
    Dim rButton As CommandBarButton
    Dim sButton As CommandBarButton
    Dim LarrysToolbar As String

    ' Give the toolbar a name
    LarrysToolbar = "UpdateClientInfo"

    ' First, delete the toolbar if it already exists
    On Error Resume Next    ' so that it doesn't stop
on the next line if the toolbar doesn't exist
    Application.CommandBars(LarrysToolbar).Delete
    On Error GoTo errorhandler   ' turns error
handling back on

    ' Build the command bar
    Set oToolbar =
CommandBars.Add(Name:=LarrysToolbar,
Position:=msoBarFloating, Temporary:=True)

    ' Now add a button to the new toolbar
    Set oButton =
oToolbar.Controls.Add(Type:=msoControlButton)
    Set pButton =
oToolbar.Controls.Add(Type:=msoControlButton)
    Set qButton =
oToolbar.Controls.Add(Type:=msoControlButton)
    Set rButton =
oToolbar.Controls.Add(Type:=msoControlButton)
    Set sButton =
oToolbar.Controls.Add(Type:=msoControlButton)

    ' And set some of the button's properties
    With sButton
        .DescriptionText = "Run all the macros to update
a presentation"   'Tooltip text when mouse if placed
over button
```

```
        .Caption = "UpdateToNewClient"      'Text if Text
in Icon is chosen
        .OnAction = "UpdateToNewClient" 'Runs the Sub
UpdateToNewClient() code when clicked
        .Style = msoButtonIcon      ' Button displays as
icon, not text or both
        .FaceId = 22

    End With

    ' And set some of the button's properties
    With oButton
        .DescriptionText = "Create the Client Name"
'Tooltip text when mouse if placed over button
        .Caption = " CreateClientName"      'Text if Text
in Icon is chosen"
        .OnAction = "CreateClientName"  'Runs the Sub
CreateClientName() code when clicked
        .Style = msoButtonIcon      ' Button displays as
icon, not text or both
        .FaceId = 66
    End With

  ' And set some of the button's properties
    With pButton
        .DescriptionText = "Create the Client Contact
Information"   'Tooltip text when mouse if placed
over button
        .Caption = "CreateClientContact"      'Text if Text
in Icon is chosen
        .OnAction = "CreateClientContact"  'Runs the Sub
CreateClientContact() code when clicked"
        .Style = msoButtonIcon      ' Button displays as
icon, not text or both
        .FaceId = 33
    End With

  ' And set some of the button's properties
    With qButton
        .DescriptionText = "Add the goals"    'Tooltip
text when mouse if placed over button
        .Caption = "CreateGoals"     'Text if Text in Icon
is chosen
        .OnAction = "CreateGoals"  'Runs the Sub
CreateGoals() code when clicked
        .Style = msoButtonIcon      ' Button displays as
icon, not text or both
        .FaceId = 52
```

```
        End With


    ' And set some of the button's properties
        With rButton
        .DescriptionText = "Skip to next slide"
    'Tooltip text when mouse if placed over button
        .Caption = "ChangePage"      'Text if Text in Icon
    is chosen
        .OnAction = "ChangePage"   'Runs the Sub
    ChangeSlide() code when clicked
        .Style = msoButtonIcon     ' Button displays as
    icon, not text or both
        .FaceId = 55

        End With


        ' You can set the toolbar position and
    visibility here if you like
        ' By default, it'll be visible when created
        oToolbar.Top = 150
        oToolbar.Left = 150
        oToolbar.Visible = True


        Exit Sub    ' so it doesn't go on to run the
    errorhandler code

    errorhandler:
        'Just in case there is an error
        MsgBox Err.Number & vbCrLf & Err.Description
    End Sub



    Sub Auto_Close()
    'This will run when PowerPoint closes and it will
    delete the toolbar.
        Dim oToolbar As CommandBar
        Dim LarrysToolbar As String
        ' Note:  MyToolbar should be the same value here
    as in the code that created the toolbar
        LarrysToolbar = "UpdateClientInfo"
        On Error Resume Next
        Application.CommandBars(MyToolbar).Delete
    End Sub
```

For each macro in the process, Larry created a button definition and a With clause in the Auto_Open routine connecting the button to the correct macro. You will need to do the same thing.

Create And Test The Add-In File

Create a copy of the PowerPoint file you have been working with. Make sure it contains a few blank slides and the macros you want in the final add-in.

Go to the VB editor and comment the code. You need to make sure when you come back next time, you understand what you did and why you did it. You can't add too many comments to code.

Save the presentation file and run the macros. This makes sure when you added the comments you didn't mess up any of the existing code.

When finished testing, remove all the slides created during testing and save the presentation one more time.

You are now ready to save the file with just the code as an add-in. Go to File → Save As. From the file type drop down list, select, PowerPoint Add-In. Notice the save location changes. PowerPoint wants to save the add-in with all the other add-ins on the computer. This is usually the place where you want to save your add-in as well. If it isn't, change the location. When you have set the location, click OK to do the save.

Why would you want to change the save location for the file? If creating an add-in for distribution, you will probably want to store a copy somewhere on the hard drive is easier to find than the add-in folder

Close the PowerPoint file. Go to Tools → Add-Ins. The new add-in may already be on the list of available add-ins. If it is, select it and click Load.

If it isn't on the list, add it to the list. Click the Add New button and select the add-in file. Once you have clicked OK and added the add-in to the list, you may still need to load it. Once it is loaded, the toolbar should appear.

| **Tip 54: Nothing happening when you click New?** | If nothing happens when you click New, check the security settings. You can run your own macros at a much higher security setting than you can load add-ins. |
| | Use the Macro Security button on the Tools → Options, Security tab to change the setting. You need it no higher than medium to run your add-ins. |

Now it is time for the final test. Close PowerPoint and re-open it. Open a new presentation and add slides so there are at least two slides. Check that the toolbar is available. Click the button that runs the shell macro, UpdateToNewClient. Did it work?

If it worked, you are finished. If it didn't, you need to

- Unload the add-in (Tools → Add-Ins, click yours and unload it)

- Open the presentation (PPT) version of the file containing the macro

- Make your changes and save the presentation (PPT) file

- Re-create the add-in, re-load it and re-test it.

Macros That Run In Presentation Mode

After all his macros were done, Larry decided it would be useful to be able to skip to the goals slide at the click of a button. He found a number of clients didn't want to see the whole presentation, just what he could do for them.

The first thing he did was add a custom show to his presentation files containing only the goals slide. He added an invisible button to his presentations allowing him to skip ahead to the goals slide.

Creating macros to use while a presentation is running is much the same as creating one to run while in edit mode. You need to decide what to do, create and test each macro, and then use the macros.

You can assign them to buttons on a slide and run them with a mouse click or have them run when a certain event occurs.

Larry created a macro that jumped to the goals custom show, which he had named Goals Only. This way, he could jump to the goals without anyone knowing it and end the presentation after showing the goals. The code for the macro is:

```
Sub JumpToGoals()
' This macro jumps to the goals custom show
' Macro created 1/20/2004 by Kathryn Jacobs
'
SlideShowWindows(1).View.GotoNamedShow "Goals Only"
End Sub
```

Next, Larry added an invisible button to his title slide and added a mouse over action setting (Slide Show → Action Setting) that called his macro. To test the macro, he started the presentation and moused over the button on the first slide.

As Larry learned more and more about VBA, he also learned how much code was already written and ready to use. Using the resources listed in Appendix A, Larry found many ways to use macros he had never thought about. He was careful to always give credit to those whose code he borrowed, whether he used it as he found it or changed it to meet his needs.

This page left intentionally blank.

18. Producer And Similar Products

Co-Authored by Austin Myers, PPT MVP

➢ Producer

➢ PowerPoint to Video (VHS or DVD)

➢ Video Capture

Remember Curt? Well, that client of his wasn't satisfied with just web versions of his presentations. They liked the information so much they now want to distribute the content via webcasts, VHS tapes and DVD-based solutions.

I really don't know what to do. I have told them I have no video or webcast experience, but they still want me to translate the materials to the other formats.

I thought about just videotaping the presentation off the screen, but that didn't work. Can you explain what I should be doing?

Let's be honest: Translating PowerPoint presentations to other media is not really a trivial task, nor one I do often. Instead of risking sending all of you off into the weeds, I recruited the expert on PowerPoint and multimedia, Austin Myers, author of the tutorial on PowerPoint and Multimedia and several other great pieces, to help explain how to transfer the presentation via various formats.

Producer

Microsoft's literature tells us that

> Producer provides users with many powerful new features that make it easier to synchronize audio, video, slides and images to create engaging and effective rich-media presentations.

What that means is Producer provides you with a way to transform presentations into HTML, but with more punch than the HTML created directly from PowerPoint. Producer provides a way to capture not just the presentation, but also any multimedia that plays during the presentation. The entire package is then delivered to other machines via streaming media.

Producer also allows the presentation and all of the multimedia files to burn to a CD for distribution when the client may not have PowerPoint or the Viewer. All they need is an Internet browser. This assures playback on just about any Windows machine.

Where Do I Find Producer?

Producer is not delivered with PowerPoint, but it is a free companion program. You can download the latest version of Producer from the Microsoft website. Information on Producer and the download links are available at either of the following URLs

For pre-2002 versions:

www.microsoft.com/windows/windowsmedia/technologies/producer.aspx

For 2002:

www.microsoft.com/office/powerpoint/producer/prodinfo/default.mspx

How Do I Use Producer?

Producer adds presentations, movies, sounds and still pictures to a project so they can be played according to a timeline you define. Producer works on any computer with Windows 2000, service pack 1 or later, or any version of Windows XP.

Producer is run like any other program on a computer. You open it from either the desktop or the start menu. When it opens, you can start a new project or continue working with an existing project. We are going to work through the New Presentation Wizard, as that is how you will most likely create new projects.

Figure 18-1: Microsoft Producer Window

Clicking OK after selecting the New Presentation Wizard brings up the Wizard's introductory screen, which gives an overview of the process. Read this screen, then click Next to bring up the template screen.

Note: As we work through this example, I will be showing you the content of the wizard pages. When you look at them on the screen, each wizard page will have a header above and buttons the area shown.

The Presentation Template screen determines what you want the background to look like, what elements you want on the Producer template, what resolution you want used for video in the presentation, whether you want the HTML elements to be moveable and how you want the audio handled. We are going to scroll down to about the middle of the list and select the Globe template, which has a small area for videos.

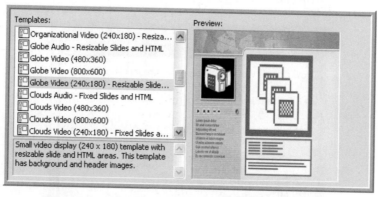

Figure 18-2: Presentation Template Window

Once a template is selected, the right side of the screen changes to a preview of the format. Click Next.

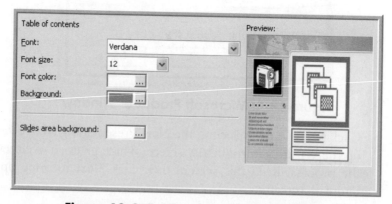

Figure 18-3: Table of Contents Window

On the Table of Contents screen, define fonts and colors for the presentation. Use colors and fonts appropriate to the color scheme for the intended presentation. Click Next.

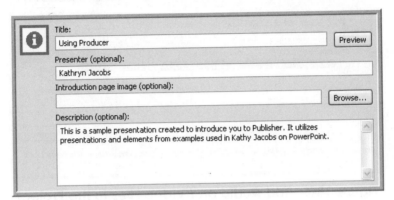

Figure 18-4: Title Window

After defining the formatting, define the Presentation Information for the presentation. This content will show while the presentation is loading.

Be careful what you type here. There is no spell checking available on this screen, although you will be able to change the content later if you notice mistakes. Once you have input the information, click Next.

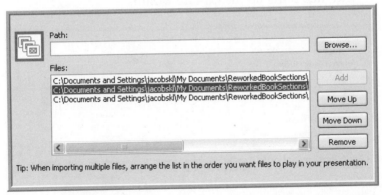

Figure 18-5: Add Presentations and Pictures to the Project

Now you are ready to add presentations and pictures to the project. Use the Browse button to navigate to each presentation file and each still photo or graphic to include. Use the Move Up and Move Down buttons to re-arrange the files if necessary. When all the files are added and in the right order, click Next.

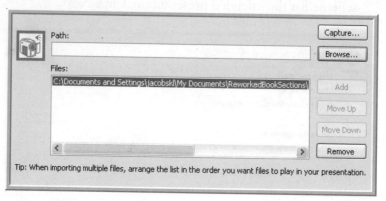

Figure 18-6: Add Audio and Video Files to the Project

The next step is to add or capture the audio and video segments for the project. Add these items by browsing to existing files on the computer or by capturing sound and audio from outside the computer.

Use the Browse button to add elements from the hard drive. Add the video and/or sound files and reorder them. To capture new video or audio, click the Capture button. Producer will add the existing content to the timeline showing behind the wizard and then bring up the capture wizard.

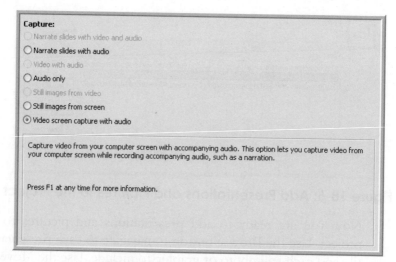

Figure 18-7: Capture Wizard

Kathy Jacobs on PowerPoint

This wizard grabs audio and video directly from the computer's screen and microphone. You are most likely to use this feature to add music or narration to the presentation.

If it seems the import into Producer is taking much longer then expected, check the following warning message has not been received – it may be hidden behind the running programs if PowerPoint is open.

Figure 18-8: Hidden Warning Message

Your screens and options may look different depending on what multimedia hardware and software is installed on the machine. Different versions of the multi-media player will also change the screens.

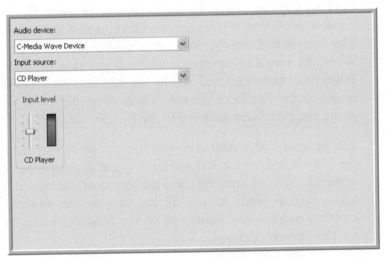

Figure 18-9: Sound Options Window

Select the source of the sounds and the volume level, then click Next.

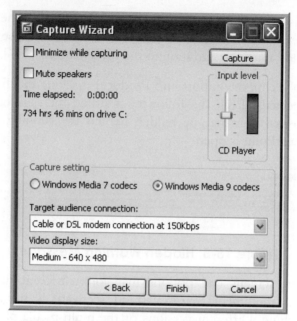

Figure 18-10: Sound Capture Window

Clicking Capture starts the audio capture process. Every time Capture is clicked, it will start the creation of a new sound file. The button will change to Stop while capture is in progress. When the sound is captured, click Stop and save the audio file. When you have captured all the sound files, click Finish and return to the Producer Wizard. When all of the sound files are in the list, click Next to move to the Synchronize screen.

The Synchronize screen asks whether you want to synchronize the sounds and/or the slides after they are imported. Select Yes and click Next to bring up the final screen of the wizard, which tells you it is ready to add all the files to the project. Click Finish. Producer will import all of the files and place them in the timeline you defined.

As the elements are added, you will be asked to synchronize the timing of the PowerPoint slides, the audio files and the video files to the slide files.

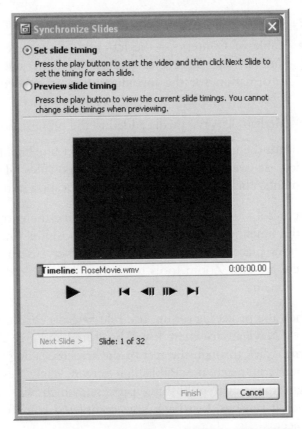

Figure 18-11: Synchronize Slides Window

The synchronize screen will show in the middle of the desktop. A preview of the first slide in the first presentation appears in the upper left corner of the desktop.

Select Preview to see what the current slide and movie timing. To start the preview, click the large triangle.

Now it is time to set the timing. Select Set slide timing and click the large triangle again. This time through, click the Next Slide button to change slides during the audio or video.

Note: Next Slide button not showing? Click the slide preview in the upper left of the desktop.

Click Finish when done coordinating the timing. You will move to the main Producer interface. The interface is organized in three tabs

- Preview – lets you see the produced project run

- Table of Contents – the left side of the screen lists each slide in the project in order; the right side shows the information for the introduction page created during the wizard

- Media – lists the media added to the presentation

Beneath the tabbed area, there is a project timeline. It shows the slides, as well as the audio and video files. To rearrange elements, click and drag them to a new location in the timeline.

There is a blue bar on the timeline showing the current position in the timeline. To review from a new position, drag the bar to another place on the timeline. This is very useful for testing. There are also Zoom tools to change the visible detail level of the timeline.

When the project is set up, use File → Save Project to save the work. Navigate to where it will be stored and give the project a name. Click through the rest of the screens, taking the defaults. When you reach the Publishing screen, click Next. This will begin the actual publishing process, which will take awhile. Once it finishes, you have now completed your first Producer project.

So, What Do I Do With It?

Now that you have the project done, you need to make it available for use. If you are just going to be running the project from your machine, you don't need to do anything. You will run the project by clicking the HTML file created by Producer.

If uploading the project to the web, move all the files created by the publish process. Link the HTML file to an existing website and you are all set to go.

How Does Producer Encode My Presentation?

Producer uses Windows Media Encoder for multimedia capture and is subject to the same best-use practices as using Windows

Media Encoder as a stand-alone application (see the section on Windows Media Encoder in Chapter 7 for more information).

Okay, So What Should I Worry About?

As with any translation from one format to another, there are trade-offs in quality and compatibility. When using Producer, you choose which browsers will be able to view the streaming media. Keep in mind older versions of the browsers can't handle some of PowerPoint's more advanced animations and transitions.

Also decide which version of the Windows codec will be used to handle the multimedia portion of the presentation. Here too, there is a trade-off. Windows Media Codec 9 will give the best results, however it also requires the client machine have Windows Media Player 9 installed. Using an older codec (version 7) will give much higher compatibility as it works with Windows Media Player 6.4 or above, but there is a loss in playback quality.

Can I Use Producer For Anything Other Than Web Delivery?

Different networks can pass differing amounts of information between machines in a single second. Curt doesn't know what kinds of networks his client has installed at their various sites. However, he does know they want to offer their employees as many options as possible. This brings up another of Producer's advantages.

When delivering content with Producer, you can adjust the data rate/quality for delivery over every type of network from a high speed LAN to a dial-up connection. Producer allows you to create multiple versions of the same presentation. With the proper server setup, you can even determine the best setup for your particular use. Remember as the data rate is lowered, it also lowers the playback quality on the client's machine.

Where Can I Learn More?

There is considerably more to using Producer. To learn more, visit Microsoft's web site, download Producer and experiment with the many ways it can be used. In addition, Microsoft's site has several examples of projects created using Producer, so you can see the capabilities of the product.

For peer-to-peer help on Producer, there is a dedicated newsgroup where you may exchange information with other users and receive technical assistance. You can access the newsgroup:

- Your newsreader:

  microsoft.public.producer

- Through Microsoft communities:

  support.microsoft.com/newsgroups/default.aspx?News Group=microsoft.public.producer&SLCID=US&ICP= GSS3&sd=GN&id=fh;en-us;newsgroups

- Or through Google:

  groups.google.com/groups?hl=en&lr=&ie=UTF- 8&oe=UTF-8&group=microsoft.public.producer

PowerPoint To Video: VHS Or DVD

Like Curt, there are times when you want to convert a presentation so it can be viewed without a computer. The most common of these conversions are to either VHS tape or to DVD.

In order for Windows to record presentations for use with VHS or DVD, additional hardware and/or software must be used to capture and record the presentation to the desired media. Apple users have this option built into PowerPoint and the Apple computer hardware.

Record To VHS Tape

Recording to VHS requires either

- A computer with a TV Out video card such as the ATI All-In-Wonder™
- Conversion hardware to take the monitor's signal and convert it into a TV signal that can be recorded.

The cabling required to do this is usually included with the vendor's video card or conversion hardware and should be used as each work a bit differently.

While the steps to record are straightforward once the hardware is connected, keep in mind there is a huge difference between a computer monitor and a television. Televisions have a much lower resolution, are easily oversaturated with bright colors and typically clip some of the image along the edges.

To make it easier, connect a television to the video recording system while creating the presentation so you can see in real-time what the image looks like. This will save untold hours going back and adjusting the presentation for proper appearance.

Tip 55: Presentation recording tutorial	Looking for Austin's full tutorial on recording presentations? Check out this URL from Sonia Coleman's site: www.soniacoleman.com/Tutorials/PowerPoint/recordvhs.htm This tutorial comes complete with full-color pictures of the equipment (including the cables), as well as a pair of drawings detailing where to put which piece of equipment when you set up the recording hardware.

Record To DVD

There are two methods available for converting a presentation for DVD delivery: Playing the presentation and using a DVD recorder attached to the TV to capture the output, or capturing the presentation on the computer and then copying the output to a DVD.

Using A DVD Recorder Attached To Your TV

The first method uses a Video Out card or converter, which is used in the same manner as recording to VHS. Complete the wiring per the video card manufacturer's directions, start the DVD recording and play the presentation on the computer. Note this method is subject to the same quality loss in the conversion process described for VHS recordings. It also is limited in that you can't edit the video in any way.

Using A DVD Recorder On Your Computer

The second method to record to DVD uses software to capture the presentation and then uses a DVD burner on the computer to create the DVD. This process is more complex but does have several benefits, the biggest being the ability to edit the resulting file. This process also allows a DVD menu to be created for playback in a standard DVD player.

Once the video is captured, save it to DVD with the software that came with the DVD burner. Test the completed DVD on a separate DVD player before distributing it.

Capturing The Presentation

There are a number of applications available to do the screen capture and record it to a video file. Camtasia (from TechSmith) is one good choice, although it does have some serious limitations. It requires re-routing the sound card wiring in order to capture audio contained in the presentation, and for this reason Austin does not recommend its use. On the plus side, it has a very clear user interface, which is why Kathy prefers it.

Austin prefers to use Microsoft's Windows Media Encoder. It is available as a free download from the Microsoft web site. While it doesn't have the most intuitive interface, it does do an excellent job of capturing the presentation along with audio without the need to re-route the machine's sound cables.

In both cases, there are some things you can and should do in order to get the best possible results. It takes a fairly powerful PC to both play the presentation and capture audio/video to a file at the same time. With this in mind, do the following before beginning your capture

- Shut down ALL other applications running in the background, including anti-virus software, internet connections, email connections and other taskbar software.

- Reduce the screen resolution to no higher than 800 X 600. You can even set the resolution to 640 X 480 and still get acceptable results for television viewing. Using this lower resolution will allow more of the computer's resources to be allocated to PowerPoint. This allows the presentation to run more along the timeline intended.

- Lower the screen's color depth, preferably to 16-bit. This greatly reduces the amount of data recorded and stored.

- Turn off video hardware acceleration. While this sounds counterproductive, it forces the video to be handled by the processor instead of the video card. If the video is being drawn by the video card, the information must then be moved back to the CPU for capture and requires much more work for the system.

- Reduce the audio capture format to the least data required for acceptable sound. For television playback there is no need for high data rates in stereo.

- Reduce the frames per second (fps) to the lowest acceptable quality. This level will depend upon what you have happening on the screen. Lots of motion requires higher frame rates to make the captured video appear smooth.

- Use a solid color for the background on the slides. A busy background, like an image, requires considerably more processor activity to capture and compress than a solid color background.

- Capture the video and sound in an uncompressed format. This reduces the workload on the processor and provides a higher quality image if you need to edit the file later.

- Use variable data rates for capture. You can set the data rate in the capture software. Variable data rates allow the capture software to reduce the file size and work load by using only the amount of data needed to produce a quality capture.

- Once the capture is completed, decide what codec will be used when saving. If transferring to a DVD, make certain the file format is compatible with the DVD burning software you will use.

- Using the Windows Media Encoder to do the capture will create a WMV file, so make sure the DVD software will be able to play WMV's. If it doesn't , you will need to add an extra conversion step.

One word of warning: Captured presentations create very large files. Make sure there is space on the hard drive for the files before starting the capture. Otherwise, you will get errors in the middle of the video capture and have to start again.

If you are concerned about having enough space or speed, do the regular disk maintenance (Chapter 8) before starting the capture process, including a defragmentation of the hard drive.

Appendix A: Where To Get More Help

➢ Group Help Sources

➢ PowerPoint Help Web Sites

➢ Template Sources

➢ Macros, Add-Ins and Other Useful Additions

Group Help Sources

Main PowerPoint Newsgroup

This on-line group can be accessed through the local newsreader, through the community web interface from the Microsoft site or through the web interface on Google Groups.

- To access via a newsgroup, set the news reader to microsoft.public.powerpoint (for PC questions) or microsoft.public.mac.office.powerpoint (for Macintosh questions)

- To access via Microsoft's Communities interface, go to www.microsoft.com/office/community/en-us/default.mspx?dg=microsoft.public.powerpoint&lang=en&cr=US

- To access via Google's web interface, go to groups.google.com/groups?hl=en&lr=&ie=UTF-8&oe=UTF-8&group=microsoft.public.powerpoint

- When searching for answers to your questions, you might try going to either the general Google site (www.google.com) or the Google Groups site (groups.google.com/advanced_group_search?hl=en) and searching there. You never know what you might find.

The Microsoft PowerPoint newsgroup is a great place for getting answers to all things PowerPoint. The experts there (including myself and the other PowerPoint MVPs) will do their best to provide answers in a timely manner, with humor and fun conversations on the side.

MSO

This is Linda Johnson's excellent question and answer group for all questions and issues related to Office. Hosted by Freelist.org, this list is a wonderful resource for both the new and experienced user. Emails come directly to your inbox. To join the list, visit www.freelists.org/webpage/mso

PowerPoint Yahoo Group

This Yahoo group is dedicated to answering PowerPoint questions of all kinds. This group is not nearly as active as the Microsoft PowerPoint newsgroup, but there are several good questions asked about PowerPoint each week.

To access this group, go to:

groups.yahoo.com/group/powerpoint

Do not confuse this with the Microsoft PowerPoint Yahoo group (groups.yahoo.com/group/microsoftpowerpoint). The microsoftpowerpoint group is virtually dead and generates quite a bit of spam.

The Office Experts

This is an on-line forum run by MrExcel. I am currently the moderator for the PowerPoint section of the forum. Questions tend to come in spurts, with answers provided by a wide variety of Office users.

To access the forum, go to

www.theofficeexperts.com/forum/forumdisplay.php?s=&foru
mid=6

PowerPoint Help Web Sites

The PowerPoint FAQ

www.pptfaq.com

www.rdpslides.com/pptfaq

Part of Steve Rindsberg's great PowerPoint site, this set of pages contains the distilled PowerPoint wisdom of the newsgroup through the years. If questions come up multiple times, Steve adds the question and answers to the FAQ. Read the *Don't use PowerPoint for anything serious until you've done this* section, then use the rest as a searchable resource.

Sonia Coleman's Site

www.soniacoleman.com

Run by PowerPoint MVP Sonia Coleman, this site is a great resource for tutorials, templates, downloads and great artwork. Sonia's site is the home of the Autorun CD programs: PowerLink Plus, PowerLink and Autorun CD Project Creator.

Echo's Voice

www.echosvoice.com

Run by PowerPoint MVP Echo Swinford, this site is the home of many tutorials you will find very helpful, including:

- Bezier Curves
- Multiple Masters
- Manual Creation of Autorun CDs

Glen's PowerPoint Workbench

www.powerpointworkbench.com/index.html

Created and written by Glen Millar, yet another MVP, this site specializes in showing how to use animation and effects to create slides. Glen specializes in making the 2D objects look like 3D objects. Add to that tutorials on round-tripping presentations between HTML and PowerPoint and animation, and you have one of the most fact-filled sites ever to come out of Australia.

PowerPointAnswers.Com

www.powerpointanswers.com/index.php

My site. It's full of articles, resources, links and other information. Additions are made quarterly. All the links from this book can be found there.

Indezine

www.indezine.com/articles/index.html

Run by PowerPoint MVP Geetesh Bajaj, this site is full of product reviews, tips, techniques and PowerPoint resources. Among the best information on Geetesh's site are his tutorials and articles on multimedia and PowerPoint. Be sure to check out his series of Flash articles.

In addition, Indezine has a great series on PowerPoint history, PowerPoint memorabilia and PowerPoint extras.

awesome powerpoint backgrounds

www.powerpointbackgrounds.com

Created and supported by TAJ Simmons, another PowerPoint MVP, this site has tips, tutorials and templates for you to peruse and enjoy. This site is also the home of the looping and linking tutorials.

PTT Inc

www.pttinc.com/ppgame.htm#PPGame

Bill Foley's on-line presence is at PTT, Inc. Bill is a PowerPoint expert, consultant, and trainer. His site is the home to PowerPoint tutorials on educational games, along with samples of his games.

The PowerPoint Magician

www.powerpointmagician.com

PowerPoint MVP Glenna Shaw's on-line presence, this site is jam packed with Section 508 of the American Disabilities Act and how to ensure your PowerPoint presentations are accessible to everyone.

The Microsoft Knowledge Base

This is the database of all questions and solutions addressed by Microsoft. The Knowledge Base contains information on all of Microsoft's products. To get to the PowerPoint-specific information, go to support.microsoft.com/default.aspx?scid=fh;EN-US;KBHOWTO and select PowerPoint from the product dropdown list.

Woody's Office Portal

www.wopr.com

Run by Woody Leonhard, this is the front page to Woody's forums, Woody's Watch (a monthly email newsletter with office tips), book suggestions and information on Woody's Office PowerPack. For more information, check out

Bit Better

www.bitbetter.com

Home of the Screen Beans clip art collection, this site is run by Cathleen Belleville and Dennis Austin of A Bit Better. Besides the static Screen Beans and Animated Screen Beans collections, there is also a PowerPoint forum frequented by several of the PowerPoint MVPs.

PPT Live

www.pptlive.com

PowerPoint Live is a PowerPoint community gathering and conference held annually by R Altman Productions. The conference is three and a half days of sessions, talk and the help center, where you can get one-on-one help for PowerPoint questions and problems.

Template Sources

Wondering how I picked the sources I did? I know these template sources best. They are companies that have been around for quite a while, have good customer service and reasonable prices for their templates. In fact, a few of the places listed even give away their templates free!

www.powerpointbackgrounds.com

ww.soniacoleman.com

www.powerpointed.com

www.brainybetty.com

www.powerfinish.com

www.powerbacks.com

www.templatecentral.com

www.presentationpro.com

www.powerpointart.com

www.power2present.com/mainframe.htm

www.inzones.com/powerpoint/index.htm

This Isn't Enough?

If you need even more template sources, go to Google (or your favorite search engine) and do a search on "PowerPoint Templates." You will get more results than you'll have time to investigate!

Macros, Add-Ins And Other Useful Additions

RnR: RDP And Reillyand, Inc.

Steve Rindsberg and Brian Reilly, two of the PowerPoint MVPs, collectively have created a great set of PowerPoint add-ins and tools to make your development life easier. Some of their tools are free, some have a small cost associated with them. Their tools include

- PPTools Starter Set and Starter Set Plus
- Prep4PDF
- PowerPoint ShapeStyles
- FixLinks Pro
- PPTMerge
- PPT2HTML
- PowerPoint Presentation Optimizer
- PowerPoint Image Exporter
- PowerPoint Palette
- PowerPoint Protect

To learn the details on the tools offered by Steve and Brian, check out their site at www.rdpslides.com/pptools

OfficerOne

officerone.tripod.com/addins.html

Chirag Dalal, a PowerPoint MVP, runs OfficerOne, a site with PowerPoint tips, techniques, and lots of macros and add-ins. Some of Chirag's offerings include

- PowerShow
- PowerKiosk
- Shortcut Manager for PowerPoint
- SecurePack
- Volume Control
- SundayStar
- Shortcuts for PowerPoint
- PowerPoint Web Browser Assistant
- Kiosk Assistant
- PowerPoint VBA Controls Assistant

- SyncViews
- Smooth Shadows
- Set Default Slide Layout
- TransparentShow
- SlideNavigator
- MultiSave
- ShowMonitor
- ShowPlus
- AutoDateTime
- Full Show 97
- Event Generator
- FaceId Explorer

OfficeTips

www.mvps.org/skp/

Shyam Pillai, also a PowerPoint MVP, runs OfficeTips. This site offers VBA tutorials and samples, as well as both free and commercial add-ins. The add-ins and tutorials on Shyam's site include:

- Handout Wizard
- Sequential Save
- Image Importer
- Unflip
- Save the Trees
- Live Web
- NoEsc
- FaceID Browser
- and many, many more

Tushar Mehta

www.tushar-mehta.com

Tushar Mehta, an Excel MVP, has a site full of Office tips, tutorials and add-ins. The three PowerPoint add-ins Tushar lists on his site are:

- PPT-Timer
- Textbox from file
- RandomSlideShow

For details on these tools, go to Tushar's site and click on the PowerPoint link in the left hand column.

Aladat

www.aladat.com

www.soniacoleman.com/Tutorials/PowerPoint/acdpc_instructions.htm

AlaDat provides PowerPoint tools. The most popular of their tools are the CD creation tools and PrezGuardPro. In addition, they also sell SlideConverter. For details on AlaDat's tools, go to Steve Hetrick's site or Sonia Coleman's site

Snag-It

www.techsmith.com/download/snagitdefault.asp

Sold by TechSmith, Snag-It is a great screen capture program that integrates well with all of Office. It makes screenshots in just a few clicks, then improve them with just a few more. Most of the screen shots in this book were created using SnagIt.

VoxProxy

www.voxproxy.com

Sold by Right Seat Software, VoxProxy adds animated talking characters to the presentation. The characters conform to Microsoft's Agent technology.

The PowerPoint Viewers

www.rdpslides.com/pptfaq/FAQ00153.htm

Microsoft provides three Viewers for watching PowerPoint presentations on computers without PowerPoint itself installed.

- The 2003 Viewer, which supports most PowerPoint 2003 features. (By extension, it also supports the features of all previous versions.)

- The 97 Viewer, which supports all PowerPoint 97 features and all earlier versions.

- The Macintosh Viewer, which supports all Macintosh PowerPoint features from 98 earlier

Looking For A PowerPoint-To-Flash Converter?

There are almost as many PowerPoint to Flash conversion programs as there are users who want to do the conversion. Three of the best converters include:

- Macromedia Breeze

  www.macromedia.com/software/breeze

- Articulate

  articulateglobal.com/presenter.html

- PresentationPro

  www.presentationpro.com/products/PowerCONVERTE R.asp

Since the field changes so frequently, I suggest you research the various tools by searching the newsgroup and the web for "powerpoint flash converter."

In addition, Impatica makes a conversion product using Java instead of Flash. It can be found at www.impatica.com

Finally, Latitude Communications makes MeetingPlace iCreate, which is based on Wanadu's conversion products. Information can be found at www.latitude.com/prod_svc/icreate

Turning Point - Interactive Audience Response

www.turningtechnologies.com/index.asp

Looking to get the audience involved in the presentation? Try Turning Point – a PowerPoint add-in that adds polling questions to the presentation and gets feedback from the audience on these questions while running the presentation.

In addition to creating questions, Turning Point also stores the audience responses for evaluation after the presentation.

This page left intentionally blank.

Appendix B: Hardware Considerations For PowerPoint

➢ What you need

➢ Primary and Secondary Monitors

What You Need

If you are going to create and run PowerPoint presentations, you need as fast a machine as possible, with as much memory and hard drive space as possible. Knowing this configuration is a dream but not a reality for all of us, the following system configuration is what Microsoft recommends as the minimum system requirements for each of the last three versions of PowerPoint.

PowerPoint 2003

www.microsoft.com/office/powerpoint/prodinfo/sysreq.mspx

PowerPoint 2002

www.microsoft.com/office/previous/powerpoint/2002sysreq.asp

PowerPoint 2000

www.microsoft.com/office/previous/powerpoint/2000tour/sysreqs.asp

Multiple Monitors

To run PowerPoint on multiple monitors, you must have the following hardware

- One video board for each monitor
- Two or more monitors

In addition, if trying to use multiple monitors in PowerPoint 2000 or earlier, it is a good idea to have software to control both monitors. The two best software solutions for these set ups are

- MultiShow Software, by Iosysoft

  www.iosysoft.com

- SundayShow, PowerShow, and PowerKiosk, by OfficerOne (Chirag Dalal, PowerPoint MVP)

  officerone.tripod.com

If using PowerPoint 2002 or later, you can use the Presenter's view to do the same thing.

In addition, there are two pages on the PPT FAQ about multiple monitors

www.rdpslides.com/pptfaq/FAQ00476.htm

www.rdpslides.com/pptfaq/FAQ00231.htm

Why Would I Want This?

There are a few sneaky tricks you can do in PowerPoint if you have multiple monitors running.

First, you can have notes showing on one monitor and the slides showing on another. This is especially helpful if you are running a presentation. Turn the screen towards you and show the PowerPoint notes interface on it. Then, project the running program on the screen for the participants to see.

Next, if using PowerPoint for a meeting where you need to pre-select or change content while the show is running, you can be working away at the slides without the participants knowing. If you do this, the changes won't show until the slide is re-started on the screen. So if editing the slide being shown, the changes won't show until you leave and re-enter the slide.

Finally, you can have two presentations running, one on each monitor. They will not actually run at the same time, but they will both be visible at the same time. (In other words, only one presentation will be active and animated, but the other one will be visible.)

This page left intentionally blank.

Appendix C: The Most Common Time Wasters And Their Solutions

➢ Not reading the FAQ

➢ Skipping the planning phase

➢ Video Drivers/Hardware Acceleration

➢ Saving to removable media

➢ Saving incorrectly

➢ Autoformat

➢ Not using masters and templates

➢ Not setting up color schemes

➢ Storing content in more than one folder

➢ Not creating a formal folder structure for your work

➢ Using the wrong fonts for distributable presentations

➢ Assuming media is embedded

➢ Not creating your own toolbar

Not Reading The FAQ

Problem

Running into a problem when you are deep into creating a presentation can be a real problem. It is worse when you know the solution is out there, but you can't find it. You check the Help files, you beat your head on the desk, you try every menu option you can think of, but still – no solution.

Solution

As the collective knowledge base for all common PowerPoint problems, the FAQ has resources and answers to many of the most common problems asked on the PowerPoint newsgroup. Chances are, if someone else has run into your problem, the solution is in the FAQ.

Bookmark the home page for the FAQ and read it. Use it as a reference tool when you run into problems. Use it to learn new stuff. Use it for entertainment. Just be sure to use it.

www.pptfaq.com

Skipping The Planning Phase

Problem

You didn't do any planning or design, so the presentation leaves the audience completely lost. You not only have wasted time, you have wasted the audience's time.

Solution

Do your planning up front and keep the planning information current. Create a storyboard or outline. Do an audience analysis (re-read Chapter 2 if you need help with this part). Find out if the presentation will be shared. If it will, plan that into the presentation. Plan the colors, styles, fonts and templates. Finally, keep good records of who you talked to, when and what about. Those notes and records will save you if there are problems later.

Video Drivers/Hardware Acceleration

Problem

Elements on the slides keep disappearing when you play the shows. The movies don't always show, the graphics look weird, there are extra lines in places you know you didn't put them and the colors are off. To make it all worse, it's a brand new computer!

Solution

Check the web to see if more recent video drivers have been released for the video card and monitor. Even brand new computers are not guaranteed to have the most recent drivers on them. The computer may be new to you, but unless you downloaded and installed the drivers yourself within the last day, the drivers could be out of date.

Some video drivers are updated as frequently as weekly. This is especially true for the drivers for higher-powered video cards and high quality monitors. Since the users of these devices depend on their content looking perfect on the screen, the device creators keep updates regularly available.

If you know you have the most recent drivers, and you are still having video problems, turn down the hardware acceleration a notch or two. You can do this from within PowerPoint using the Slide Show → Set Up Show dialog. Or, you can do this from the desktop by right-clicking to bring up the Properties, going to the Settings tab and clicking the Advanced button.

If everything is working great when you test the presentation on the computer, don't change anything until after you give the presentation. Sometimes a new driver breaks things instead of fixes things. If you update, be sure to test again.

Since installing new software on a machine can also break things, be sure to check the presentation still runs if you install any software that might influence your presentation. This includes fonts, printer drivers, multimedia programs, graphic programs and anything that might change the file associations.

Saving To Removable Media

Problem

Sometimes, the presentation just disappears. The file becomes un-readable or just appears to be gone. Usually this happens at the worst possible time.

Other times, you try to save your presentation and get a message the device is full, even when you think it isn't.

Solution

Never try to save the file to anything but the hard drive. If you need to carry the presentation from computer to computer, save it to the hard drive, close PowerPoint then copy the presentation file to the floppy drive, CD, USB drive, network drive, etc.

PowerPoint doesn't work well saving directly to non-permanent drives. It tries to create and use temporary space in the same place as it saves the main file. If working from a diskette, there probably isn't enough room for both the presentation file and the temporary space.

On a network, saving to network drives instead of the local hard drive will create a lot of network traffic as PowerPoint accesses not just the real file, but the temporary files as well. This increases the chances file pieces will get lost. Things get even worse if the network connection goes down while PowerPoint is accessing one of its files on the network drive.

Don't save directly to the CD drive, either. It, too, may cause problems The only time PowerPoint can write directly to the CD drive is when you are running PowerPoint 2003 on a

Windows XP system with a CD writer and doing a Package to CD. Even then, just because PowerPoint is able to do it doesn't make it a good thing to do. It's probably wiser to use Package for CD's Copy to Folder on the hard drive and then burn those files to the CD.

Saving Incorrectly

Problem

There are a whole range of ways you can save the presentation file incorrectly The most common of these are

- Back saving – saving for use in a previous version

- Leaving Fast Saves on

- Not saving often enough

- Not saving a backup

All of these problems can cause you grief. The first two will give you large files are likely to corrupt easily. The last two will cause you to lose data. Remember, there are two kinds of computer users: those who have lost data and those who will.

Solution

First, turn off Fast Saves (Tools → Options → Save tab). Next, don't save the presentation for use in a previous version unless you need to open the file in PowerPoint 95. Every version of PowerPoint since 97 uses the same file format. You don't need to back save unless you are sharing data with a very old version. (By the way, if you are sharing your presentation with a computer that only has PowerPoint 95 on it, you will run into many more problems than the file size.)

Save the file on the hard drive frequently. Save it with a new name at least once for every hour of work you have into the file. If you can't remember to save the file with a new name, get the Sequential Save add-in and use it.

www.mvps.org/skp/seqsave.htm

Autoformat

Problem

You paste an object or text and the size changes. Or you paste and the layout of the slide changes.

Solution

Turn off the three parts of AutoFormat. The options can be found in Tools → AutoCorrect Options. Turn off all three pieces – AutoFit title text to placeholder, AutoFit body text to placeholder and Automatic layout for inserted objects. You worked hard to decide how you want the presentation to look. Don't let PowerPoint overrule your decisions.

Not Using Masters And Templates

Problem

Making and keeping all the slides looking consistent is taking forever. Every time you have to change something, you have to go back and change every slide by hand.

What's worse is, when the overall look of the presentation needs to change, you have to go into all of the other PowerPoint files in this project and make the changes by hand.

Solution

Every presentation should be based on a template. If you keep the templates clean and usable, changing the look of presentations will be much easier. In addition, the more of the design work kept on the master slides, the easier it will be to make presentation-specific changes.

In PowerPoint 2002 or later, take advantage of the multiple masters feature. If you need to have some slides follow the same pattern as the rest, but with a certain element always in the same place, make a master just for that series of slides. Changing the slides will become much easier.

Not Setting Up Color Schemes

Problem

You go to change the text of a presentation, but when you click in the placeholder, the text disappears. Or, when you add autoshapes to the presentation, the colors clash with the background. Worst of all, when you insert a graph, the colors of the bars fade into the background.

Solution

Set up the color schemes. Make sure the background color works with the title and text colors, even if you have a graphic as the background. Make sure the eight main colors in the presentation work well together.

Storing Content In More Than One Folder

Problem

You link to a sound file on the computer. When you move the presentation to another computer, the links break and the presentation no longer has sound. This also happens to movies.

Solution

Put a copy of each sound file and movie file into the same folder as the presentation before you link to it. Same goes with linked graphics or other elements. The time you save by moving the file first more than makes up for the chance you might end up with duplicate files on the hard drive.

By the way, if you didn't insert the link while the movie or sound was in the same folder as the presentation, you can't just move the linked file to the folder after the fact. You need to move the sound or movie file, remove the old link in the presentation, and create a new link – in that order.

If the links do break, check out the FAQ entry on fixing links:

www.rdpslides.com/pptfaq/FAQ00155.htm

Not Creating A Formal Folder Structure For Your Work

Problem

You created a really great demo for a client. Now, if you could just remember where you put it. You checked the My Documents folder, but it didn't jump out at you.

Solution

Create a folder structure that tells you who the presentation was created for, what the presentation is about and maybe even when you made it. Create new folders when you start a new project.

Most people like to store things in the My Documents folder. That is fine. Just create the working structure inside the My Documents folder.

In my main folder, I have a folder for each client I have worked with. Inside those folders, I have separate folders for each project or revision of a project I worked on.

For example, the content for this book is all in one folder. Inside that folder are folders for each of the presentations I used to create the screen shots for each chapter. There are also folders for any correspondence about the book and a folder for the PDFs as they were sent out for review. The whole structure not only makes it easier to find the things I create, it ensures I put all my linked files for a particular presentation in the same folder as that presentation.

Using The Wrong Fonts For Distributable Presentations

Problem

You worked days to get the presentation just right. Then, you sent it to your boss to review it. The first thing you hear back from her is the slides look terrible. The letters are too small, the lines are cramped together and some of the characters don't even show. Turns out, you used a font your boss doesn't have and you didn't embed it.

Same presentation, round two. This time you embed the fonts. Better, but now you hear from your boss she gets an error message when she opens it in PowerPoint 2003. The file is not able to be edited because the font is not fully embedded.

Solution

First, try to always use the standard fonts. If you need to use a font that isn't standard, be sure to embed it. If you do embed it, make sure you test the presentation on another computer to be sure it looks right.

If you need a refresher course on choosing and embedding your fonts, re-read Chapter 4.

Assuming Media Is Embedded

Problem

You created a presentation with pictures and music from the latest school concert and sent it to the other participants. When they try to play it, they see all the pictures, but they don't hear any sound.

At the end of the presentation, you put a movie of the group. It doesn't play, either. But the animated logo you put in does.

Solution

The only type of sound files embedded are WAV files. They only embed if they are smaller than the size set in Tools → Options.

If the sound files aren't WAV files, you need to send them along with the presentation in order for others to hear them.

Other types of media are never embedded – they are always linked. If you put movies in a presentation, the original movie files must be sent with the presentation.

So, why did the animated logo work? It was an animated gif. Gifs are considered graphics, not media, so they embed just fine.

Not Creating Your Own Toolbar

Problem

You need to do a certain function over and over. You know it is in the menus somewhere, but you hate trying to find it.

Solution

Customize your version of PowerPoint. Create toolbars for those activities you use most frequently. You can even create extra menus if you prefer to use menus instead of toolbars.

Just remember the new toolbar resides on your computer only. If you switch computers, you will need to set up the environment all over. Or you can use the Save My Settings wizard. Go to Start → All Programs → MS Office Tools → Save My Settings Wizard.

Index